IMAGES
of America

FLORENCE

ON THE COVER: The Cluv Filarmonic de Florence takes a break on the Pinal County Courthouse steps in 1894. Earlier, in 1888, the *Florence Enterprise* announced the formation of a different band, the Florence Brass Band, whose "unmusical toot toot toot will waft the length and breadth of the town." Brass bands were popular across the country, but apparently there was at least one critic in Florence. (Courtesy Pinal County Historical Society.)

IMAGES *of America*
FLORENCE

Pinal County Historical Society

Arizona Historical Foundation

ARCADIA
PUBLISHING

ISBN 978-0-7385-4899-9

Published by Arcadia Publishing
Charleston, South Carolina

Printed in the United States of America

Library of Congress Catalog Card Number: 2007923092

For all general information contact Arcadia Publishing at:
Telephone 843-853-2070
Fax 843-853-0044
E-mail sales@arcadiapublishing.com
For customer service and orders:
Toll-Free 1-888-313-2665

Visit us on the Internet at www.arcadiapublishing.com

To Della Arcadia Redondo Meadows, whose unbounded energy and love of Arizona helped preserve its history.

Contents

ACKNOWLEDGMENTS

The five authors from the Pinal County Historical Society who contributed their experience and skills to this history of Florence are Margaret Truman Baker, Louise Clark, Patricia Faux, H. Christine Reid, and Lynn Smith. We could not have created this work were it not for the Pinal County Historical Society Museum's extensive archives, especially the Della Meadows Collections. Any photographs not otherwise credited appear courtesy of the Pinal County Historical Society Collection.

We deeply appreciate the following individuals and families who shared their photographs and memories: Margaret Truman Baker, Dorothy Borree, Rik Carter, Frank A. Celaya, Judy Clark, Cindy Cluff, Bookard Dooley, Barbara Clemans Eidson, Susan Fordyce, Richard C. Guerrero, Glenn Guild, Tara Harmon, Amos Hawkins Jr., Ron Joaquin, Dennis Lease, Celeste Mandell, Joyce Pratt, John Swearengin, Alfred and Freida Brunenkant Westfall, James and Edwina Van Haren Westfall, Fredric G. White III, Natalia White, and David Winchester.

Not every undertaking is so privileged as to include contributions from noted photographers such as Pedro E. Guerrero, Dixie Legler, and Louise L. Serpa. We deeply appreciate them.

We also thank the following for their contributions: the *Apache Junction Independent*, the Arizona Historical Society, the *Casa Grande Dispatch*, the Dorothy Lease estate, the Earl Moore estate, the Don Stillman estate, the National Park Service, and Tucson Trade Engraving.

INTRODUCTION

Why does anyone build a town in the middle of the desert? To most people, a desert is barren—a place to go through quickly, not a place to make your home. Surprisingly Florence's Sonoran Desert is rich with a variety of wildlife. Even though rainfall cannot always be ensured, there is the Gila River, an important source of water and the major natural feature of the area. The town of Florence originally grew up on the south bank of the river at nearly equal distances from present-day Phoenix and Tucson. However, Florence's founders were not the first people to live in this valley.

Over 1,000 years ago, an agrarian civilization inhabited the Gila River Valley. The Native Americans who were living in this region when the Spanish came called these ancient natives the Hohokam, commonly translated as "those who have vanished."

The Hohokam Indians led a subsistence life that included plant gathering, hunting, and farming. The soil was fertile, but they needed water for their corn, beans, and squash to grow. Therefore, with no beasts of burden and only digging sticks, they created an extensive canal system that is believed to be the most complex irrigation system ever created in ancient times in North America. The Hohokam, situated on major trade routes, exchanged parrots, seashells, obsidian, rare minerals, salt, feathers, and pottery. Late in their known history, the Hohokam built platforms and multi-storied buildings, one of which became a landmark near present-day Florence. Then the Hohokam disappeared.

No records exist of anyone living along the Gila River from 1450 to 1680. The first reports mentioning the bands of Native Americans—the Akimel O'odham, "river people," and the Tohono O'odham, "desert people"—occurred after 1680. Did these people evolve from the Hohokam, or was there an abandonment and then a return to this river valley? The Akimel O'odham, still commonly known as the Pima Indians, believe they are in fact descended from the Hohokam. A Jesuit missionary first recorded the presence of the multi-storied Hohokam building. Other Jesuit missionaries who came with the Spanish explorers reported seeing Native Americans tending irrigated fields. The missionaries introduced wheat seed, horses, and iron plows to the Pima.

In 1821, Mexico won its independence from Spain. During this unstable time for the region, there were only a few reports from trappers and travelers who journeyed along the river. In the late 1840s, during the Mexican War, soldiers found only desert and some scattered Native American villages. The 49ers that traveled the southern route to California provided information about the Pima. In fact, the Pima Indians impressed these 49ers by providing them with much-needed wheat and corn. By the 1850s, Mexican families were ranching on the land south of the Gila River.

On June 29, 1854, the Gadsden Purchase brought those living in the southern Gila River Valley into the United States. Still, there was no rush to settle in the region. People traveled west along the river, but few remained in the area.

The Arizona Territory was separated from New Mexico Territory in 1863. On March 2, 1866, Esteban Ramírez filed the first recorded local homestead claim, marking the beginning of Florence. Ramírez had to register his claim in Prescott, Arizona Territory, because a land office would not be established in Florence until 1873, when the town's central location made it a good site.

Location was as important to Florentines in the mid-19th century as it had been to the much-earlier Hohokam. With a settlement built on the bank of a river on a broad plain with foothills and mountains not too far away, Florence residents had water for their farmland, grassland for cattle ranches, and minerals from the nearby mountains. Apache Indians also lived in those mountains surrounding the town. The federal government established forts, Indian agencies, and reservations. Early entrepreneurs of Florence contracted with the government to supply hay and livestock purchased from local farmers.

In 1875, a major silver mine was discovered in the mountains. Miners and wagon trains needed protection from vandals. Florence became a supply center for farmers, ranchers, miners, and the military. Entrepreneurs built stores, saloons, hotels, and other commercial enterprises.

Florence, because of its location, became the county seat of the newly created Pinal County in 1875. County residents needed to come to Florence for any government business. By 1909, Arizona Territory had moved the territorial prison from Yuma to Florence. Florence's central location and its fertile land were considerations behind the decision. The prison could hopefully become self-sufficient.

The boom did not last. Florence was bypassed by the mainline railroad, and a major highway was built west of town. Located in the center of ranch country, Florence became the rodeo town it still is today.

The Pima and Maricopa Indians are members of the nearby Gila River Indian Community. Adjacent to the town of Florence is a small community of Tohono O'odham. This village and Florence cooperate and sustain a positive working relationship.

With a blend of farmers, ranchers, miners, entrepreneurs, and cowboys, Florence is a community enriched by its diversity. Many residents are descended from immigrants to the New World who migrated north from China, South America, and Mexico. In the early years when soldiers and miners headed west (or east from California) without families, many of them married daughters of the Mexican families who were living in the area. Therefore, very few families are all Anglo or all Mexican, and that is the way the people of Florence like it. With a rich heritage that derives from many different cultures, Florence is proud of its past and hopeful for its future. At this time, the surrounding river valley is being planted with subdivisions and people from near and far. May they, too, appreciate the town of Florence's history and become part of it.

One

Those Who Came Before

Fr. Eusebio Kino, a native of Italy, spent most of his New Spain missionary career in the region of the northern Pima Indians. In 1694, Father Kino's record of Casa Grande became the first report of the ruins by a European. He was fascinated by the crumbling ruins of the ancient four-story Hohokam structure located just south of the Gila River. During his 24 years in the area, he returned six times to the building that he named the "Great House," or Casa Grande.

Anthropologists believe that the Hohokam's construction of multi-storied buildings around the year 1300 signifies the concentration of power in the hands of the few. Pima Indians living in the area reported that a chief, years before, had constructed the building and had ruled over the inhabitants. Today some believe the Salado Indians from the north were an influence. It is unknown why Casa Grande was built. Was it constructed for religious reasons or rather for protection?

Florence resident Rev. Isaac T. Whittemore alerted the federal government that the ruin was melting away because of the material of its construction: caliche mud. Mainly because of Whittemore's visionary actions, money was provided to preserve the building. In June 1892, the Casa Grande Ruins became the first archaeological site established by the federal government. After a national park system was set up in 1916, the Casa Grande Ruins became a national monument.

The monument has remained a presence in the lives of Florence residents. In the last decades of the 1800s, the ruins were a destination for outings and picnics. The ruins later hosted an annual historical pageant performed for four years.

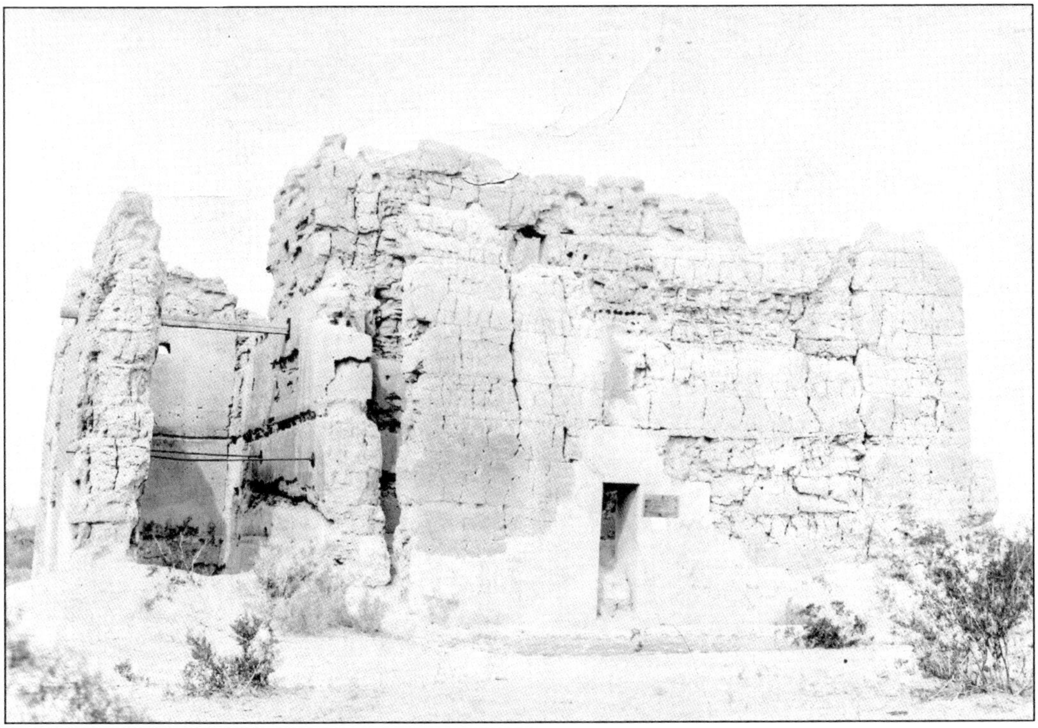

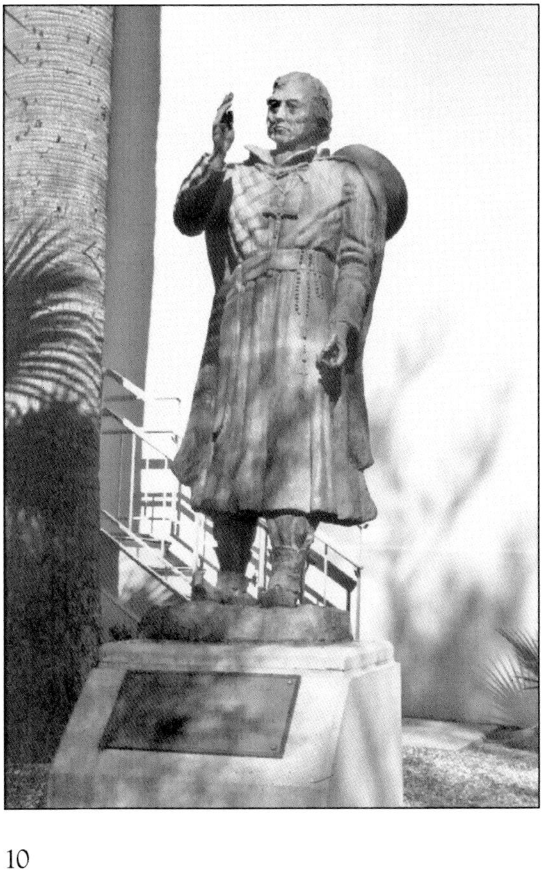

Casa Grande was situated to allow sweeping views of the Gila River and the mountains. This late-1880s photograph shows very clearly that Casa Grande was deteriorating. By this time, any wood that had been used for roof beams and lintels had been torn out and carried away. A model of the ruin, looking much as it does here, was exhibited at Chicago's Columbian Exposition of 1893.

Fr. Eusebio Kino preached to the Pima Indians along the Gila River but was unsuccessful in establishing a mission near the Casa Grande ruins. In November 1697, he and his soldier escort camped beside the ruins. After fasting all day, Kino celebrated Mass. There is no contemporary portrait of Kino, but a statue like this represents Arizona in Statuary Hall in the Capitol.

Isaac T. Whittemore, a native of New York, was a Presbyterian minister in Florence and a missionary to the Pima Indians. He tried unsuccessfully to secure the water of the Gila River for them, even traveling to Washington to plead their case. When he lunched with the Arizona Presbytery within the Great House walls in 1889, he realized vandalism had taken its toll and something had to be done to preserve Casa Grande.

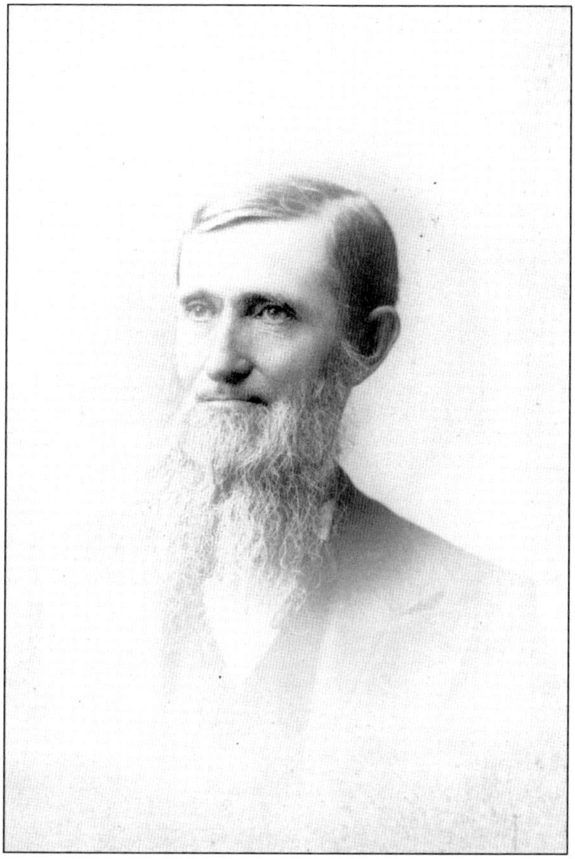

Here Reverend Whittemore stops at the ruins on one of his missionary trips to a nearby town. After Whittemore appealed to the federal government, Cosmos Mindeleff was sent to assess the status of the ruins and produce plans for potential excavation. Some money was appropriated for work at the site. In 1889, Whittemore was appointed uncompensated custodian. He was later paid $480 a year.

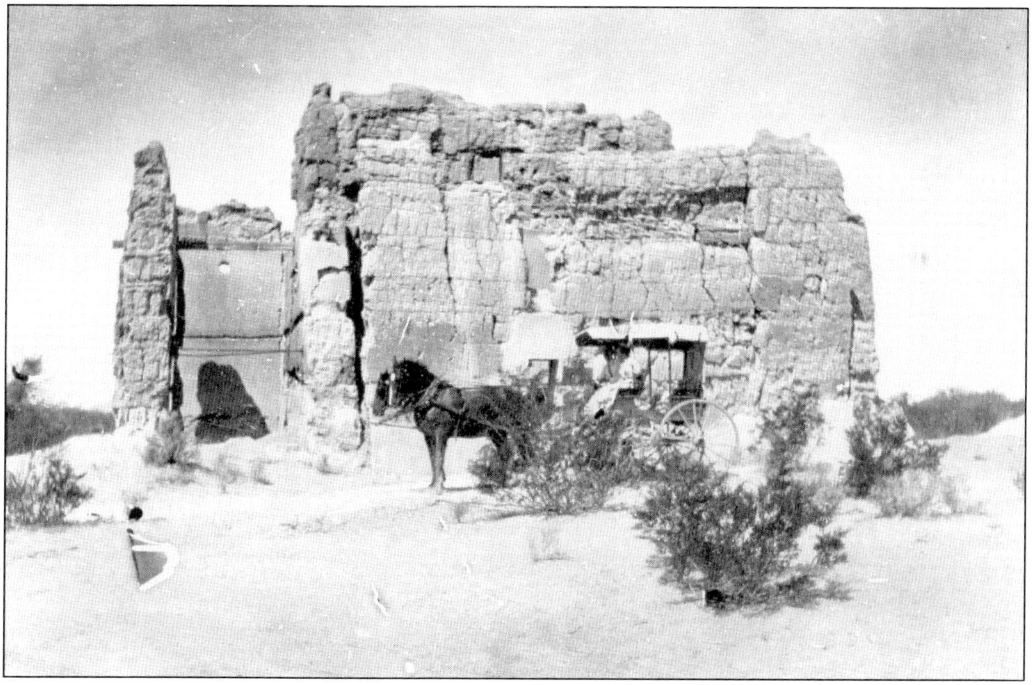

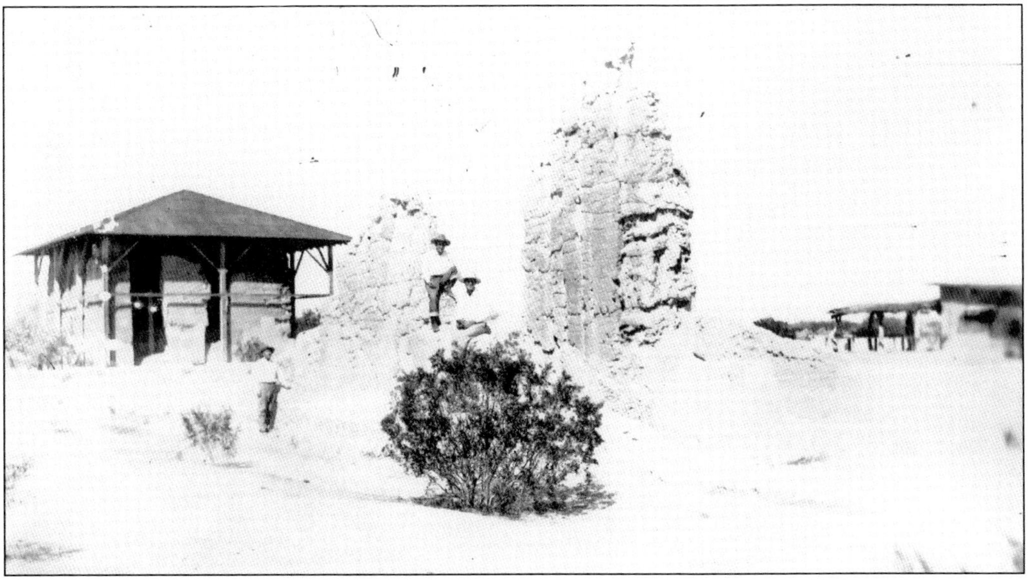

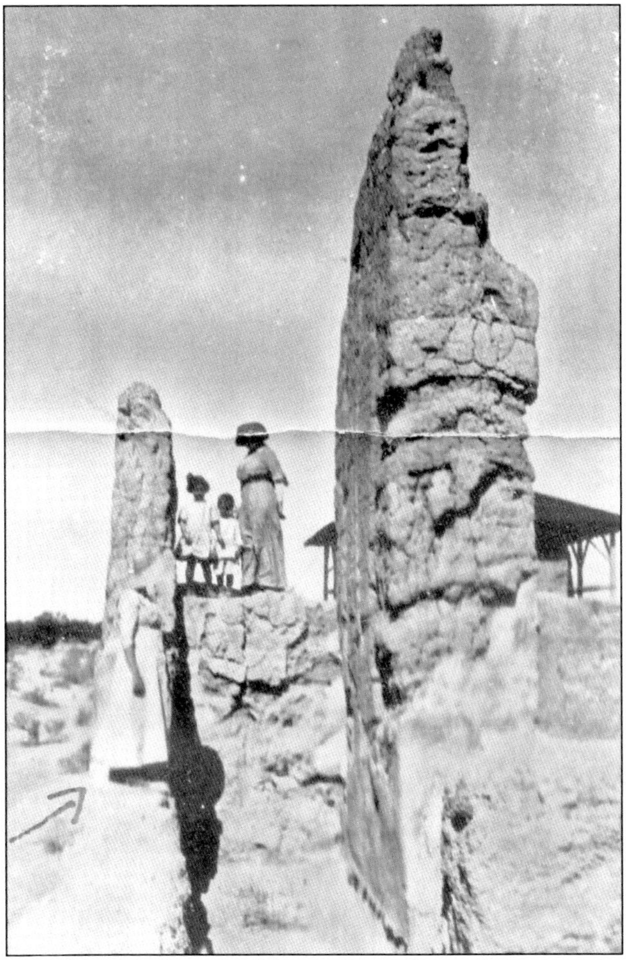

It was not until much later that visitors to the Casa Grande Ruins National Monument were constrained from rambling throughout the site. Behind the visitors is the first protective roof built over the Great House. Made of wood and corrugated iron painted red, the roof partially obscured the ruins.

Members of the Frederic G. White family of Florence enjoy an outing at the ruins. Although the government was working to preserve the structure, visitors often drove off the entrance road onto archaeological sites. These visitors were allowed to roam freely, as can be seen. The preservation area amounted to 480 acres, including the Great House in Compound A and other mounds and ruins in Compound B.

Frank Pinkley became superintendent of the Casa Grande Ruins National Monument in 1901. Called "The Boss," Pinkley had responsibilities such as recovering artifacts, repairing walls, and stabilizing the ruin itself. Pinkley left this job to serve one term as state senator but was prevailed upon to return as superintendent in 1918, remaining until his death in 1940. He was a founding member of the Florence chapter of the Masonic Order. (Courtesy National Park Service.)

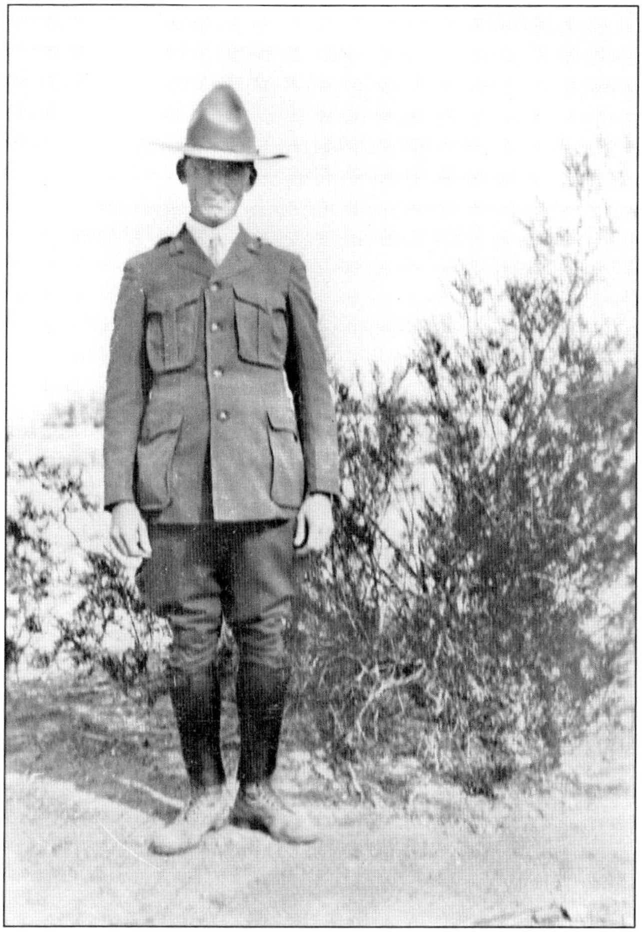

Here John and Martha White of Florence visit with the Pinkleys' daughter Nancy (right) at the ruin. Pinkley lived with his wife, Edna, in a tent on the grounds until finally building a home himself. On his own initiative, he constructed a few shelves and arranged artifacts in a corner of the Great House itself as a museum.

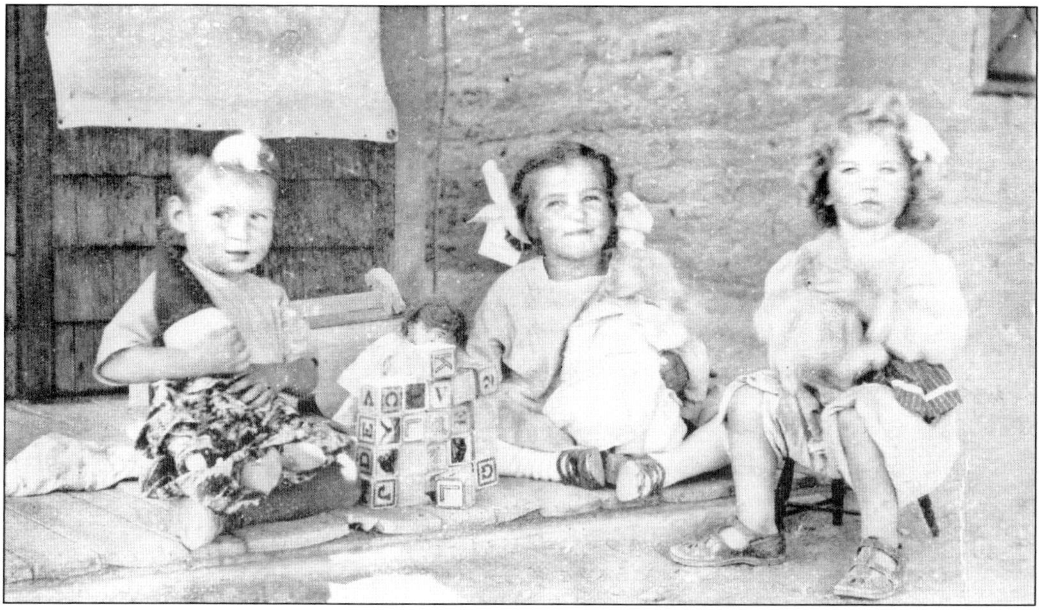

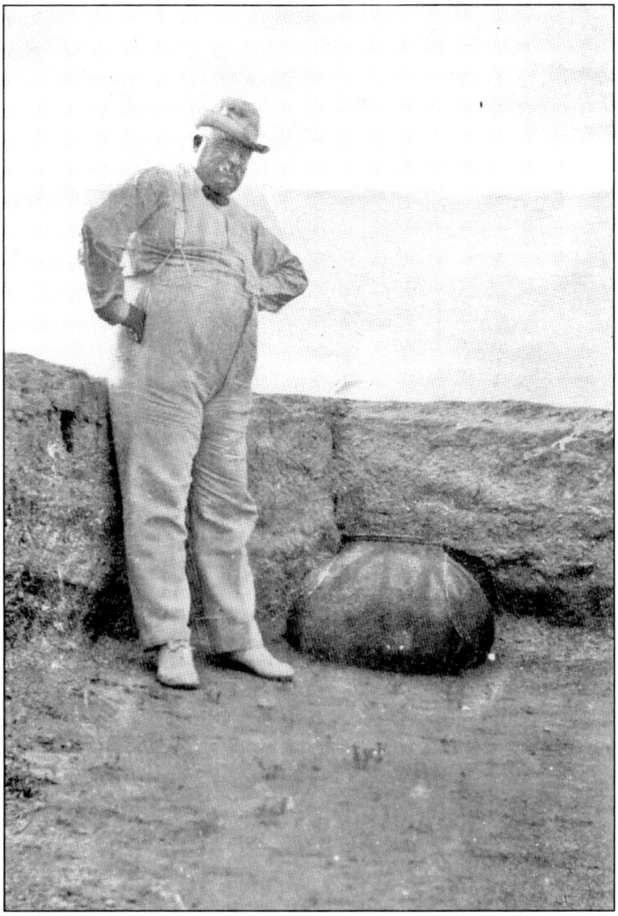

Gov. George Wylie Paul Hunt was the first and longest-serving governor of the new state of Arizona, having been elected seven times. He visited Florence while on numerous campaign trips. Here Governor Hunt looks at a Hohokam pot at the Casa Grande Ruins in 1914.

In 1932, Frederick Law Olmstead Jr., the son of the designer of New York City's Central Park, designed the steel roof that today protects the Casa Grande from the elements. The roof allows a clearer view of the ruins than the 1903 roof and is now an artifact in its own right. Interestingly the color used to paint the roof and its supports is a special shade named Ruins Beige.

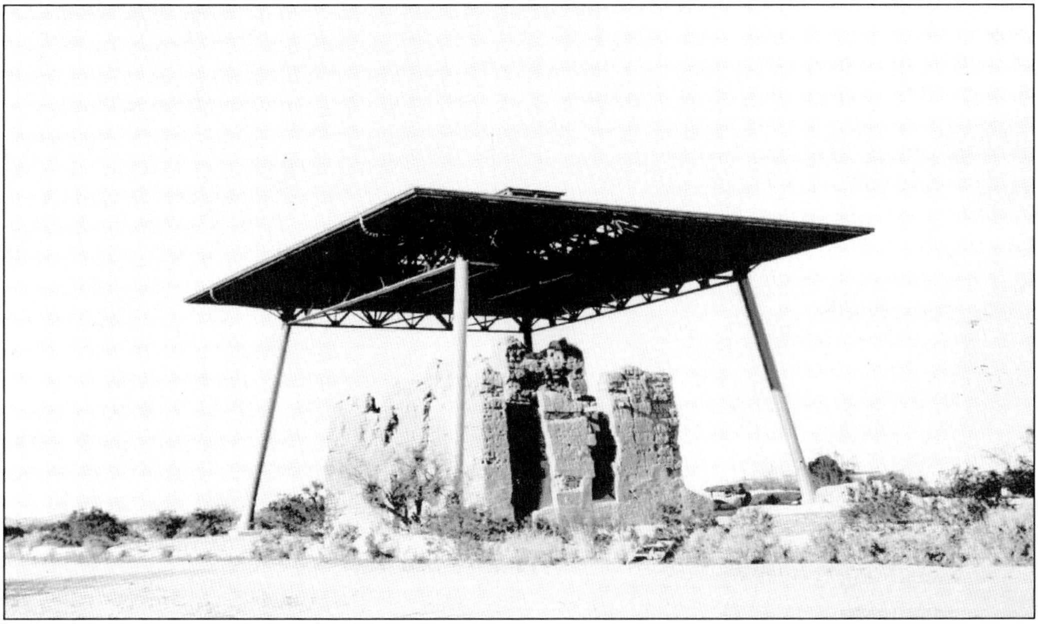

Two

A Town Is Built

According to the memoirs of early town official Richard Elihu Sloan, his newly arrived wife wrote her mother in the East that she "had gone to housekeeping in a 'mud' house!" A relative sent to Florence reported that the house was a "two-story adobe structure, quite the best in the place."

Charles Debrille Poston was one of the Florence pioneers who made his mark on the larger stage of Arizona and the country. Florence's founding fathers were entrepreneurs or workers with special skills such as engineering, blacksmithing, and carpentry. Levi Ruggles, Joseph Collingwood, William Clarke, Jean Baptiste Michea, Daniel Clinton Stevens, and Peter Rainsford Brady are all remembered and even have descendants still living nearby today.

To be the up-to-date community Florence wanted to be, the following had to be accomplished: a courthouse constructed for the newly established Pinal County, schools built, and a dependable water supply secured. In 1878, the first courthouse was built on the corner of Fifth (now Ruggles) and Main Streets. In 1872, the Arizona legislature established a system of public schools in the territory. At first, there were separate schools for boys and girls, but when the roof of the boys' school collapsed, a new building accommodating both genders was constructed in 1885. Canal companies were started for securing water. Often they dug canals where the Hohokam Indians had established canals centuries earlier.

Florence was growing, and because of a silver strike in the mountains east of town, it was becoming a boomtown. However, it could have all been lost because of one man: James Addison Reavis, the "Baron of Arizona." Through his diligent effort and outstanding ability as a forger, Reavis laid claim to much of central Arizona, from west of Phoenix to the Silver City, New Mexico, border. He almost succeeded in defrauding all the land and mine owners in the Florence area, along with the railroad to the west. With help from a Florence citizen, the fraud was discovered. Although shocking in the 19th century, the "Reavis Affair" has now faded from memory.

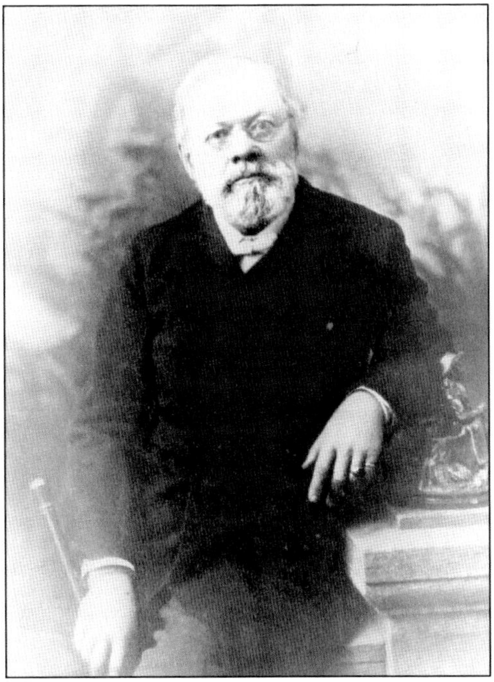

Charles Debrille Poston is known as the "Father of Arizona" for convincing Congress to separate Arizona from New Mexico Territory. He had explored the Gadsden Purchase of 1854 and could envision cities, prosperous mines, and ranches where others saw desolate deserts and rough mountains filled with marauding Apache Indians. Later he developed a silver mine, wrote books and poetry, served as a government agent, traveled worldwide, and became Arizona's first territorial congressman. (Courtesy Arizona Historical Society, No. 1777.)

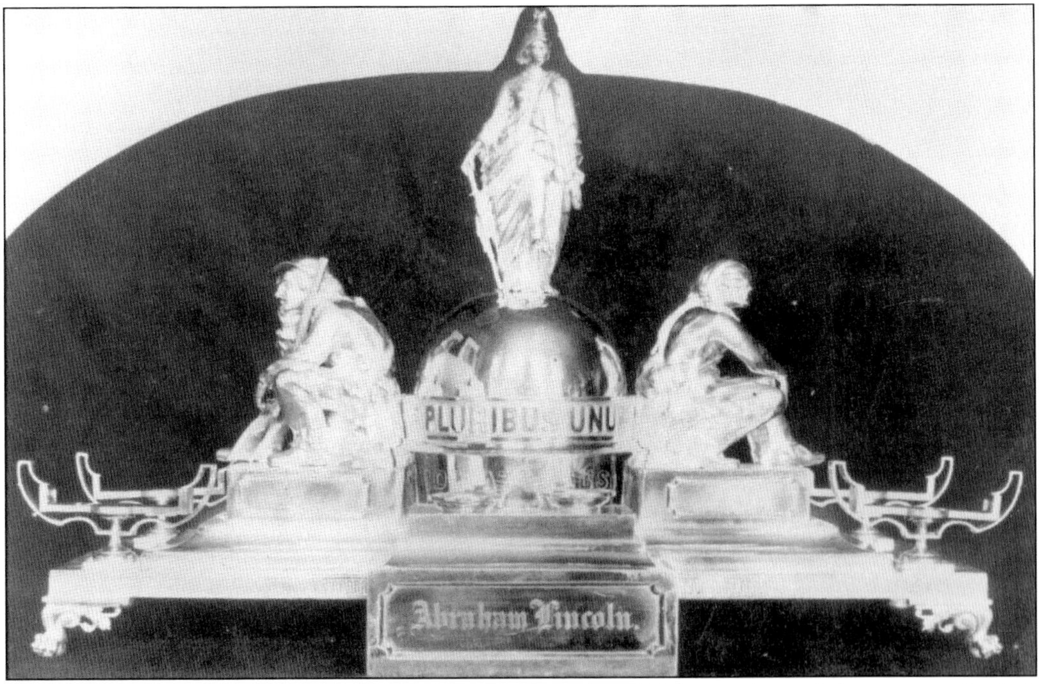

Poston presented Pres. Abraham Lincoln with this silver Tiffany inkstand for signing the bill creating Arizona Territory on February 24, 1863. Along with the congressmen he had lobbied, Poston met with Lincoln. He told Lincoln of Arizona's mineral wealth—much-needed for the Civil War effort. When the bill passed, the lame duck politicians divided up positions in the new territory as they celebrated with an oyster supper. (Courtesy Arizona Historical Society, No. 1944.)

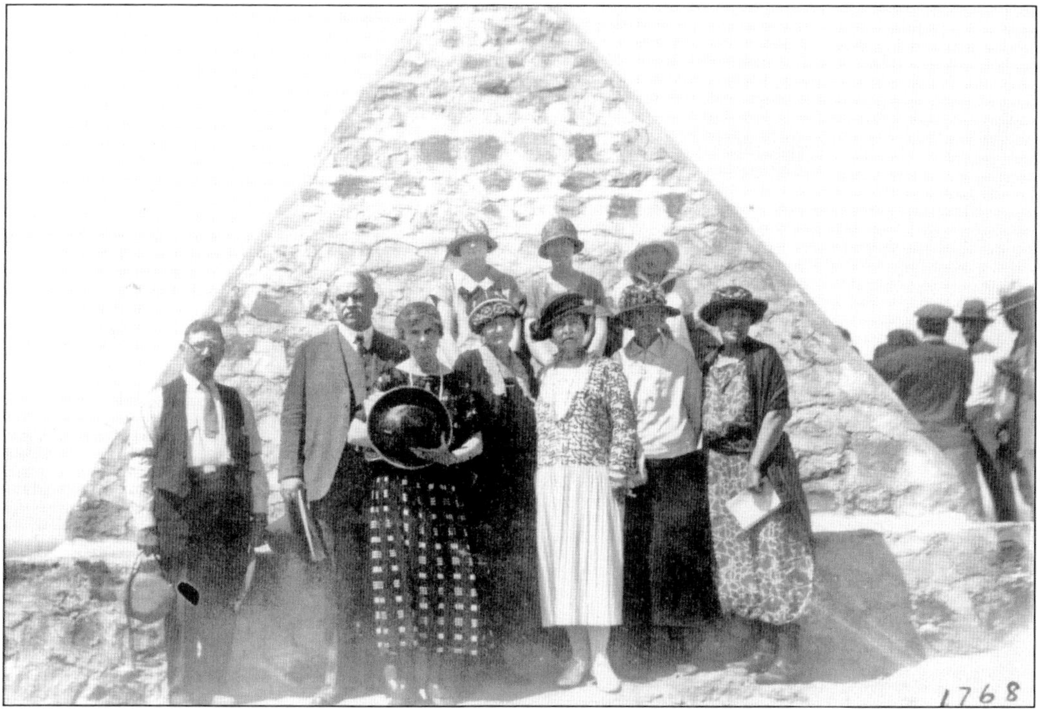

Poston's final resting place, under a stone pyramid atop the butte near Florence now named after him, was dedicated on April 24, 1925, thirteen years after his death. As a follower of Zoroastrianism, while a land agent in Florence he imagined building a temple to the sun on that butte. At left is C. M. Clark, president of the Arizona Pioneers Association, of which Poston was a founder. (Courtesy Arizona Historical Society, No. 1768.)

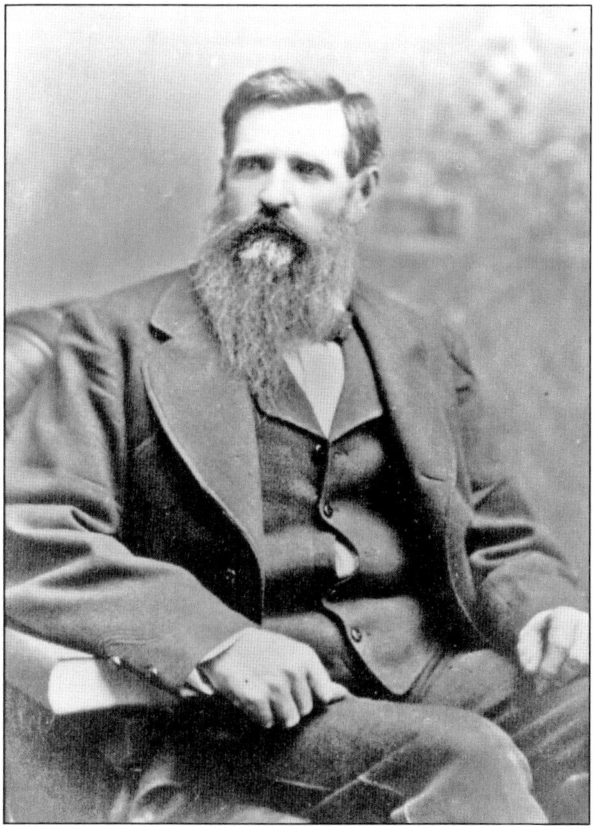

In 1857, Granville Henderson Oury came to Arizona, where he became an attorney, mine owner, judge, and statesman. A staunch Confederate, he represented the territory in the Confederate Congress and even joined the Army of the Confederacy. Later pledging allegiance to the United States, he became Arizona Territory's representative to the U.S. Congress. Around 1884, he moved to Florence, where his house still stands. He died in 1896. (Courtesy Arizona Historical Society, No. 14310.)

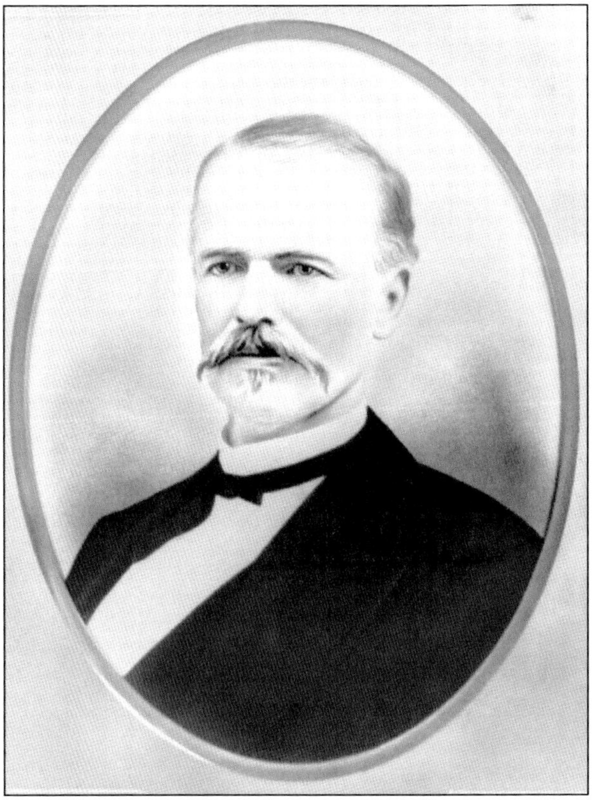

Levi Ruggles arrived in the area in 1866 as an Indian agent. Eager to pursue his vision of a town on the Gila River, he purchased land and laid out a town plan known for unique 125-square-foot plots and 60-foot-wide streets. He held many careers, including that of a politician, merchant, land developer, federal land agent, and justice of the peace. Ruggles is acknowledged as Florence's founder. (Courtesy Arizona Historical Society, No. 26261.)

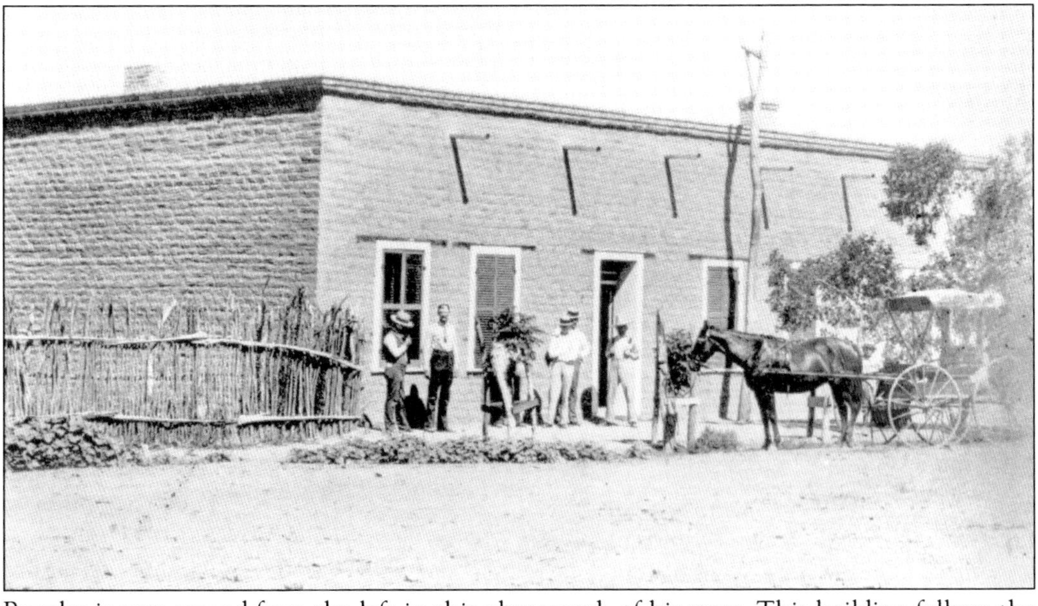

Ruggles is seen second from the left in this photograph of his store. This building follows the Sonoran tradition of architecture and is made of thick adobe brick. Notice the canales jutting out from the roof to drain rainwater, the ocotillo fencing, and the irrigation ditch with planted trees. Utilizing materials from the desert, this style of architecture was designed to survive the desert climate. (Courtesy Arizona Historical Society, No. 44664.)

Joseph Collingwood traveled to town about 1866 from his hometown of Florence, Ohio. Here he established a branch of the Tucson-based Edward Nye Fish concern and then bought the business. Fish extended credit to local Mexican farmers, who then provided crops for his federal contract obligations. Historians regard this endeavor as the basis for the economic foundation of Florence. Collingwood died in 1882, leaving his wife, Elena Barragán, and three young daughters. (Courtesy Arizona Historical Society, No. 23802.)

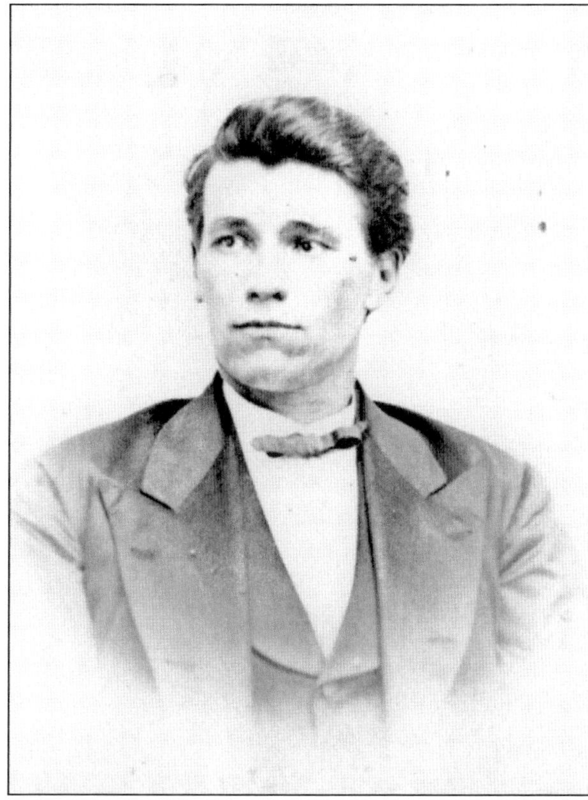

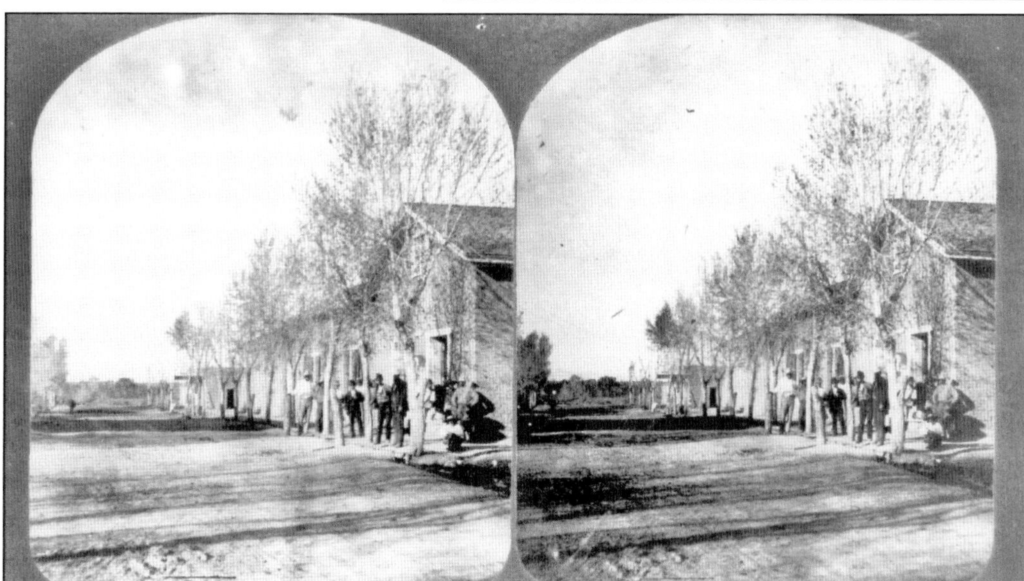

This George Rothrock stereoscope, taken in 1874, shows the second E. N. Fish store. Fish, like many Tucson merchants, realized the economic potential of boomtown Florence and set up a branch store. Wells Fargo had an office in the building and a yard for the wagons behind. Joseph Collingwood managed and eventually bought full interest in the store. The Collingwood Store was a hub of supplies and activity for the town. (Courtesy Arizona Historical Society, No. 57249.)

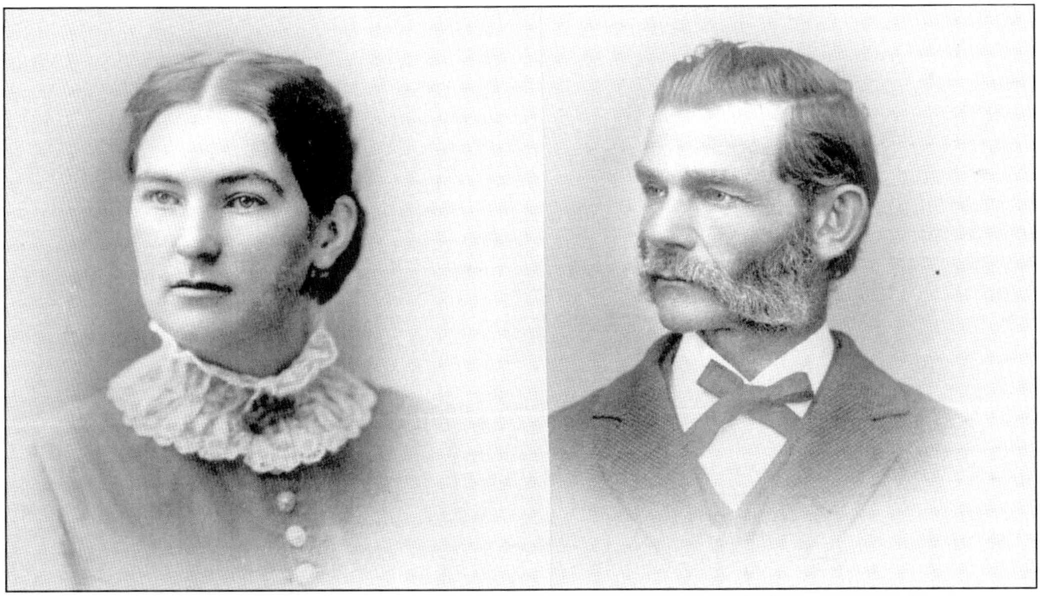

William Clarke and his wife, Ella, are pictured here in portraits. Clarke came to Arizona as a surveyor but, like so many new settlers, turned to mining. Soon he divided his time between Florence and the Silver King Mine, where he worked as an engineer. Their son Abraham Lincoln Clarke died in 1915. Ella was appointed postmaster in 1910 and served 15 years. William died in 1925 and his wife in 1940.

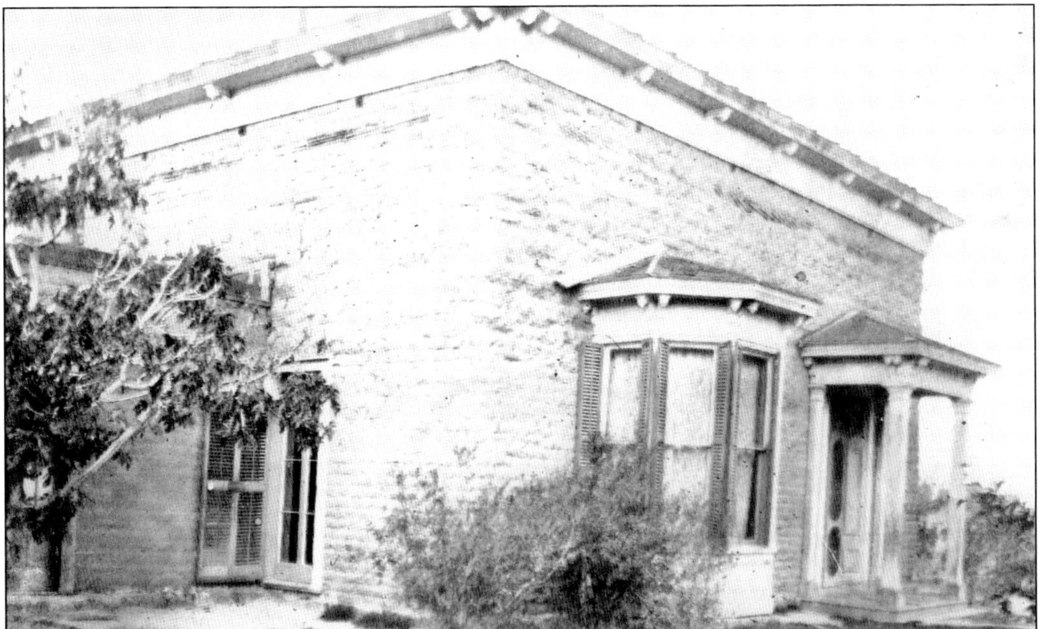

The 1884 William Clarke house was built as a wedding present for Ella. The home became a cultural center of town, hosting concerts, recitals, tea parties, and ice cream socials. Ella taught piano on an imported square grand piano. A crawl space in the attic, reachable only by ladder, provided a hiding place during Apache raids. The Indian Wars ended after Geronimo's capture in 1886.

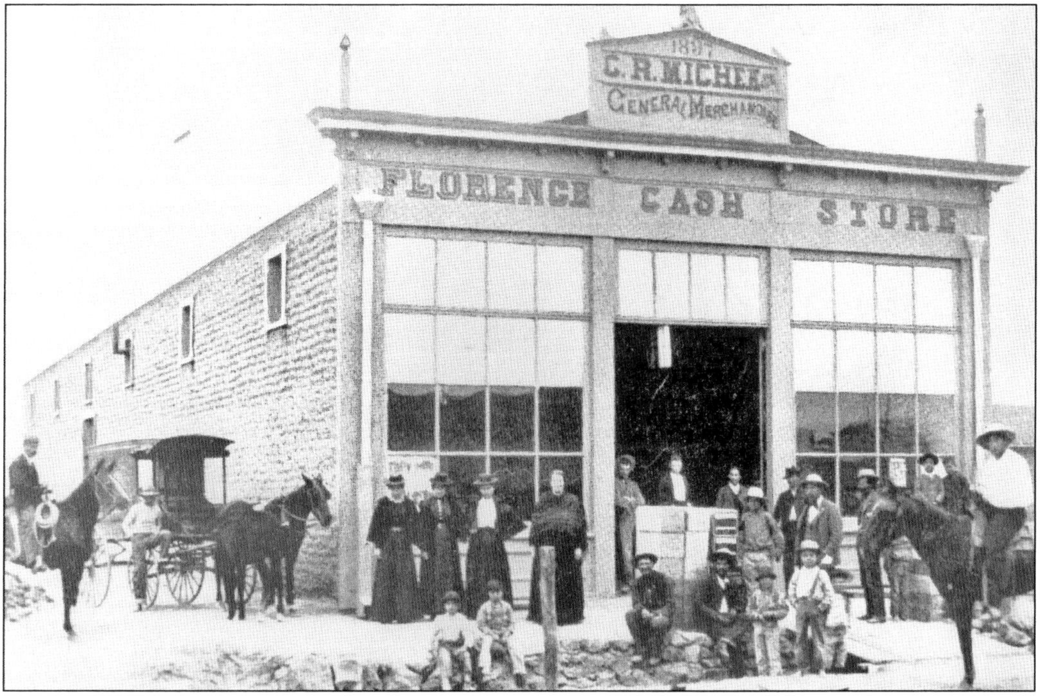

This building housed many different mercantile stores over the years. Here widow Carmen Robles Michea stands to the left of the entrance of her C. R. Michea Florence Cash Store in 1897. Carmen was a businesswoman and homemaker. Her husband, Jean Baptiste Michea, had been a French soldier with Emperor Maximilian in Mexico. He came to Florence after the French were defeated and started the Lone Star Store at another location.

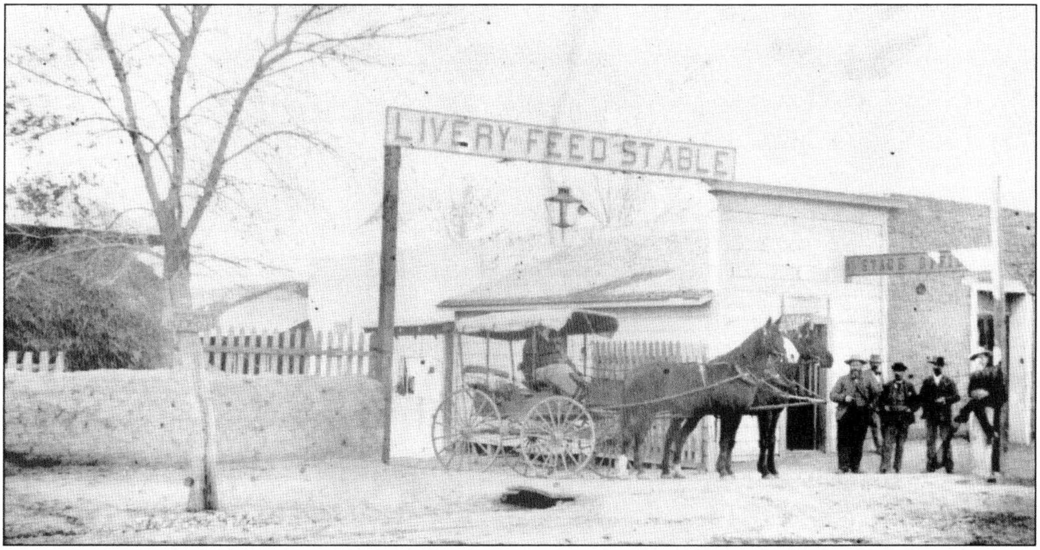

Daniel Clinton Stevens poses outside his livery stable and stage business on Main Street. After serving for the Union in the Civil War, he left his home state of Ohio for the West. For decades, he was widely known for his involvement in stage lines. In Florence, he held public offices and other business interests. A widower himself, Stevens married the wealthy widow Doña Elena Barragán Collingwood de Bamrick. (Courtesy Arizona Historical Society, No. 721.)

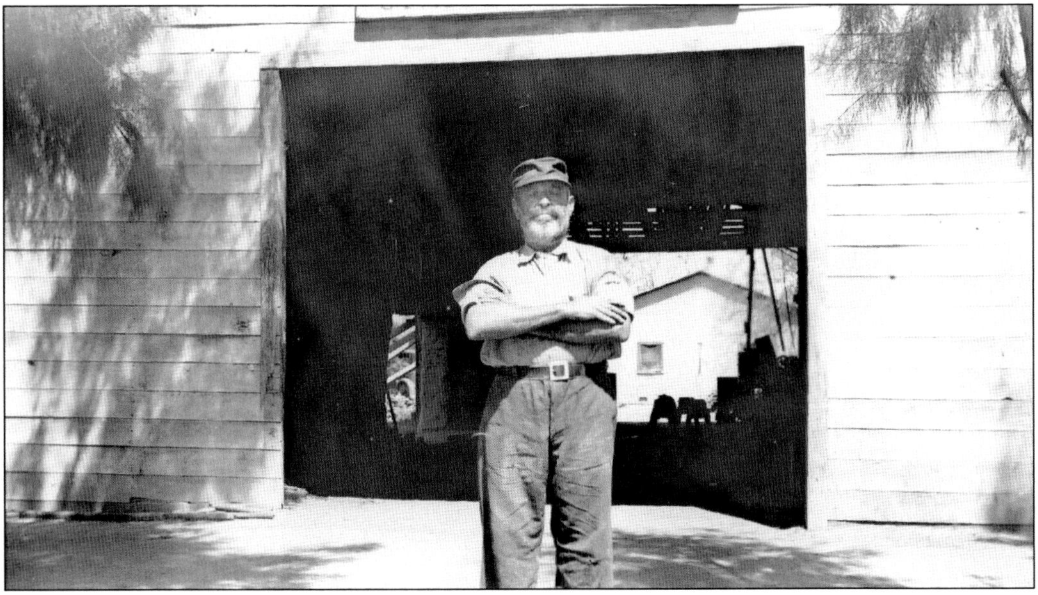

Alex Gay Sr. emigrated from Switzerland in 1864. In 1874, he married Encarnación González in Florence. His son Alex Gay Jr., pictured here, operated a blacksmith shop from 1892 to 1952. A genius with metal, Alex could fabricate just about anything needed by the town. Many humorous stories are told about this colorful and inventive character.

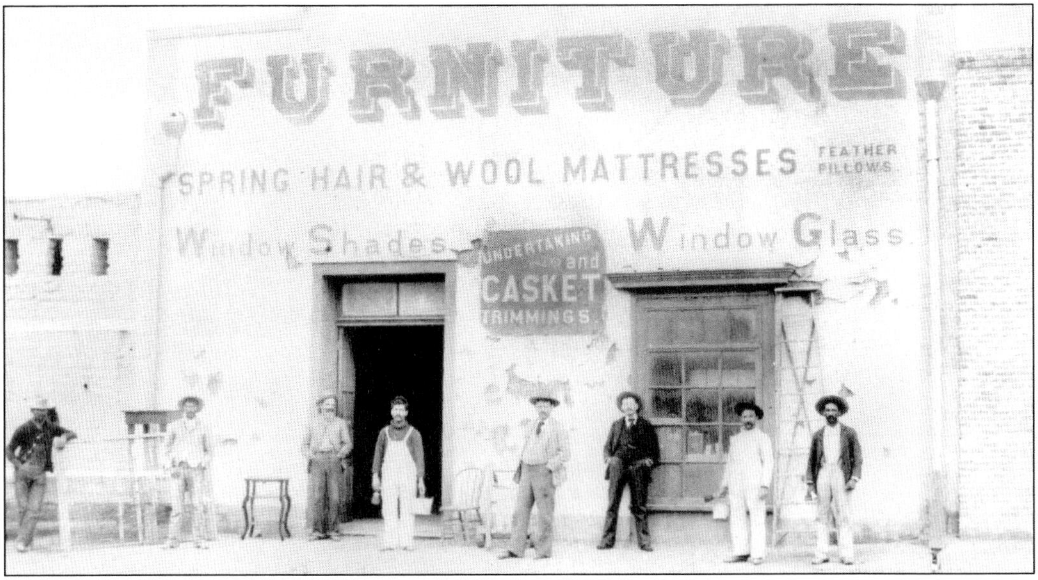

New Yorker Charles Tillman came to Florence in 1881 after working as a miner and carpenter in California and New Mexico. These unidentified men stand outside his shop at Ninth and Bailey Streets. His carpentry skills were also used to build caskets advertised as "made to order and trimmed." Tillman married schoolteacher Flora Nesbitt, built a home on Willow Street, and became the first in town to have an indoor bathroom. (Courtesy Arizona Historical Society, No. 715.)

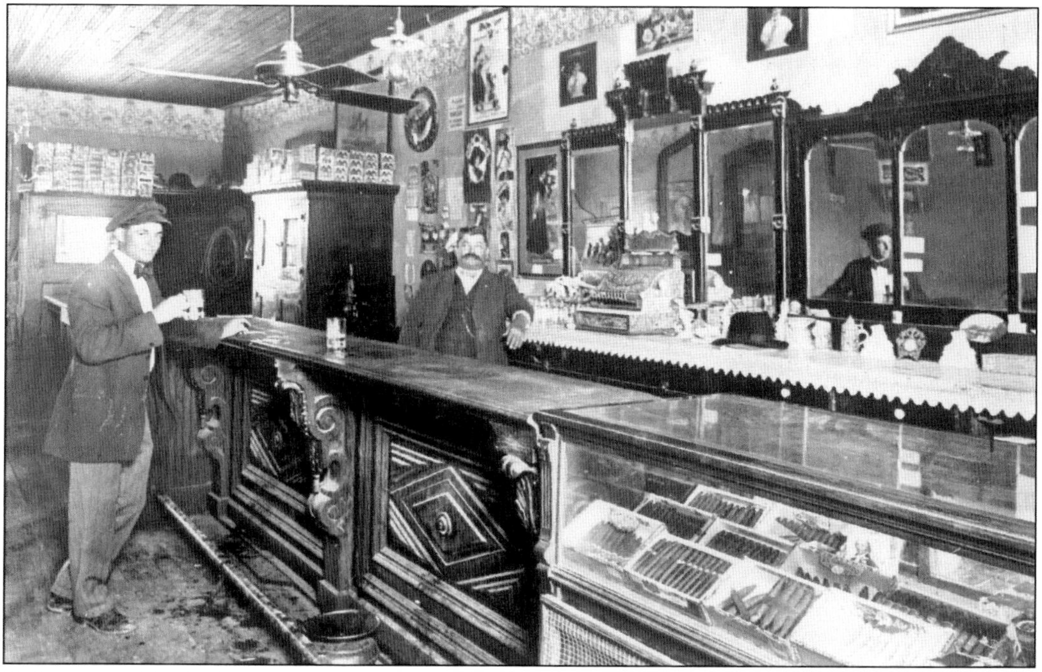

This unidentified saloon is typical of many drinking establishments of early Florence. Fine spirits, imported cigars, and games of chance were available here. In 1888, the town issued 28 liquor licenses, which were quite expensive to acquire. In 1891, William Charles Truman paid $30 for a gambling license and $570 for a liquor license. Peter Will's brewery offered the finest beer in the territory.

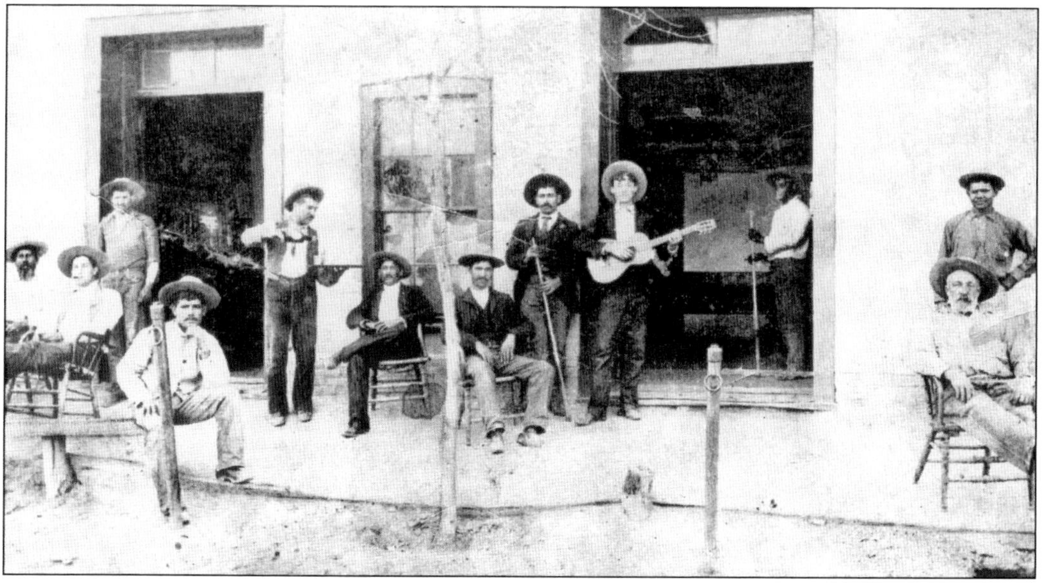

Shown in this 1872 photograph of La Paloma Cantina are, from left to right, Jesús López, Francisco Contreras, Juan Michea, Victoriano López, Pete Avenente, David Encinas, Joe López, Simón Syrian, Nick Avenente (with guitar), Chris Cano, Juan Avenente Sr. (seated), and Sam Bostick. Juan Avenente Sr. was the proprietor of this gathering spot where one could play pool, have a cool drink, and hear a little music.

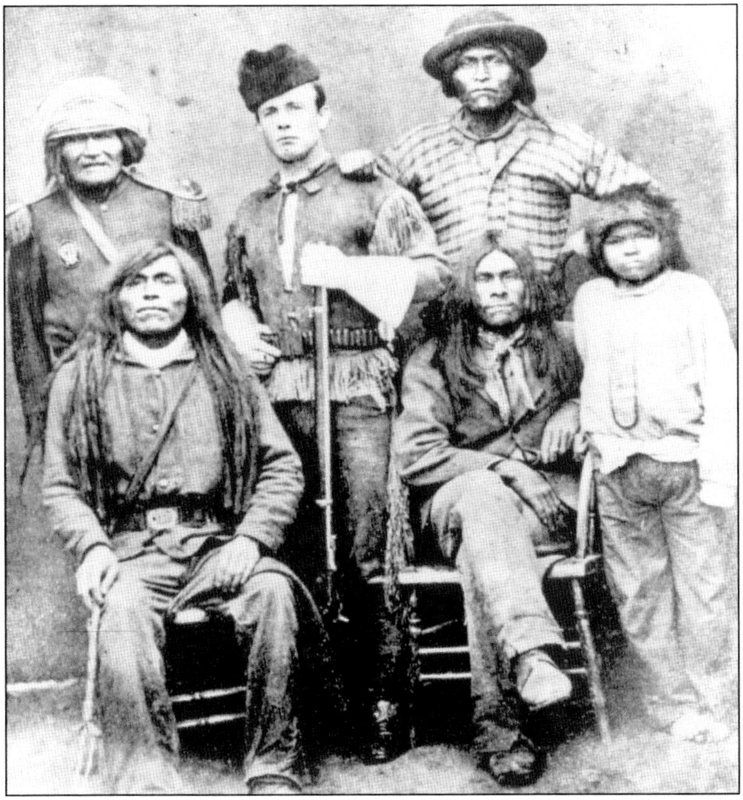

John P. Clum, wearing a fur hat, stands with Apache Indians. While serving as Indian agent at San Carlos, he resigned over his superior's resistance to his policy of Native American self-policing and government. He then came to Florence and studied law. Admitted to the bar in 1877, he preferred journalism and started newspapers in both Florence and Tombstone. While mayor in Tombstone, Clum befriended Wyatt Earp. His Florence home still stands. (Courtesy Arizona Historical Society, No. 982.)

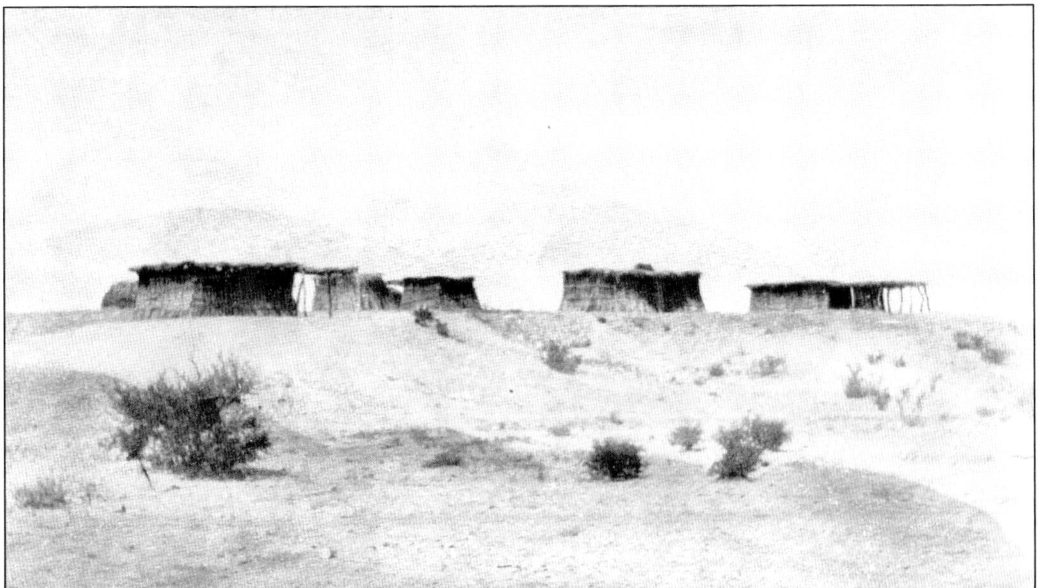

The Pima Indians lived in villages and farmed along the Gila River. Their homes were made of alternating layers of saguaro ribs and mud. A *ramada*, or arbor, was situated outside their doors for cool shade and outdoor cooking. The Pima were on friendly terms with the Anglos and would band together against their common enemy, the Apache.

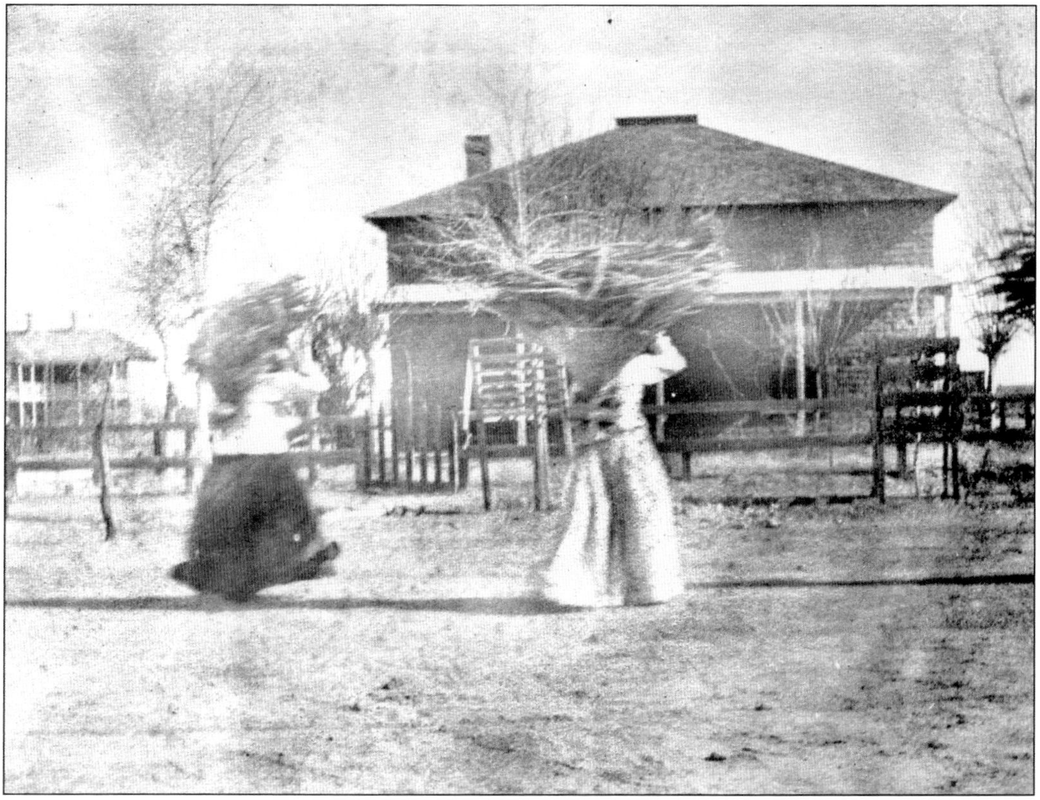

Pima Indians frequently came into Florence to sell their wares. Recently arrived women from the East, frightened at the sight, grabbed their children and hurried indoors. Soon they quelled their fears and purchased clay water jugs (*ollas*), baskets, and firewood from the Pima women.

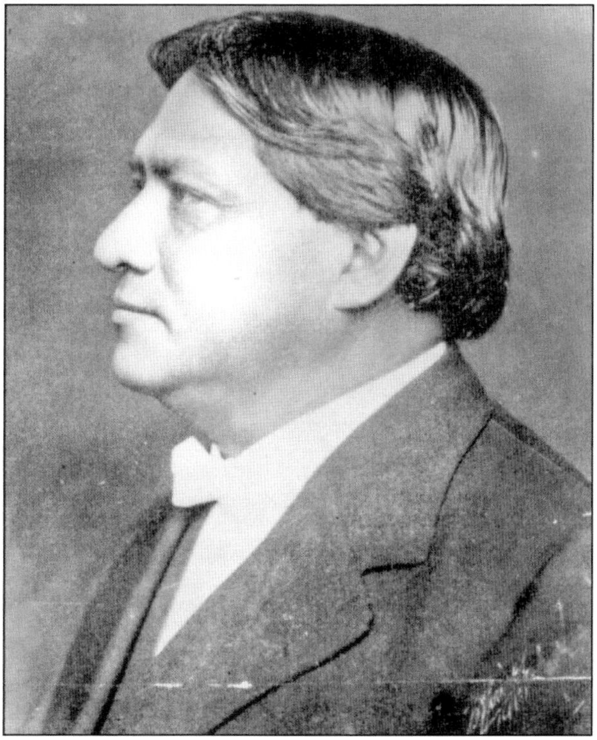

Carlos Montezuma was born in 1866 as Wassaja, a Yavapai Indian. When the Pima raided his tribe and sold Wassaja near Florence, photographer Carlos Gentile took pity and bought him for $30 silver. He changed his name and took him East to be educated. Carlos Montezuma became a famous Chicago physician but always championed Native American rights. In 1923, he died of tuberculosis in Arizona among his people. (Courtesy Arizona Historical Society, No. 53644.)

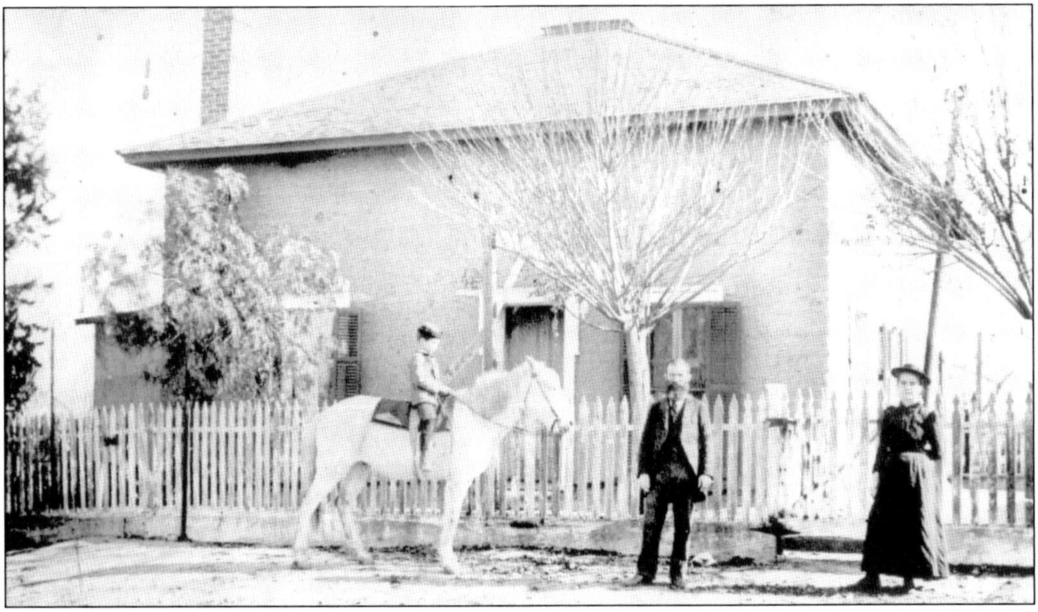

Pinal County treasurer Emerson O. Stratton is pictured with his children Edith and Elmer in 1897. Edith recalled that Florence boys would serenade young ladies for amusement. This ended for her when she compared their singing to a pack of coyotes. In 1925, Edith Stratton Kitt joined the Arizona Pioneers Historical Society and for the next 22 years organized and compiled Arizona history for what became the Arizona Historical Society. (Courtesy Arizona Historical Society, No. 760.)

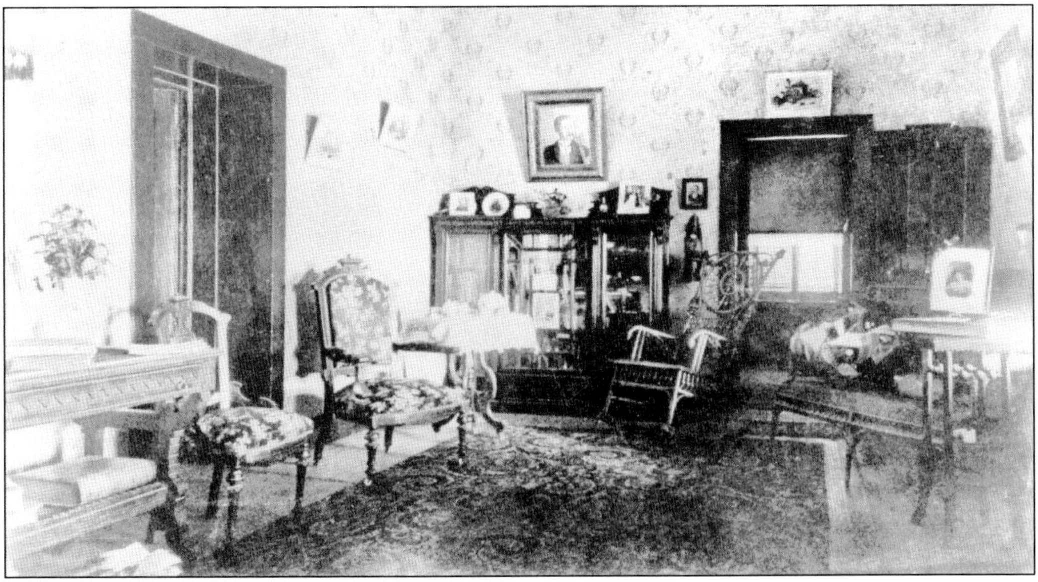

The Fletcher Doan residence was a large house called Casa Loma with palm trees lining the entrance. The living room interior shows the elegance and refinement of a wealthy Victorian home. Doan served as the county district attorney and later as the supreme court judge of the Second Federal District. He traveled between Florence, Tombstone, Phoenix, and Solomonville to hold court. In 1903, the family moved to Tombstone, where Doan practiced law. (Courtesy Arizona Historical Society, No. 28740.)

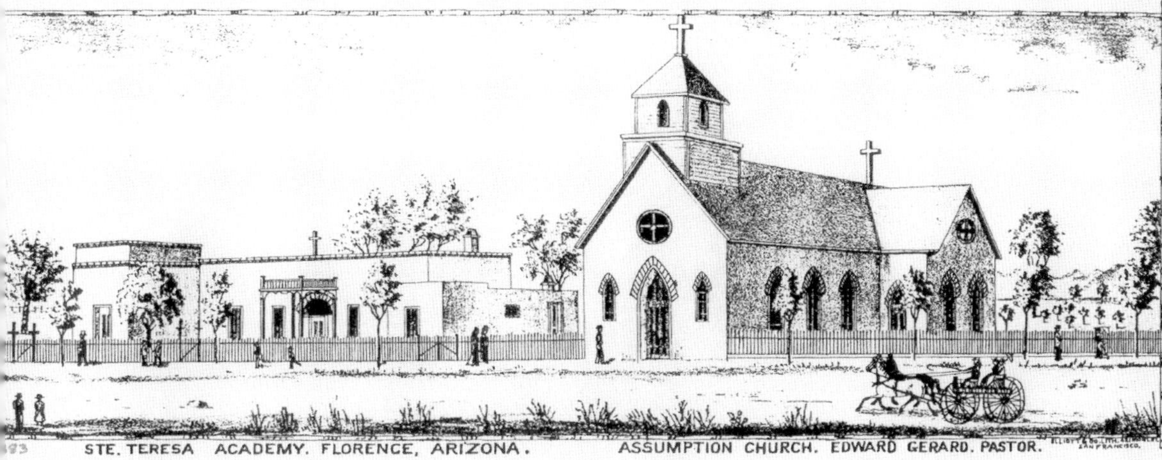

On August 25, 1870, Fr. André Eschallier contracted for a "church lot" of 600 square feet at the center of town. By December, the 60-by-22-foot Capilla de la Gila, "Chapel of the Gila," was completed (far left portion). St. Teresa Academy, the schoolhouse addition to the chapel, was constructed in the mid-1870s, and the chapel was subsequently renamed Assumption of the Blessed Virgin Mary Catholic Church. Bishop Salpointe of Tucson presided over the blessing and administered the Stations of the Cross. Fr. Edouard Gérard, the second Florence priest, traveled to the Phoenix area and established the mission churches of Our Lady of Mount Carmel, Tempe, and Immaculate Heart of Mary, Phoenix, making Florence's Assumption Church the mother of those parishes. By 1882, the population increase necessitated the building of a larger Gothic-style adobe (right), which was consecrated by Bishop Salpointe in 1884. This structure burned down in 1893, and the original Chapel of the Gila was once again used for services. (This and the following two images are from *History of Arizona Territory with Illustrations 1884*, Wallace W. Elliott and Company, San Francisco.)

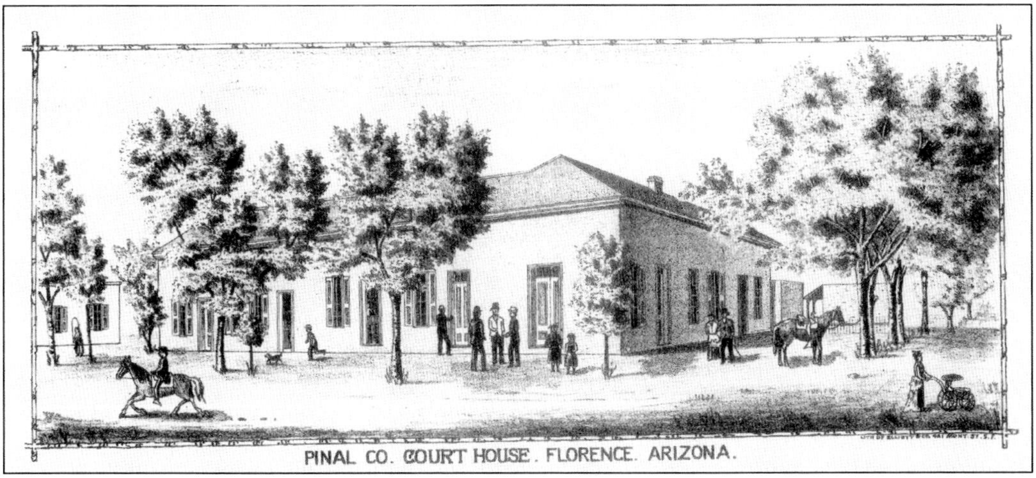

This 1884 lithograph of the first Pinal County Courthouse bears the caption, "The Court House is built of adobe, and although plain is commodious. It stands on the corner of a square surrounded by cottonwoods." The building served many functions, hosting trials, dances, church services, and an occasional lynching. Now McFarland State Historic Park, it hosts programs and events of a calmer nature.

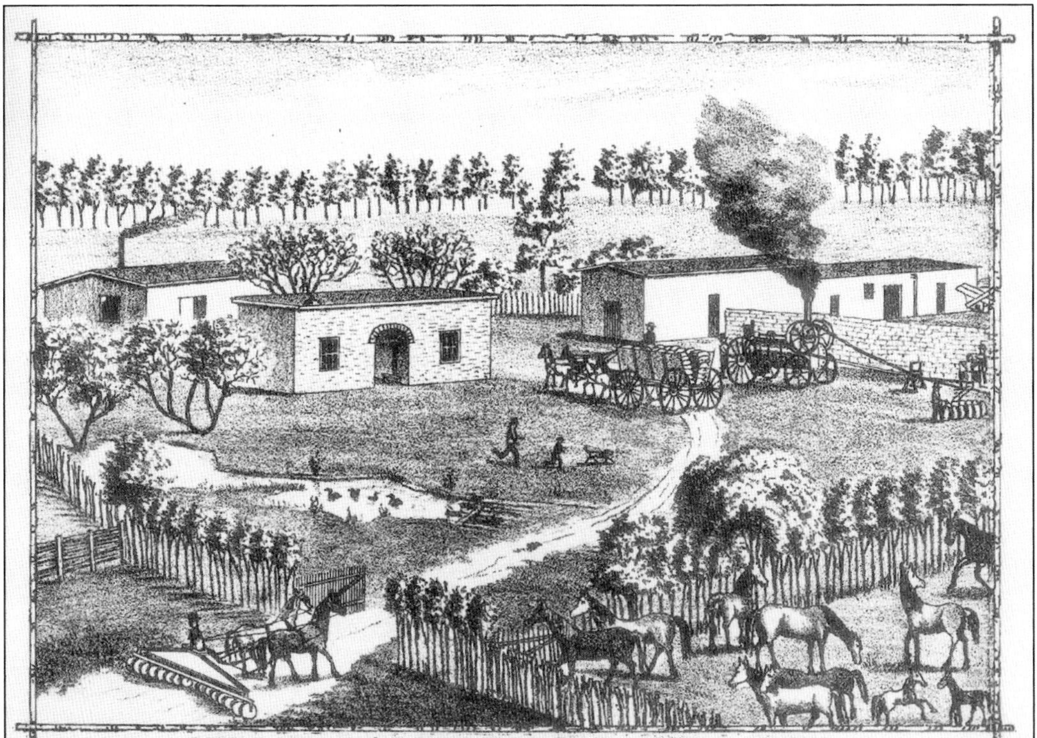

The Patrick Holland Ranch is depicted in this 1884 lithograph. The caption states, "Patrick Holland, one of the Board of Supervisors, has a large tract of land east of Florence. He employs quite a number of hands. He is a prominent citizen and deals quite largely in hogs in addition to farming, supplying some of the neighboring mining camps with pork." His Holland Ditch was an important early irrigation canal.

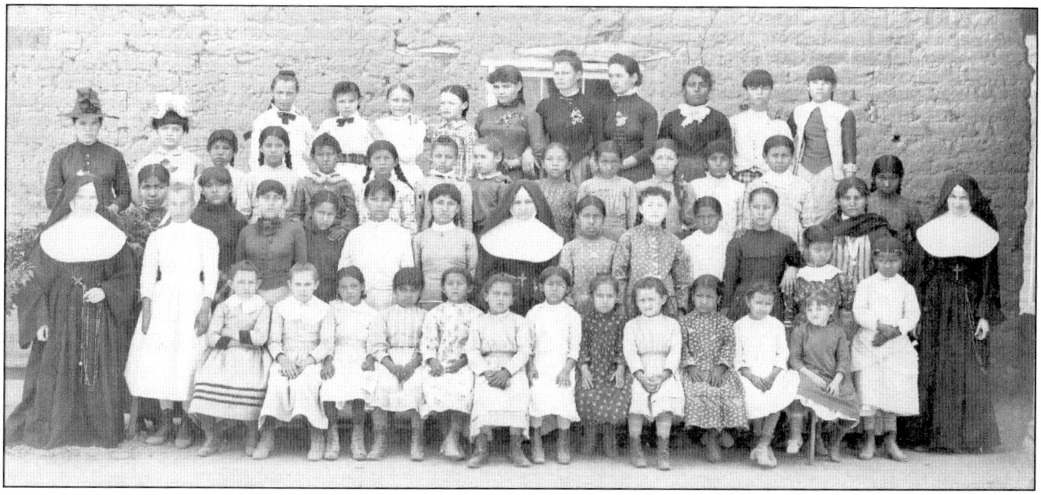

Fr. Edouard Gérard founded St. Teresa Academy, the Sisters School, in the 1870s with the St. Joseph Carondelet Sisters. Sister Agnes (center) and Sister Barbara (right) taught English, Spanish, religion, arithmetic, and music. Worn habits were woven into braided rugs for the dirt floor of their adobe convent. Clothing and shoes were shaken out each morning to dislodge scorpions and centipedes. Student tuition was paid in produce.

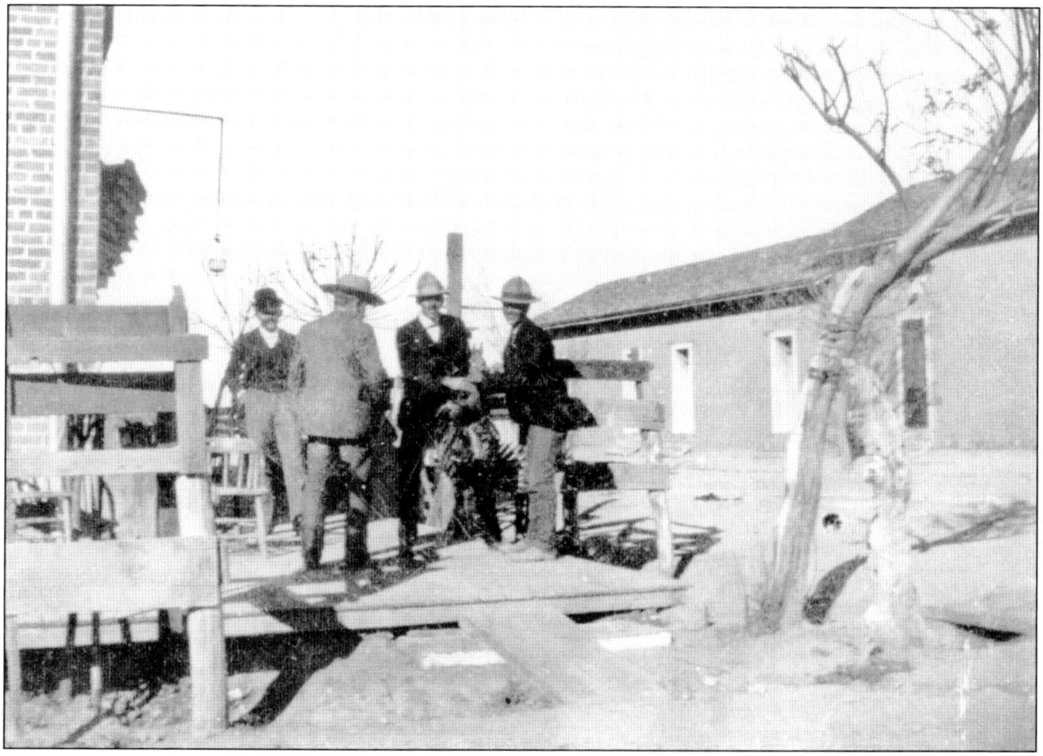

In this undated photograph, men gather at the corner of the Silver King Hotel. The wooden boardwalk is clearly visible over a small ditch. Canals crossed town and allowed water from the Gila River to irrigate the trees lining Florence streets from as early as the 1880s. Perhaps the forlorn tree here is evidence of the long, severe drought the area suffered from 1891 to 1904. (Courtesy Arizona Historical Society, No. 747.)

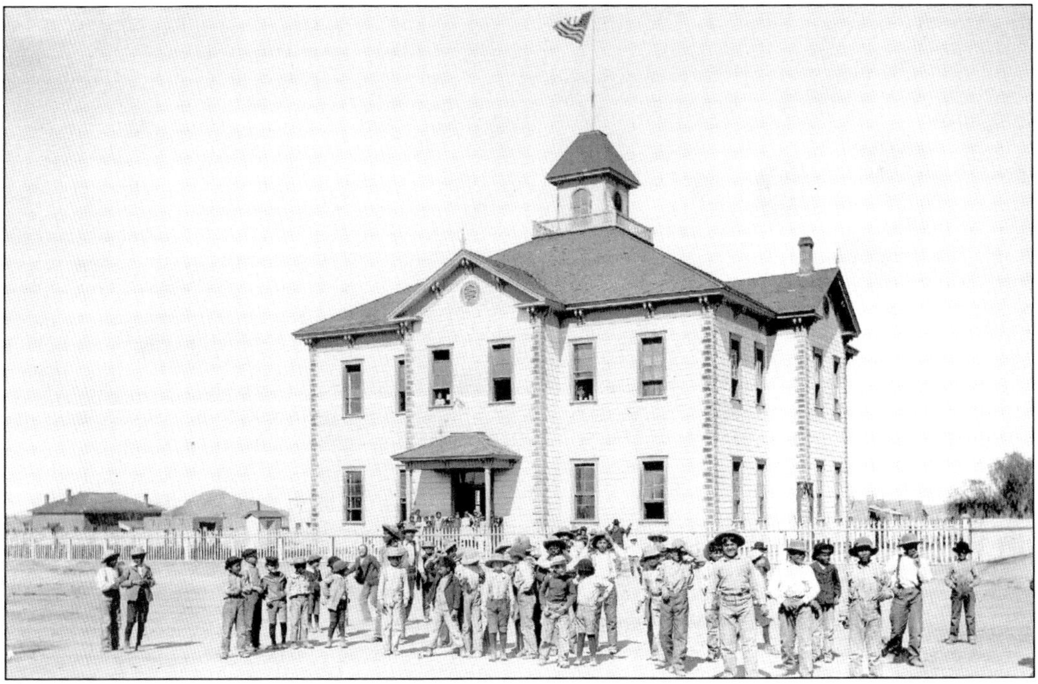

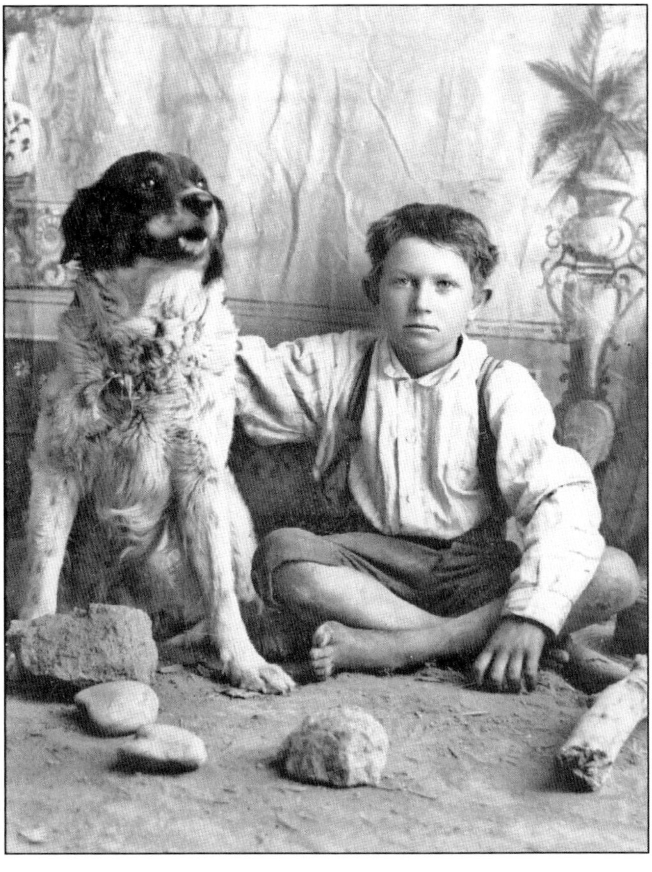

This 1885 American Victorian schoolhouse was built on the original public square of the town for $12,000. The wood frame structure was demolished in 1912 to build the next schoolhouse, which would later burn down. In front of the building, schoolboys illustrate typical antics for the camera as the girls watch from the windows and porch. As was the fashion of the day, all men, boys included, wore hats.

Young Roy Guild poses in front of a painted canvas with his pet spaniel. His father, William E. Guild, ran the telegraph line to the Silver King Mine. William's wife, Josaphine, was the sister of Ella Clarke. The couple purchased John Clum's house and became neighbors to the Clarkes. Josaphine Guild died when Roy was five and his older brother, Nott, was nine. William then married schoolteacher Emma Monk.

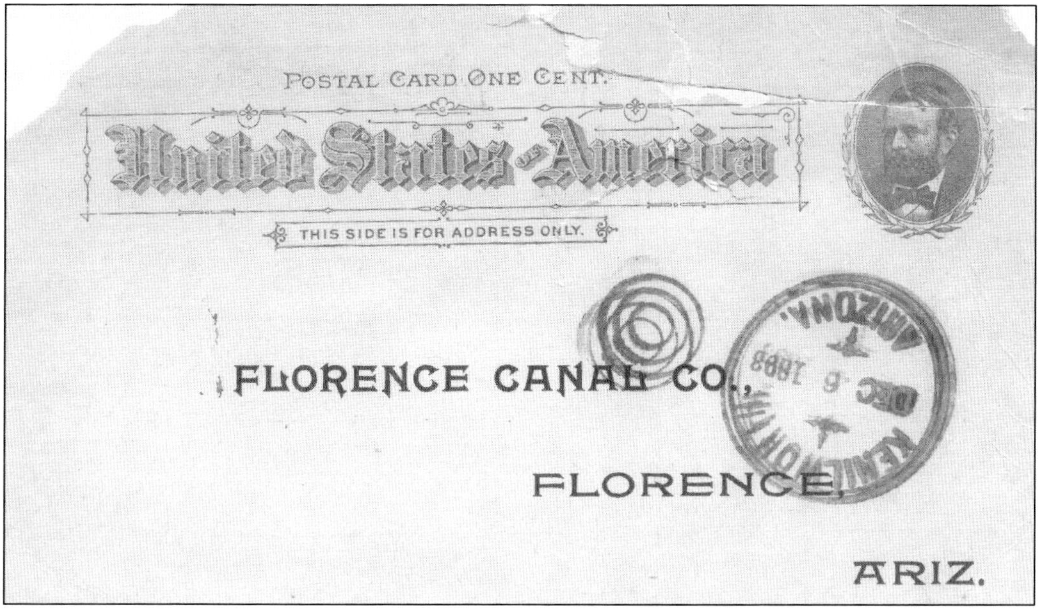

Above, this 1893 postcard water bill for irrigation echoes the 1884 description of Florence as "a pretty little town, with its shady cottonwoods and verdant alfalfa fields." Below, a *zanjero*, also called a ditch rider, was the water master of the canal, regulating and assessing the water flow to the fields for the canal companies. Troughs cut from the main canals helped irrigate trees, making Florence a welcomed oasis in the desert. Water rights issues and lack of maintenance eventually brought the companies' demise.

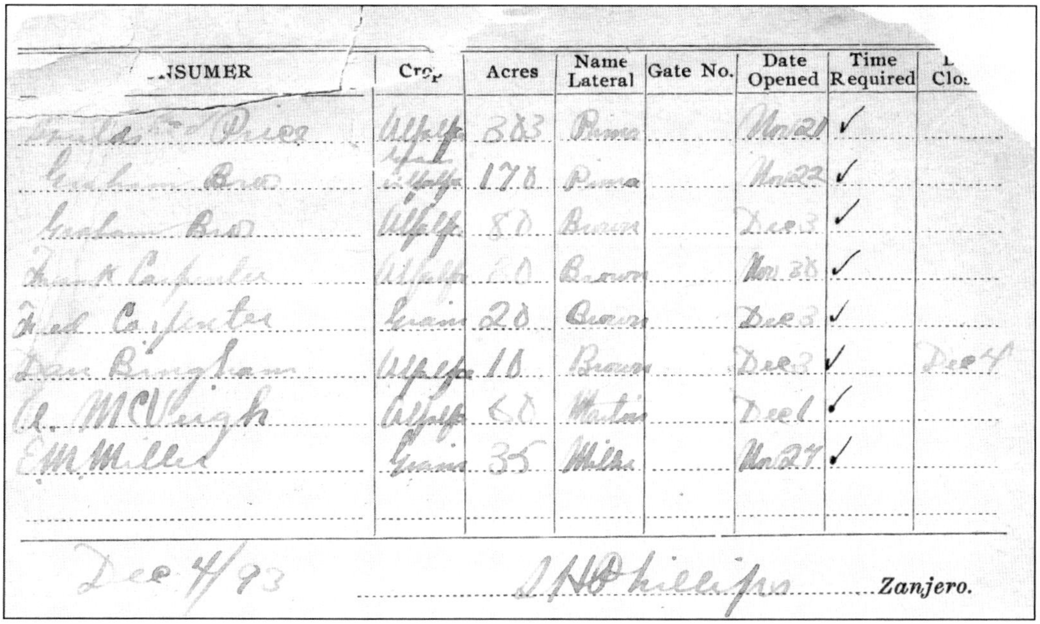

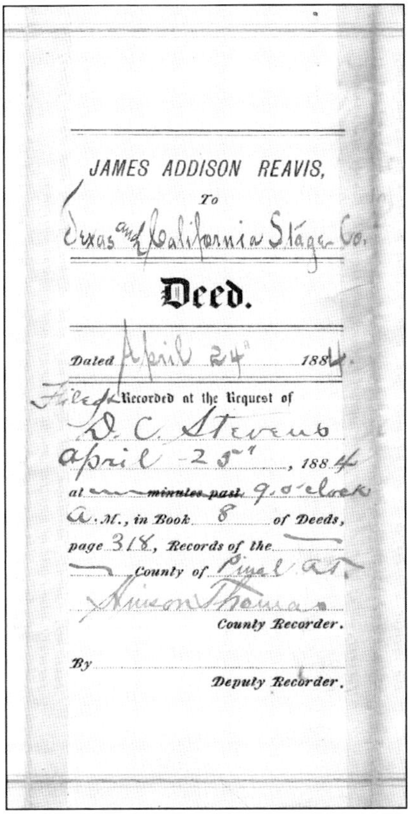
JAMES ADDISON REAVIS,

To

Texas and California Stage Co.

Deed.

Dated April 24 1884.

Filed Recorded at the Request of

D. C. Stevens

April 25th, 1884

at minutes past 9 o'clock

A. M., in Book 8 of Deeds,

page 318, Records of the

County of Pinal AT.

Anson Thomas

County Recorder.

By

Deputy Recorder.

James Addison Reavis, as the Baron of Arizona, claimed he owned 12 million acres of central Arizona reaching into New Mexico. He had forged documents to prove his old Spanish land grant. Frightened settlers and industrialists had to pay Reavis for being in his barony. Daniel C. Stevens received this deed (left) for his Texas and California Stage Company. He paid $25 for his own land, and Reavis kept the water rights. Below, Reavis's signature was accomplished with a flourish, but his life as royalty would soon end. The watermarks and printed typeface were discovered not to be of the 18th century. Reavis was sent to federal prison in Santa Fe.

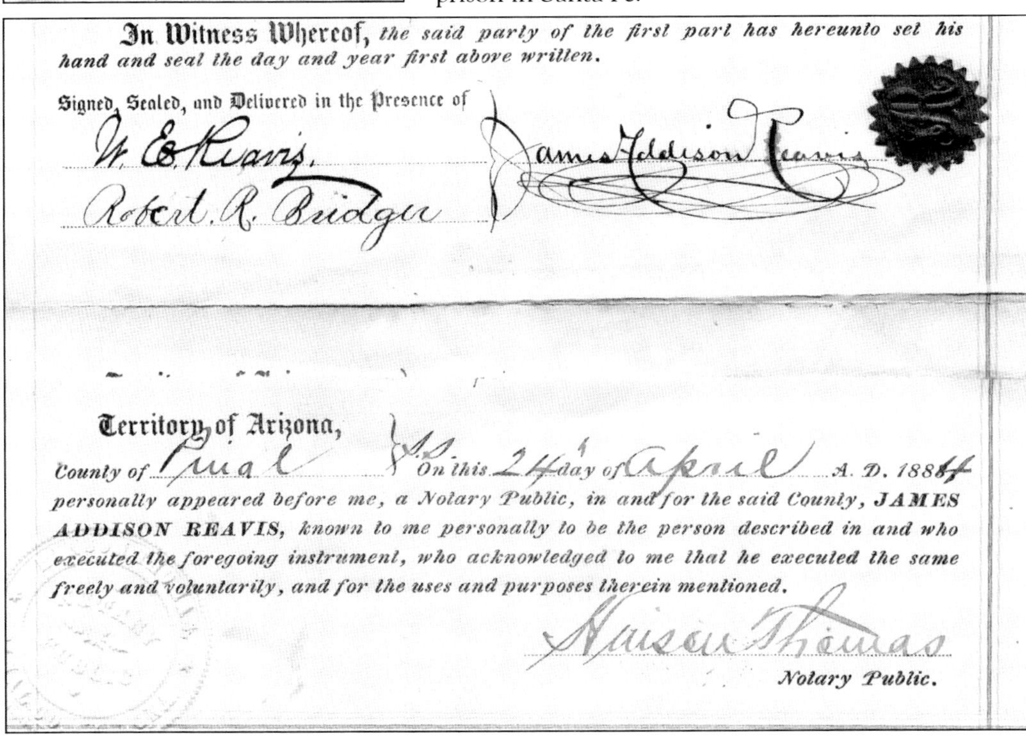
In Witness Whereof, *the said party of the first part has hereunto set his hand and seal the day and year first above written.*

Signed, Sealed, and Delivered in the Presence of

W. E. Reavis.

Robert R. Bridger

James Addison Reavis

Territory of Arizona,

County of Pinal } ss. *On this* 24th *day of* April *A. D.* 1884 *personally appeared before me, a Notary Public, in and for the said County,* **JAMES ADDISON REAVIS,** *known to me personally to be the person described in and who executed the foregoing instrument, who acknowledged to me that he executed the same freely and voluntarily, and for the uses and purposes therein mentioned.*

Anson Thomas

Notary Public.

Three

THE REAL WILD WEST

Combine cowboys, miners, lawmen, outlaws, wagons rattling through town in every direction, saloons, and gambling establishments, and you will have early Florence—a real Wild West town. Florence's dusty roads were busy. From the Silver King Mine 35 miles from town, wagons loaded with ore at first and then with shipments of silver bars and concentrates, headed to the railroad at Casa Grande. Stages with the payroll headed through Florence, then through the mountains to the mines. Over 100 mines peppered the mountains surrounding the town. Men came to Florence for a stake or a job, while miners already employed or working a claim traveled to town for supplies and recreation.

Florence's nearby ranches supplied the community with beef. Cowboys were hired to help with the endless work of running cattle. All came into town at one time or another to buy supplies and, just like the miners, enjoyed imbibing or gambling, or both, at one of the many saloons. With the transitory population of miners, prospectors, and cowboys added to Florence's entrepreneurs, there were bound to be some people who operated outside the law. The mountains, canyons, and caves surrounding town were great places for outlaws to hide. Aravaipa Canyon became notorious for renegade Apache and even murders, leading a corral in the canyon to be described as haunted. Pinal County had many stage robberies—especially on the road from Florence to Globe. Because the county courthouse and jail were in Florence, miscreants were brought to town for trial or safekeeping until they could be sent to the Arizona Territorial Prison in Yuma.

The 20th century did not diminish Florence's role as part of the lawlessness of the real Wild West. The haunted corral was part of news stories again, and Florence's location near major thoroughfares made it a mark for criminals on their way to somewhere else.

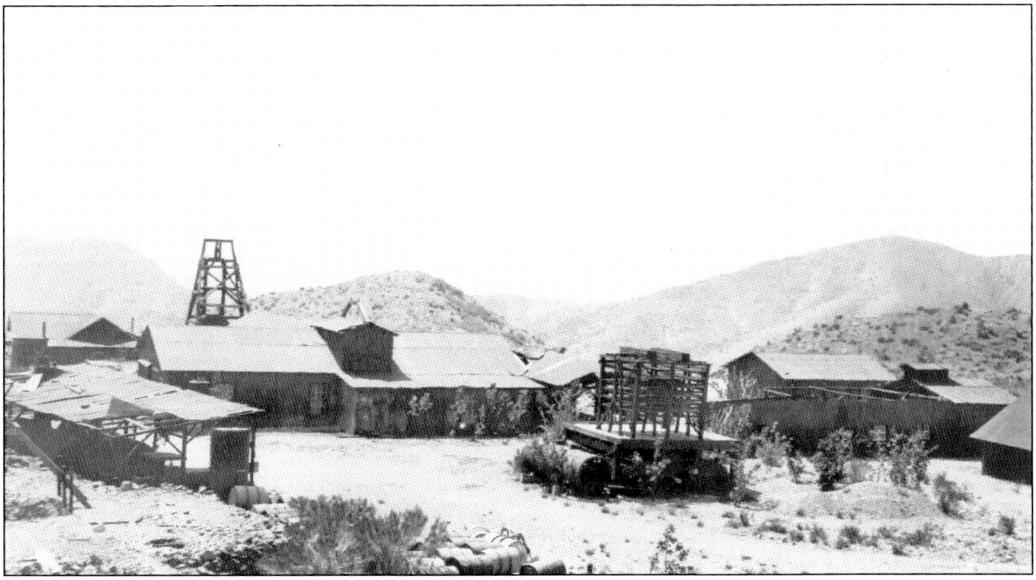

While building Stoneman's Grade in the mountains east of Florence in 1875, a soldier known only as Sullivan found rocks that proved to be silver ore. He told Florence citizen Charles Granderson Mason about his find. The intrigued Mason headed to the hills along with William Long, Benjamin Reagan, and Isaac Copeland and discovered what would become the Silver King Mine. A camp, also called Silver King, soon covered the mountainside.

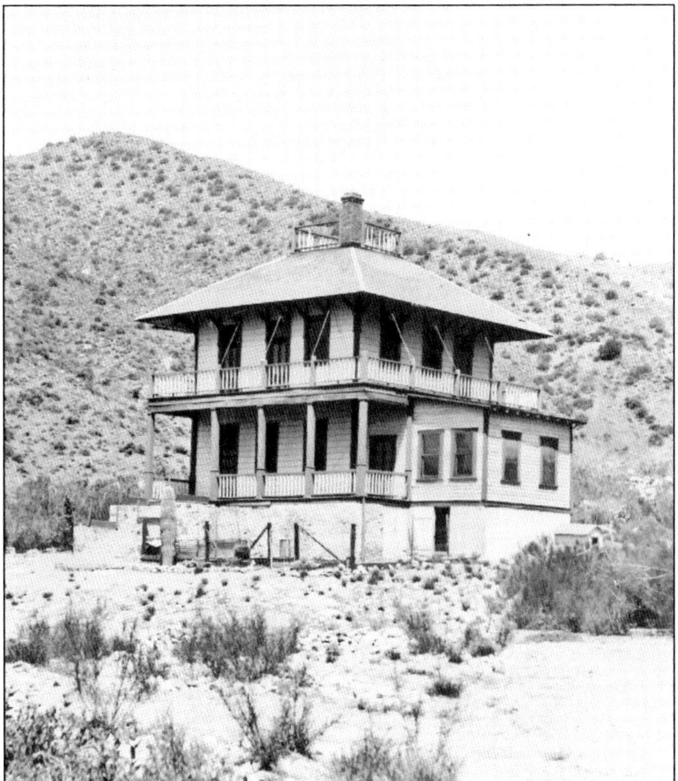

Businesses, including saloons and hotels, crowded the main street of Silver King Camp. This photograph shows the hotel reserved for the mine's visiting dignitaries. The town of Florence boomed at this time as well. Partners in the Silver King took advantage of this and diversified. They invested in dry goods stores, the smelter, and the Silver King Hotel in Florence. Output from the mine came to nearly $17 million.

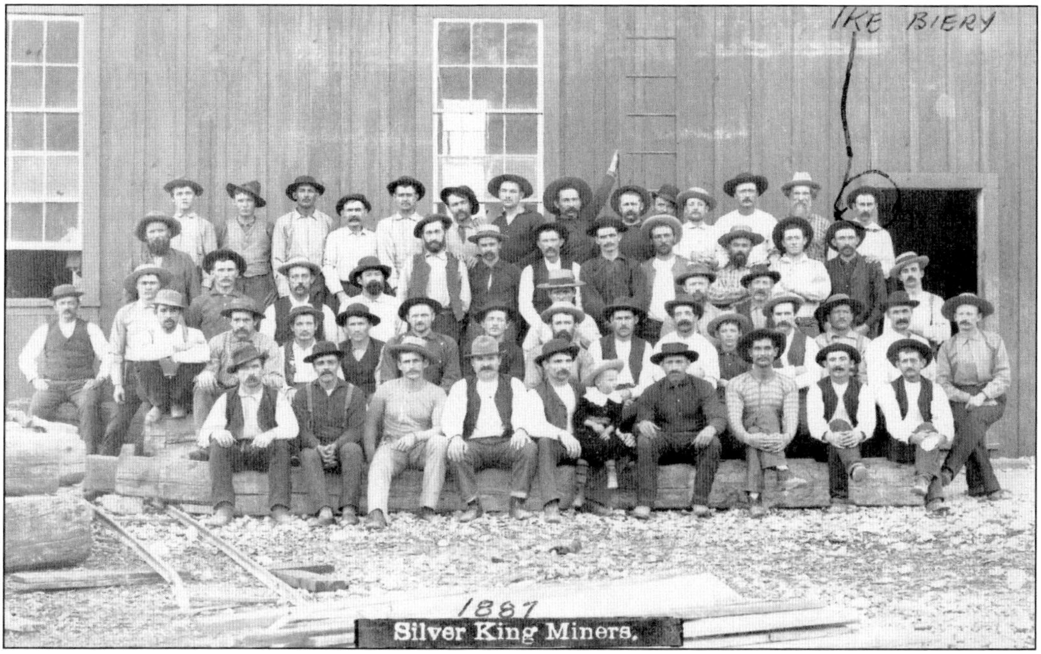

According to one source, "The ore was lousy with silver." The Silver King created many mining jobs. One day, a man walked into the busy camp while it was operating at its peak. The man, actually the same Mr. Sullivan who had first found the silver, was given a job as a common laborer! Silver King miners are shown in 1887, when the pay rock was thinning out.

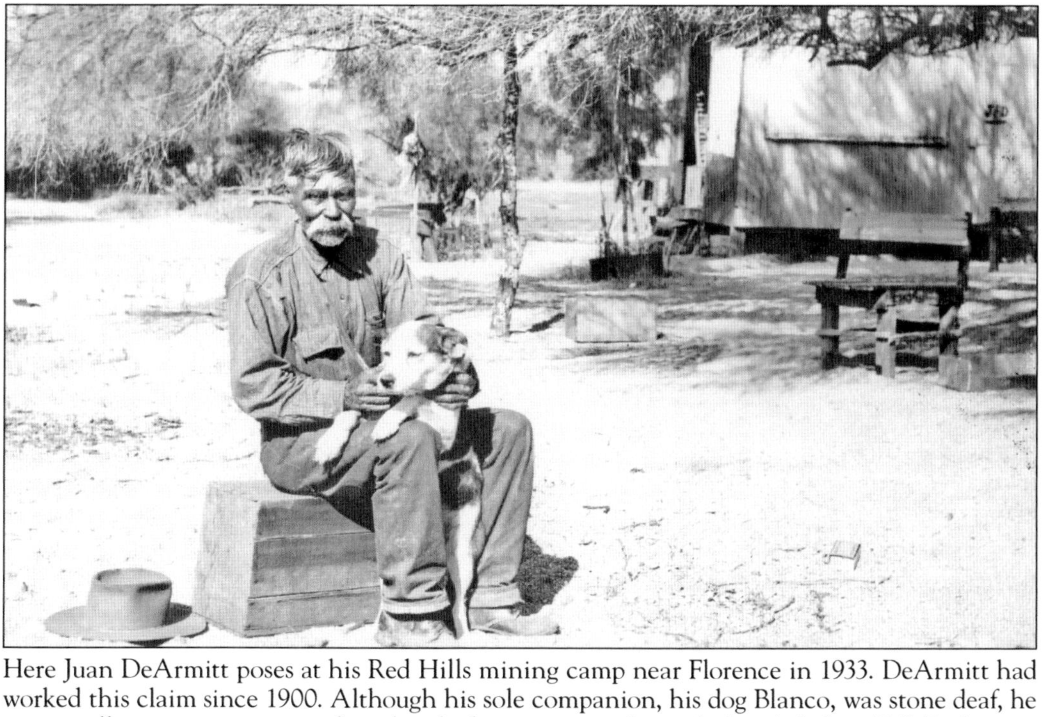

Here Juan DeArmitt poses at his Red Hills mining camp near Florence in 1933. DeArmitt had worked this claim since 1900. Although his sole companion, his dog Blanco, was stone deaf, he was excellent at cornering rattlesnakes for his master to dispatch. Juan's father, Hill DeArmitt, served as a Pima County sheriff in the 1860s and moved his family to Florence in 1869.

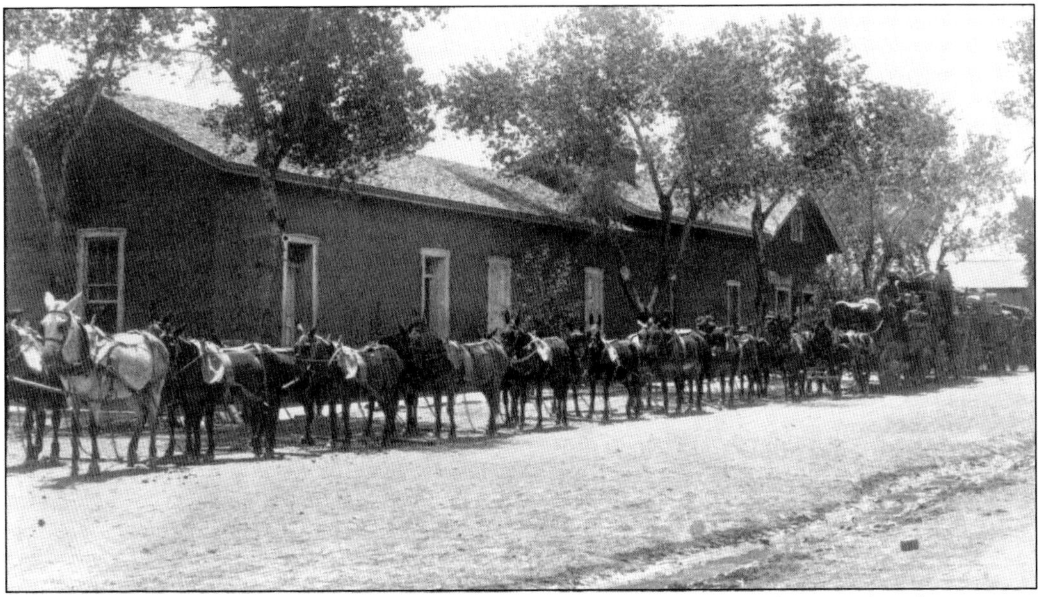

This 20-mule team, seen in a rare photograph, waits at the Joseph Collingwood and Company building to be loaded with mail, foodstuffs, equipment, and supplies for the mines. After reaching the mines and unloading, the freight wagons were loaded with silver, gold, and copper to be brought back to Florence and shipped to San Francisco and other cities. (Courtesy Arizona Historical Society, No. 719.)

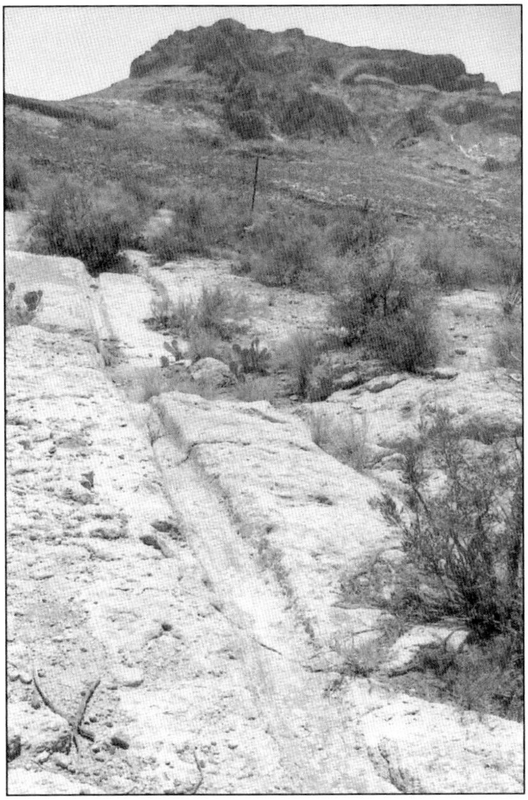

Stamp mills were constructed 10 miles southwest of the mine in Pinal, originally called Camp Picket Post. Soldiers were stationed there as lookouts because Apache Indians in the mountains watched everything waiting to attack. Shown here are the wheel tracks of the mule trains that hauled ore down the steep grade to the mill. By 1882, bars and concentrates were being shipped by stage to Casa Grande, then by railroad to San Francisco.

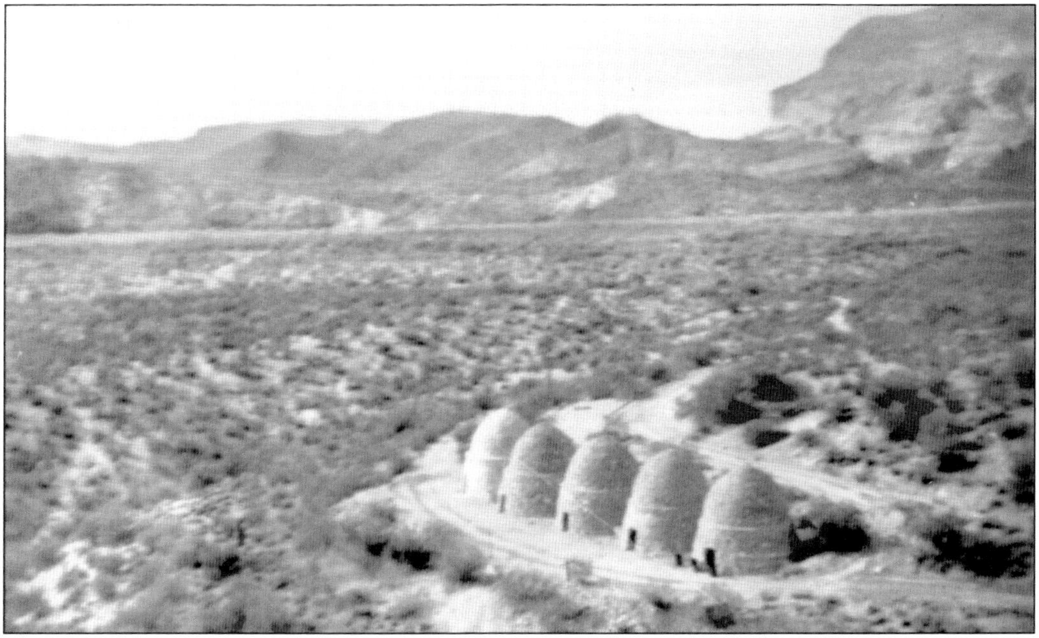

Somewhat mysterious to those who come upon them are these "beehive" ovens located east of Florence on the north bank of the Gila River. These coke, or charcoal, ovens were built in the late 1880s to supply charcoal to mining companies' smelters. Silver ore from the nearby Silver Bell and Columbia Mines was reduced to base bullion before being transported to San Francisco for further refining.

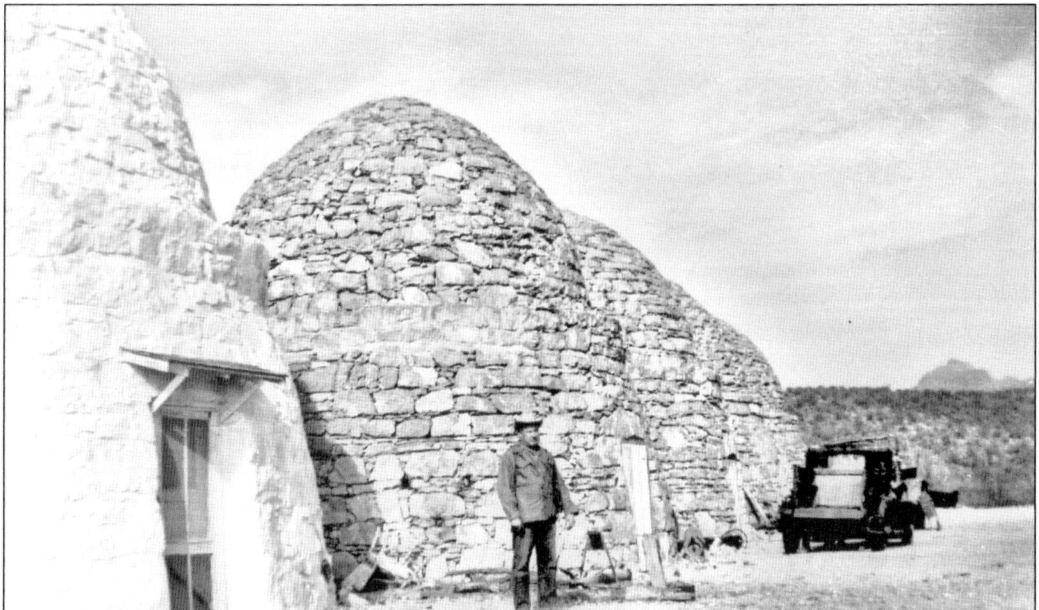

In the early 1900s, two of the ovens, which are 32 feet high and 72 feet in circumference, were made livable. Two women occupied the ovens for a time, and Buttercup Violet Ramses was raised there by her homesteader father. People used the ovens as a refuge when the river was high and the weather bad. The ovens are listed on the National Register of Historic Places.

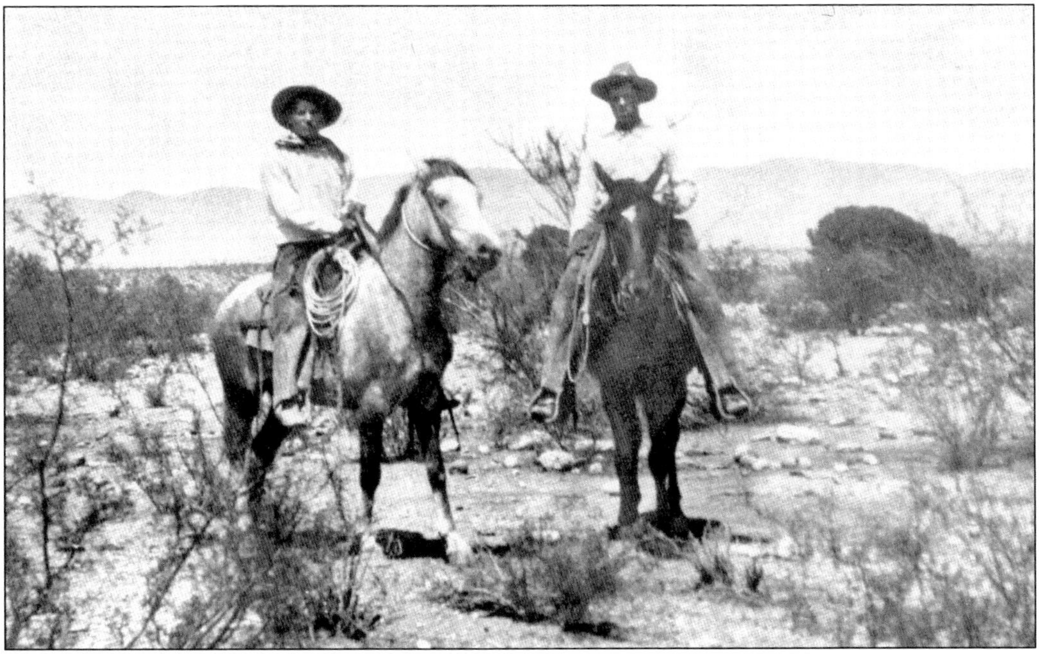

Phil Redondo (left) rides the range with a fellow cowboy. Redondo worked for many different outfits until he bought and developed the A Diamond Ranch at age 28. Redondo was so knowledgeable about running cattle, he was said to "know where his cattle were going, and where they'd come from without seeing them." He sold the ranch in 1944.

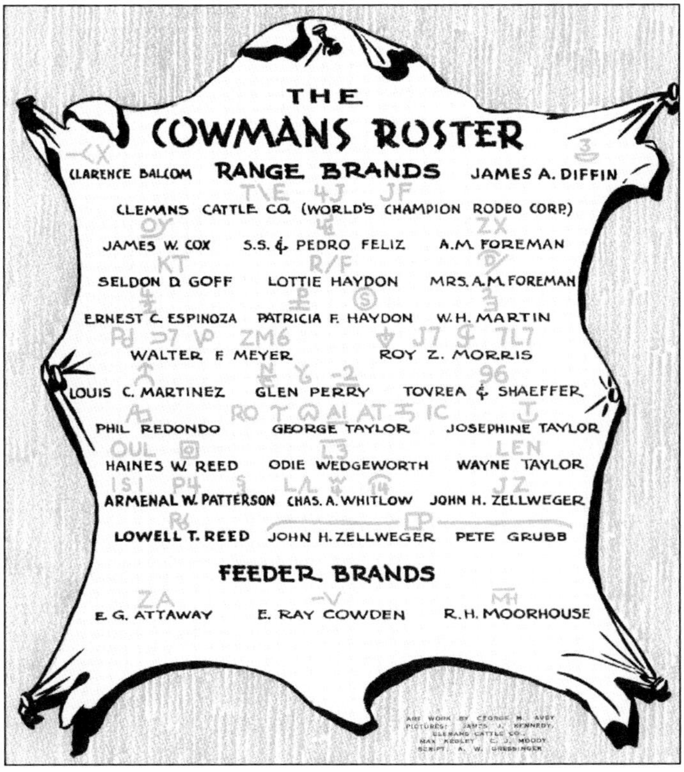

This drawing, published in a c. 1940 promotional pamphlet titled *Florence, Arizona: South of the Gila—on the Old Spanish Trail*, shows major brands (or owners' marks) of Florence-area cattle ranchers. Pictured are brands such as Patricia Haydon's Circle S, Tovrea and Schaeffer's 96, and Haines W. Reed's Box O. To prevent duplication, the Live Stock Sanitary Board was charged with registering brands starting in the late 1800s. (Drawing by George M. Avey.)

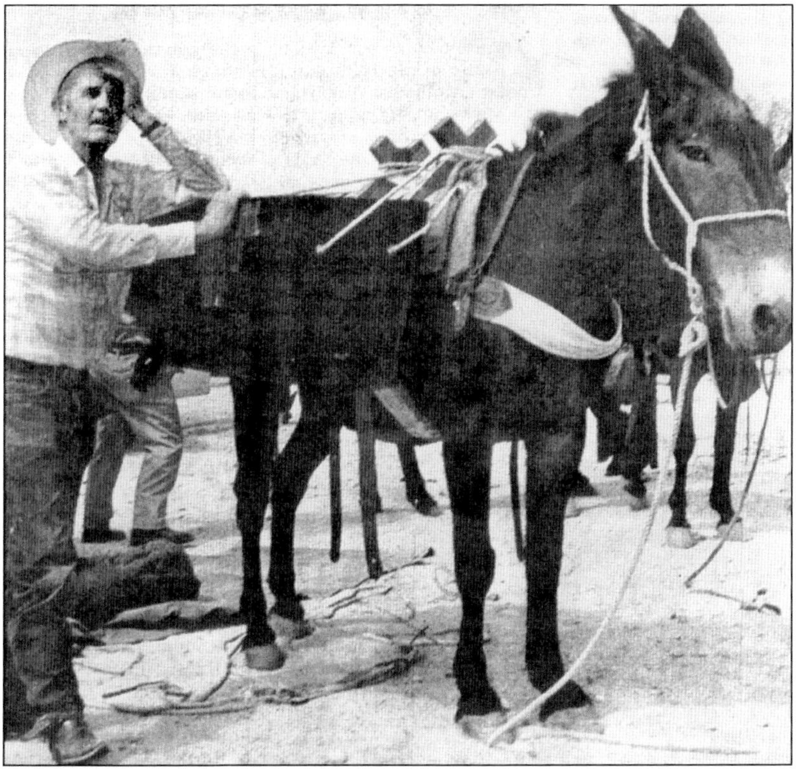

The son of William Hawkins, a cook with John Wesley Powell's expedition down the Colorado River, Amos Hawkins Sr. continued the legacy of his father's adventurous life by becoming a law officer and expert tracker. Here Amos, who knew the Superstition Mountains better than anyone, has just found his prospector friend Al Morrow dead after a long search. (Courtesy *Apache Junction Independent*.)

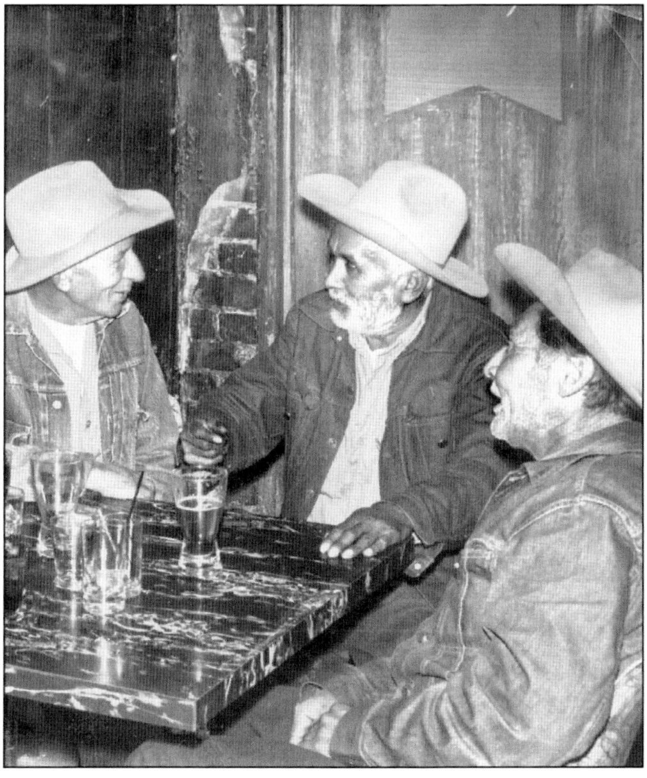

At one time, the Clemans Cattle Company was one of the largest cattle operations in the industry, with ranches in various parts of the state. To feed the herds, Clemans farmed about 3,000 total acres in two sections at Arizona Farms and the Adamsville area, both near Florence. Company cowhand Santiago Sáinz (center) and unidentified friends relax at Florence's La Paloma Restaurant in the 1960s.

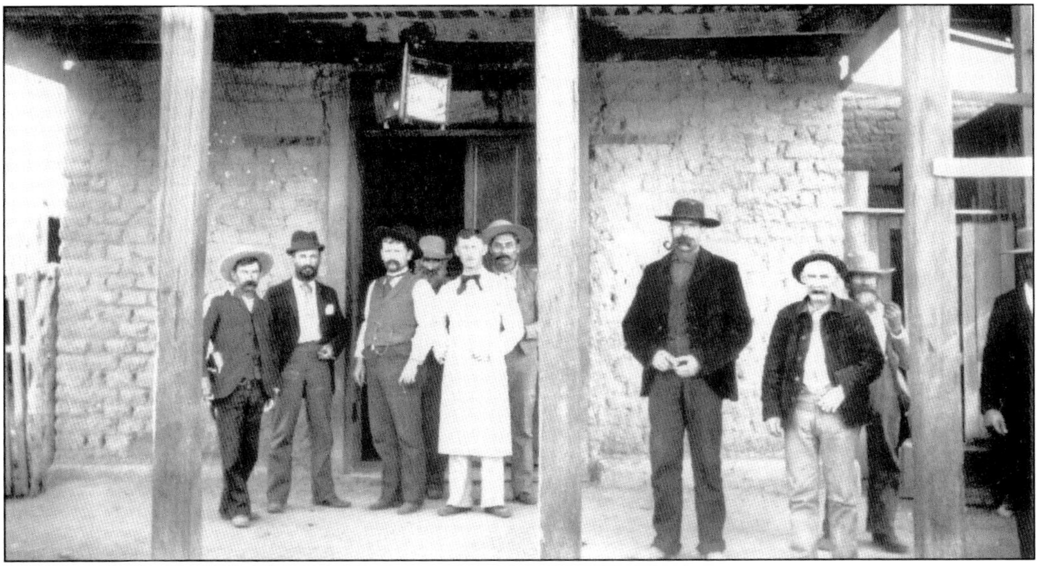

The Tunnel Saloon had an underground drinking room where patrons could escape the heat of the day. It was here that the shoot-out between Peter Gabriel and Josephus Phy began. The saloon changed locations on Main Street many times. Pictured from left to right are Jessie Browe, George E. Truman, John J. Keating (saloon proprietor), Patrick Morgan, Joe Lazure, Frank "Indian Frank" Merrian, unidentified, William Woods, and Peter Johnson. (Courtesy Arizona Historical Society, No. 61016.)

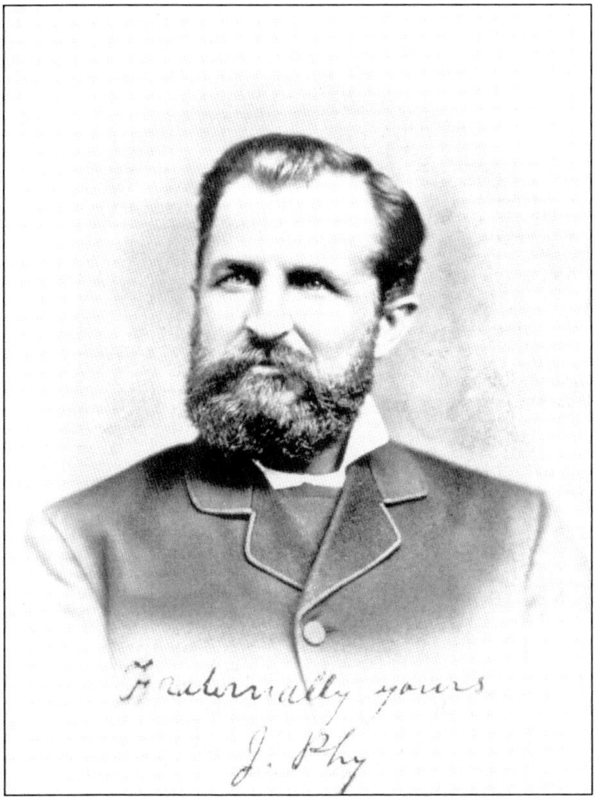

Respected lawman Josephus Phy was hired by the equally respected Sheriff Peter Gabriel to be his deputy in Florence. By 1888, politics and personality differences had produced animosity between the two that erupted in a gunfight at the Tunnel Saloon. Both men were critically wounded; Phy died while Gabriel survived. Told more often as legend than fact, the story does illustrate the wild and fierce climate of boomtown Florence. (Courtesy Arizona Historical Society, No. 249.)

The most notable stagecoach robbery near Florence was committed by flamboyant Pearl Hart and her partner, Joe Boot, in 1899. Pearl smoked cigars, drank whiskey, used "colorful language," and enjoyed publicity. Captured by Sheriff William C. Truman (seen here with Pearl on the courthouse steps), she and Boot were tried in Florence and sent to Yuma Prison. After early release, some believe she eventually settled quietly not far from the crime scene.

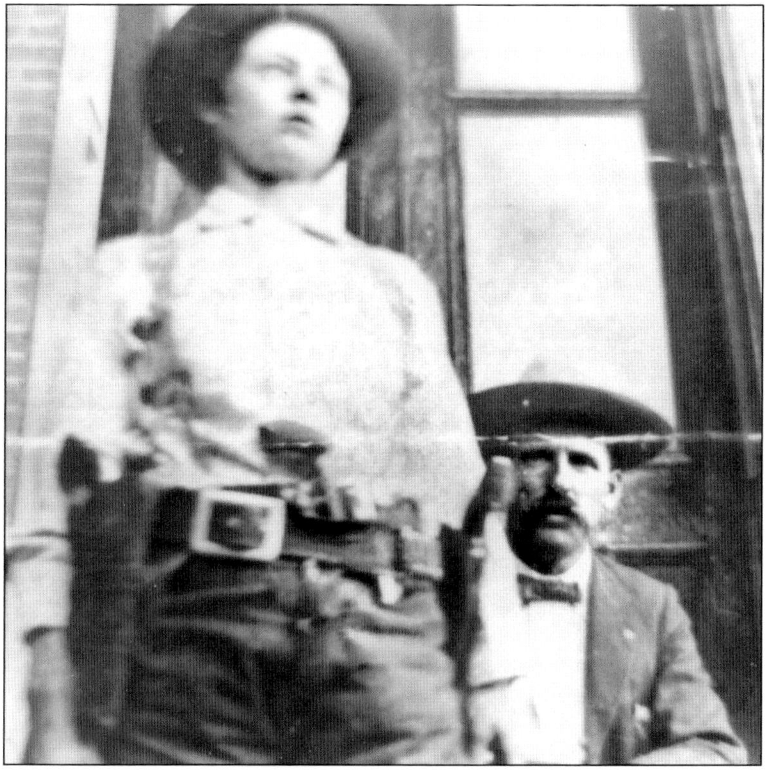

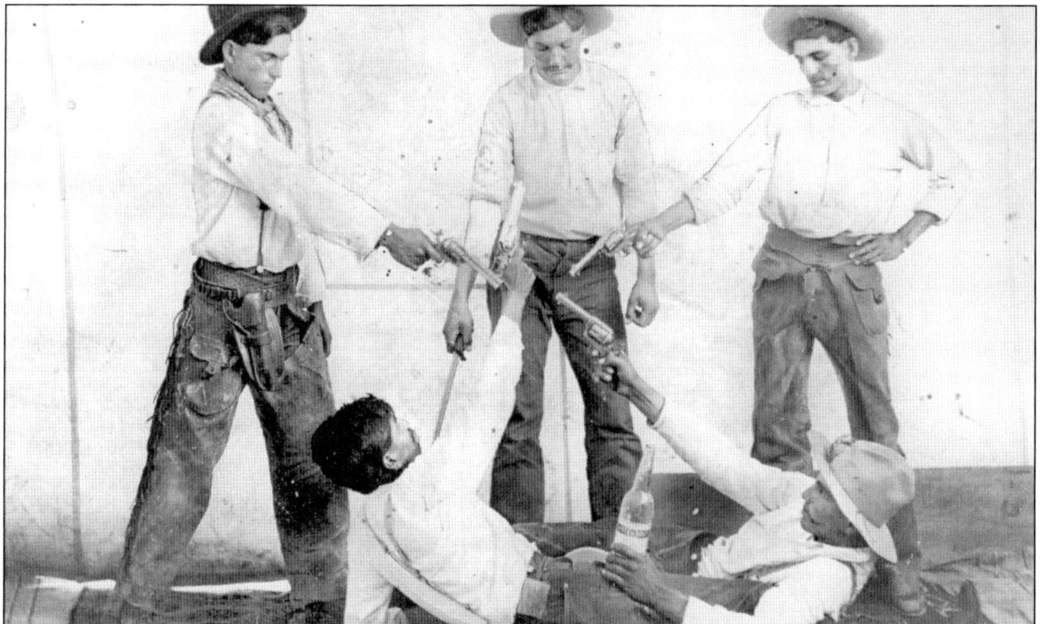

In the early 1900s, a group of Florence youth plays Shootout. Children did not have to depend on movies and pulp magazines to tell them how to reenact gunfights. All they had to do was listen to the old-timers telling stories. The "victim" on the ground at right is a young Edward Van Haren.

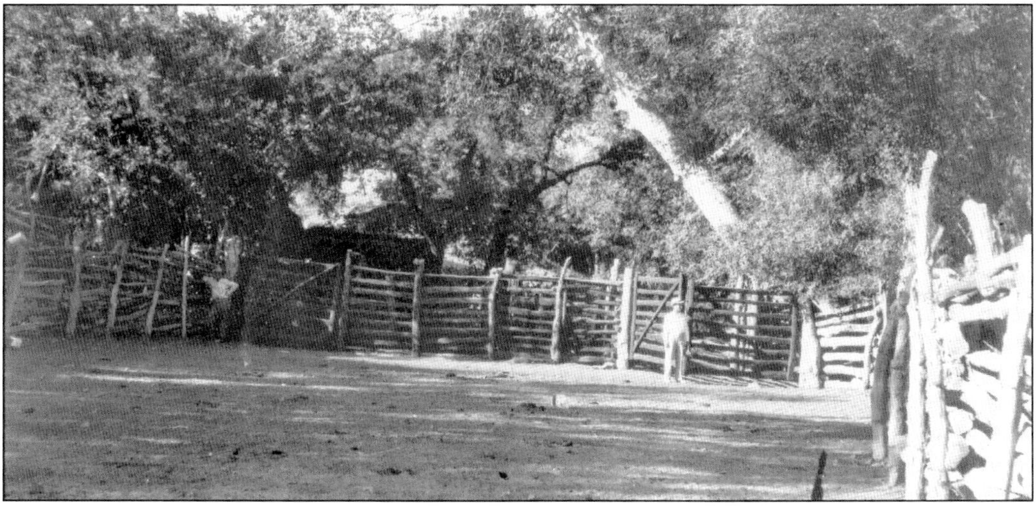

This corral, pictured in the mid-20th century, is located southeast of Florence in Aravaipa Canyon. Used by Native Americans since prehistoric times, the canyon and its secure corral became a hideout for renegade Apache in the late 1800s. Stories of the Aravaipa Apache and lost gold treasure made it a fabled site even before events in the 1880s and 1890s led to its nickname of the Haunted Corral.

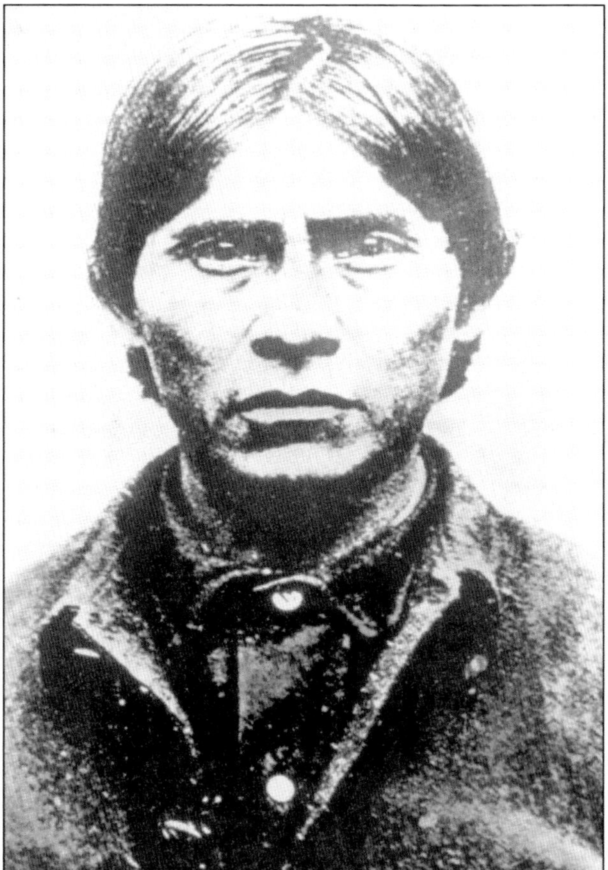

Apache Kid, a former army scout, reportedly avenged the murder of his father by killing the man he thought responsible for the crime. In 1889, Kid was found guilty of murder and sentenced to Yuma Prison. While being transported under heavy guard, his cohorts killed three guards and all the prisoners escaped to Aravaipa Canyon. The renegade Kid was never captured and became a legendary figure. (Courtesy Arizona Historical Society, No. 15755.)

After living in the area for some time, George Apsey and his family moved into Aravaipa Canyon in 1890. Apsey's livestock herds grew unnaturally, and itinerant cowboys hired as help soon disappeared. Apache scouts smelled flesh burning at his camp and remarked, "Pigs don't wear boots." Human bones were found scattered around the Haunted Corral. In Florence, Apsey was convicted of manslaughter and sentenced to Yuma Prison.

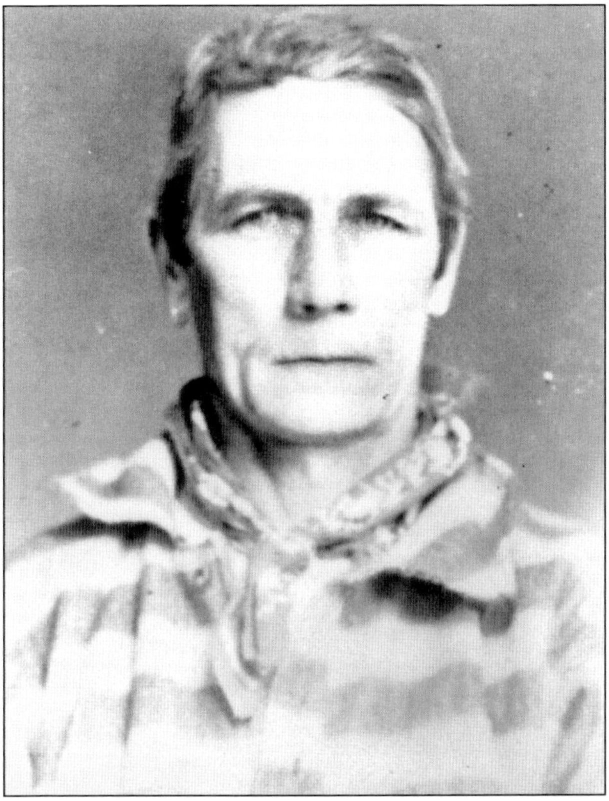

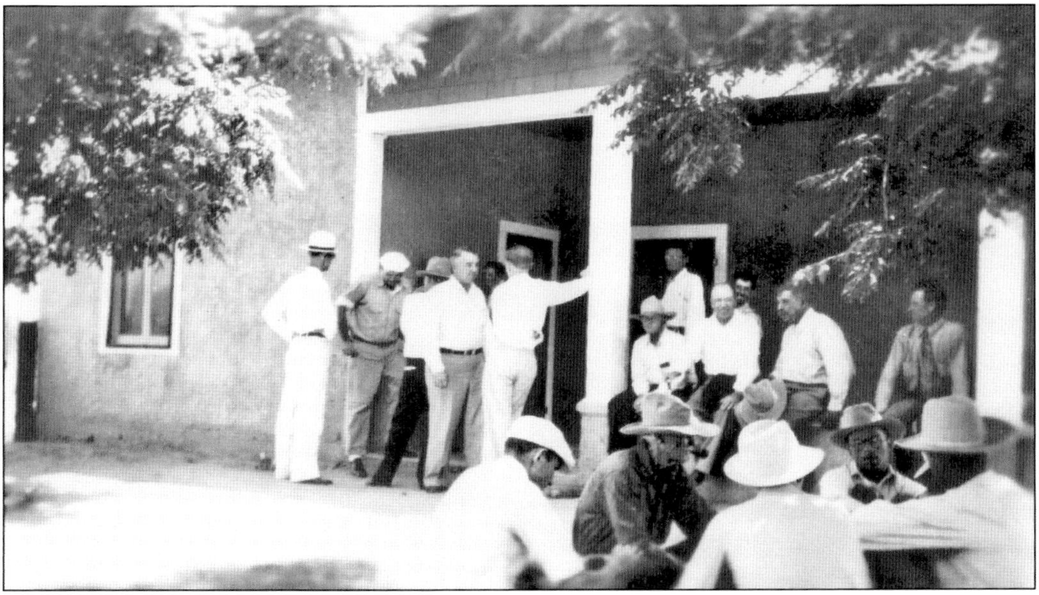

Jo Flieger bought land adjacent to the Towner brothers, the owners of the Haunted Corral. Cattle rustling became a problem and feuds broke out; Flieger suspected the Towners. When Henry Towner was murdered in the late 1930s, Flieger was accused and brought before justice of the peace Roy Guild. Here townspeople take a break during the pre-trial. Another man would later confess, leaving Flieger a respected citizen.

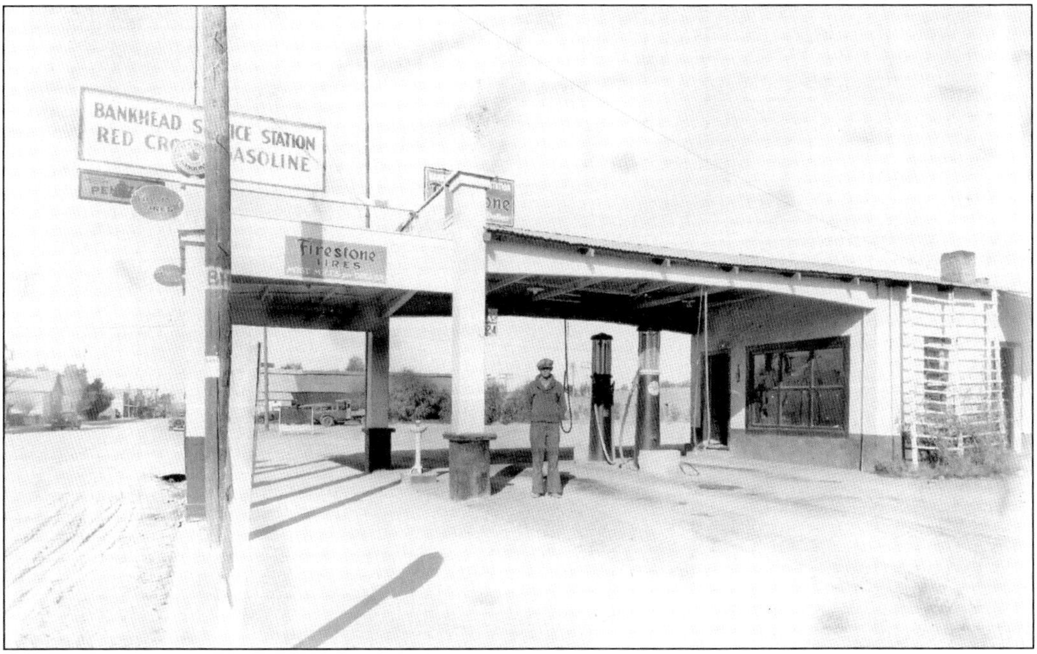

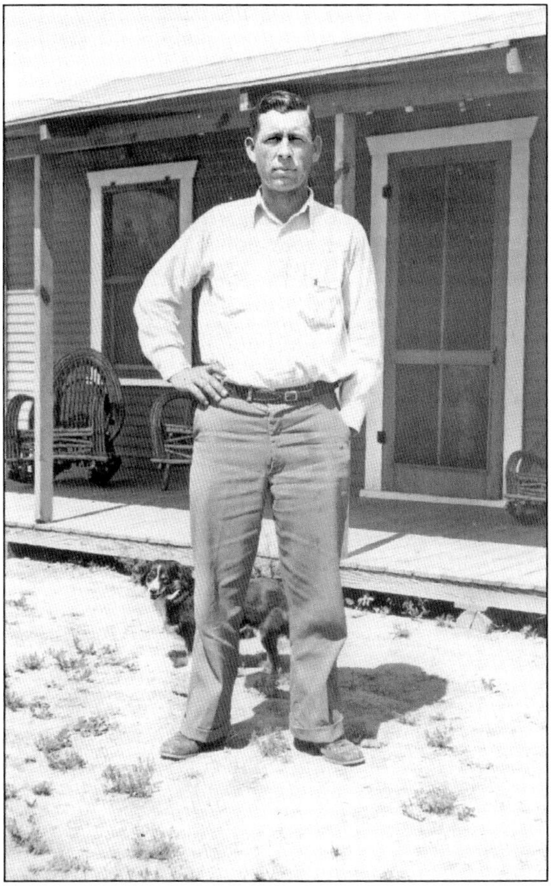

Running through Florence, the Bankhead Highway was a major route from Savannah, Georgia, to San Diego, California. At this service station in 1930, desperados fleeing a Pennsylvania robbery and highway patrolman killing kidnapped Florence deputy Joe Chapman and began a cross-country chase ending in a shootout in Chandler, Arizona. Irene Schroeder, the lone woman of the gang, was electrocuted in Pennsylvania for her crimes.

Chapman conceals his left hand in this 1933 photograph. After his hand was shattered by a bullet in the kidnaping shootout, it looked like a scorpion's pincers, earning him the nickname "Alecran," Spanish for scorpion. As a young cowboy, Joe had worked for the Cananea Cattle Company in Mexico and remained one of the best cattle inspectors west of the Mississippi in his later years. He died in 1967.

Four

FLORENCE FLOURISHES

When the families of early settlers came to town, they were often daunted by the barren desert surrounding Florence. Eventually, many grew to love it. Families lent a new tone to the community of miners and cowboys. Homes were built, some showing an eastern U.S. influence in their architecture.

Many people recorded their families and pets with the new technology: photography. Townspeople enjoyed celebrating holidays such as Independence Day and Cinco de Mayo with parades and fireworks. The 400th anniversary of Columbus Day was celebrated with daytime and evening programs.

Community was expressed through Florence's many organizations. Women started a society to encourage town improvements, later known as the Florence Woman's Club. With the women came the churches. The Roman Catholic church was the first place of worship in town. Rev. Isaac T. Whittemore of Casa Grande Ruins became the founding minister of the Florence Presbyterian Church. Fraternal organizations such as the Masons, the Elks, the Ancient Order of United Workmen, and the Alianza Hispano-Americano formed, as well as service clubs such as Rotary International and Lions International. After bands and orchestras were established, music filled the air on Bailey Street in the evenings.

Florence was not only the wild and woolly West, but also a town with a rich history and social life. Some people of the time were prescient enough to collect information about the town, its citizens, and its history. Florence owes them a debt of gratitude for what they saved.

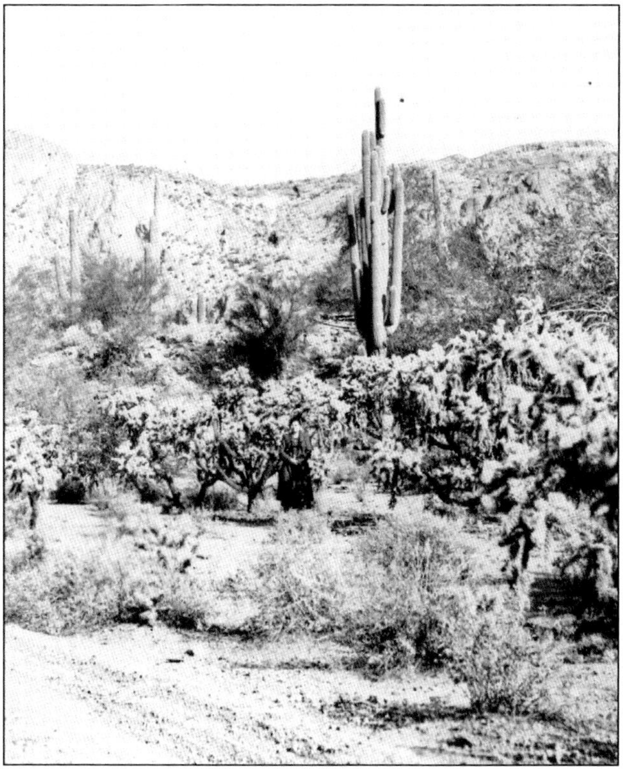

Dwarfed by the surrounding cacti, an unidentified woman poses near Box Canyon. The giant saguaro is native to the Sonoran Desert surrounding Florence. The stubby cholla was used by a Florence artisan to make furniture and curios. The most available wood in the area, cactus "wood" was used in the original adobe structures.

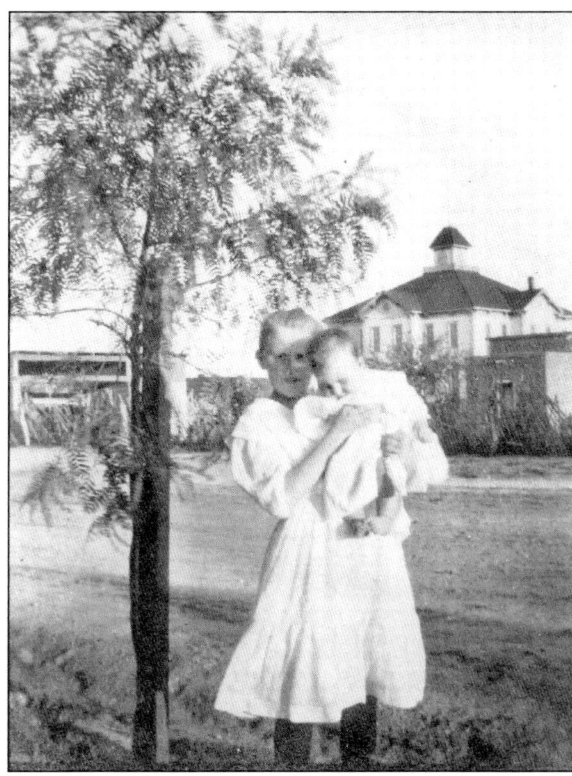

Frederic G. White came to Florence from Boston in 1900 and married Natalia Michea, the daughter of Jean Baptiste Michea and Carmen Robles. Their oldest daughter, Martha, holds an unidentified infant in the yard of the Michea-White home on Ruggles Street. Visible in the distance is the large frame schoolhouse that was torn down in 1912.

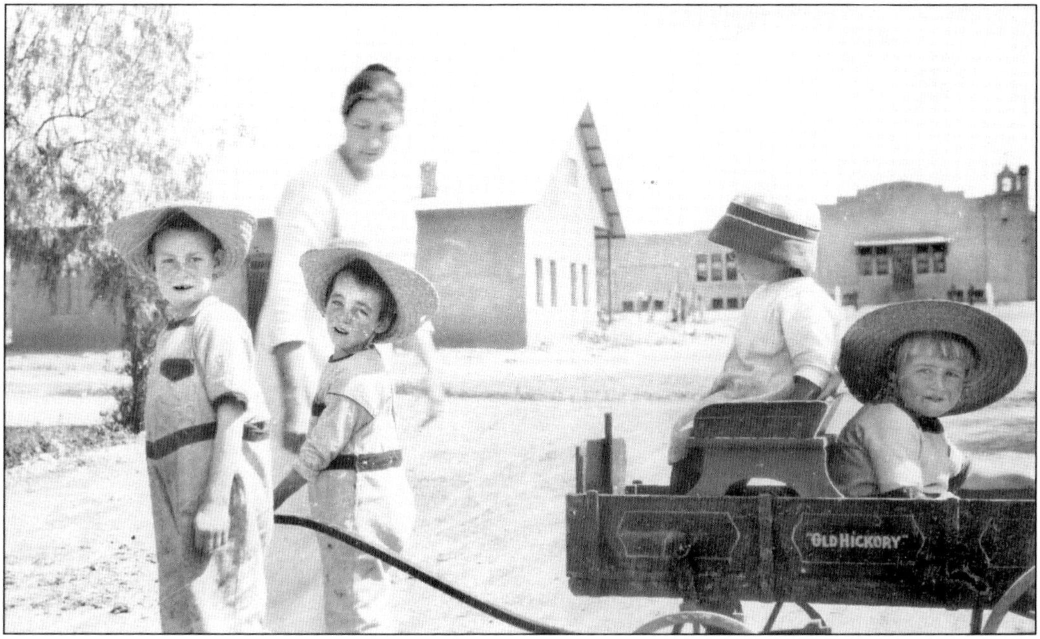

Natalia Michea White, known as "Mom White," appears with her sons John (left), Eugene (second from left), and Benjamin (right); an unidentified child is seated with Benjamin in the wagon. The frame schoolhouse has been replaced with a building in the Spanish colonial revival style, a popular design at the time. Behind it, the Assumption Catholic Church steeple can be seen.

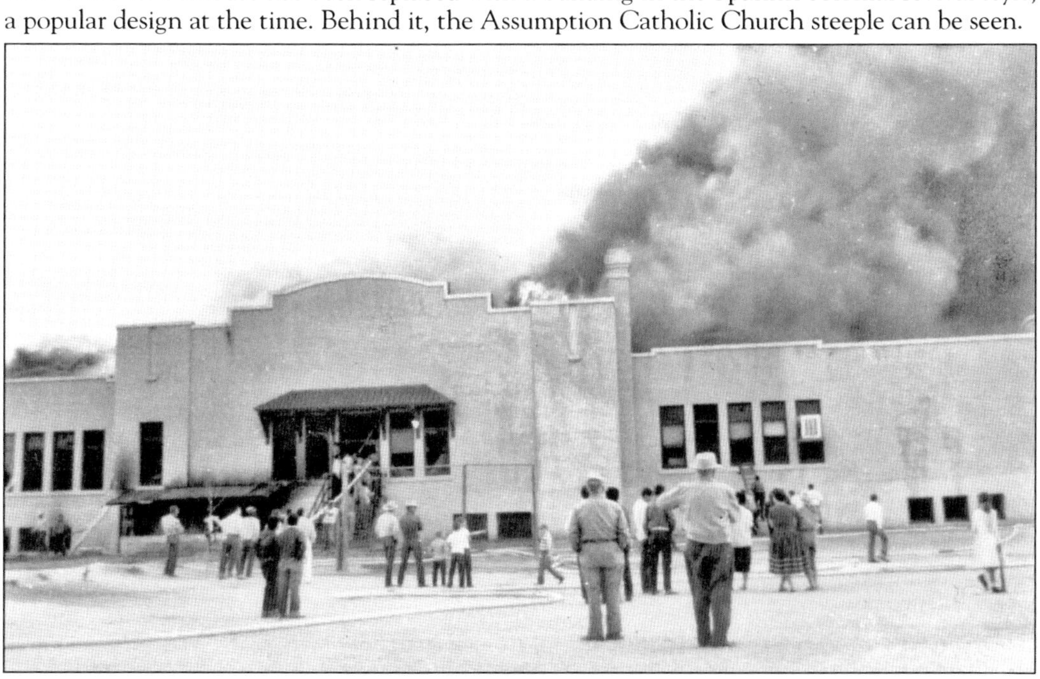

In January 1957, this elementary school (now known as Old Main) was destroyed. The fire may have started in the heating plant near the lunchroom. Teacher Mrs. W. C. McConnell saw smoke and notified Principal Fernando Ortega, who summoned firemen. School staff checked rooms for children until driven back by smoke. "The school was built in 1912 and there had been suggestions to replace it with a modern structure," reported the *Florence Reminder*.

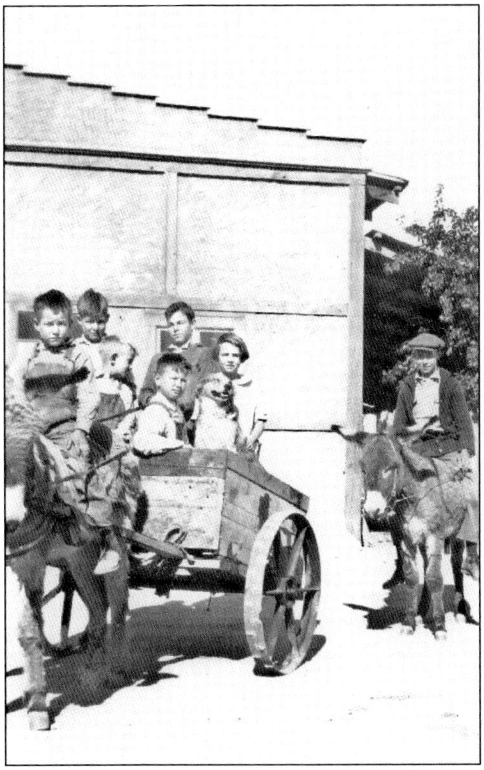

Frederic G. White's children and dog Hobo have piled into a donkey cart at the east end of the family home. It also was the site of their father's business, the Lone Star Store, where he sold lumber and painting supplies. Still standing today, the two-story adobe held many parties and dances upstairs.

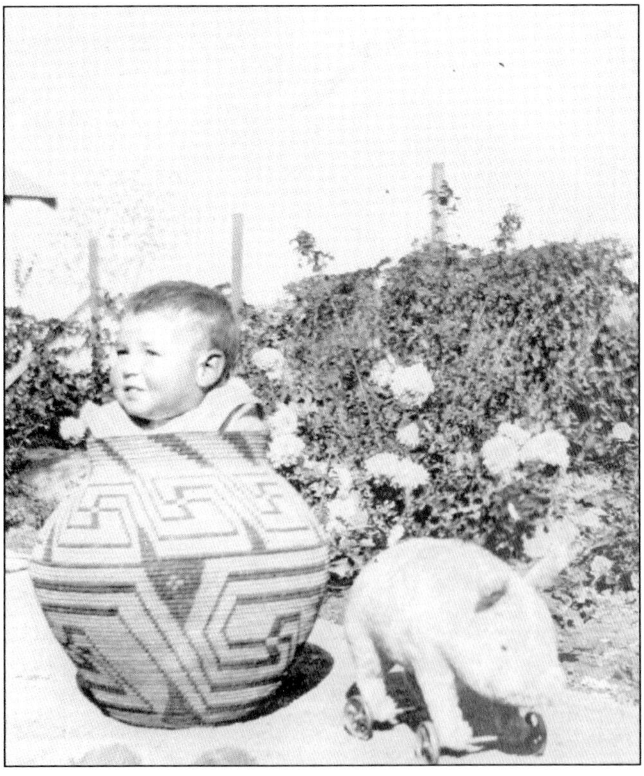

Mom White has tucked one of her babies into a large Pima Indian basket. To the right is a toy pig mounted on wheels that is almost as big as its owner. This pull toy would have been an expensive purchase. Although Florence was a small rural town, almost anything could be ordered from catalogs and arrive by train.

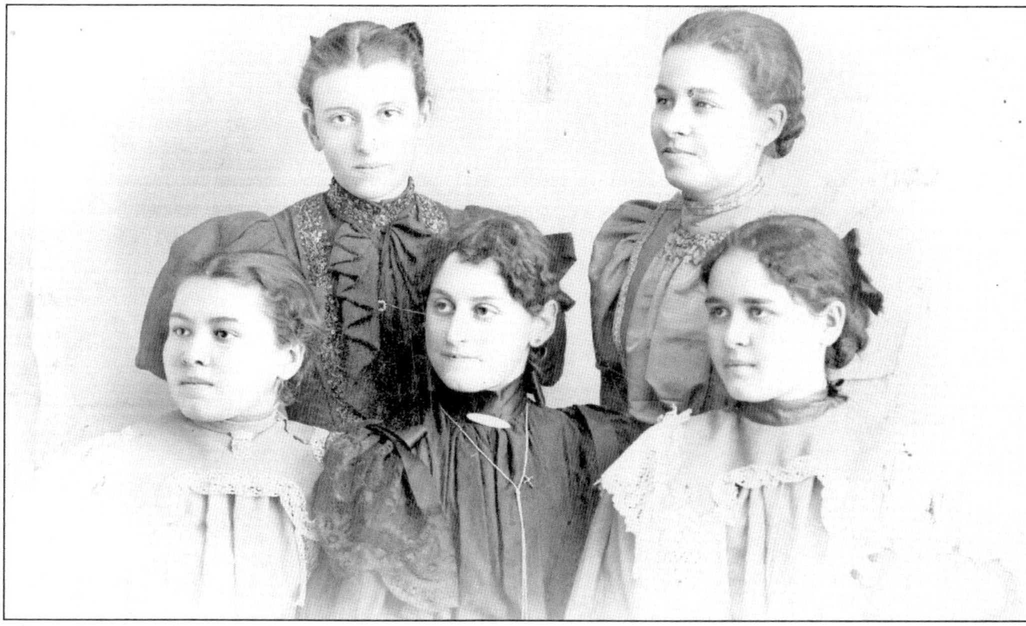

This photograph is simply labeled "the Spinas girls." Swiss-born Joseph Spinas was a prominent Florence rancher who also built one of the first irrigation ditches. He married Susanna Andrade, who died when their children were young. Daughters Nellie and Katie spent much of their time at the St. Mary's Convent in Phoenix. Joseph had two brothers, so these girls may be Spinas cousins or they may be stepsisters.

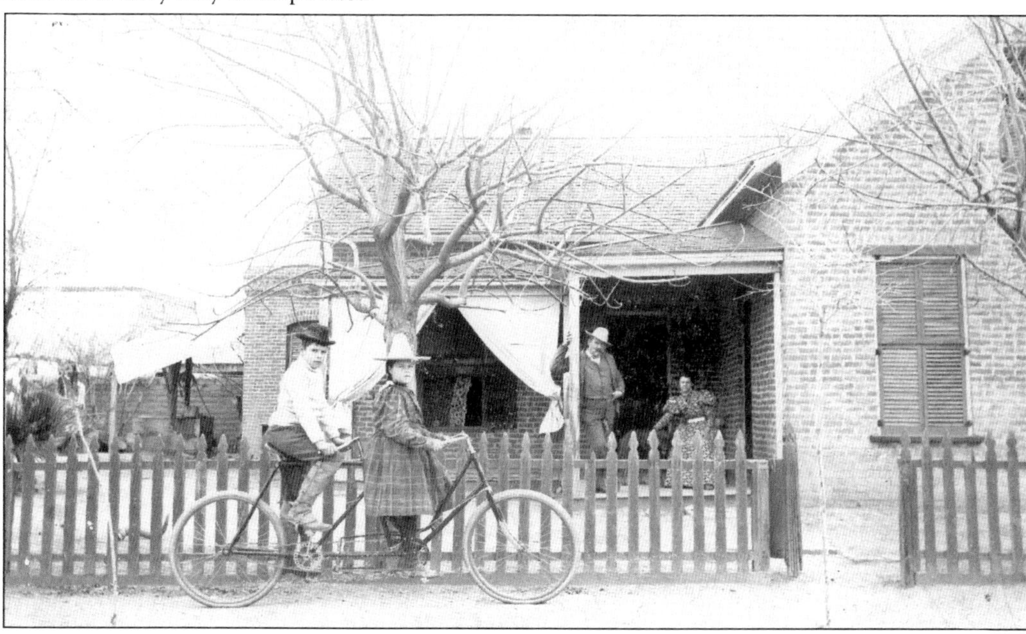

Ted and Marion Stone prepare for a ride on their tandem bicycle while their parents, William and Kate, look on. William Stone worked as a mining attorney and later as Arizona Territory's district attorney. Kate helped organize the Episcopal Sunday school, Literary Society, Woman's Club, and Music Club. The curtained sleeping porch of their Main Street home provided relief on hot summer nights.

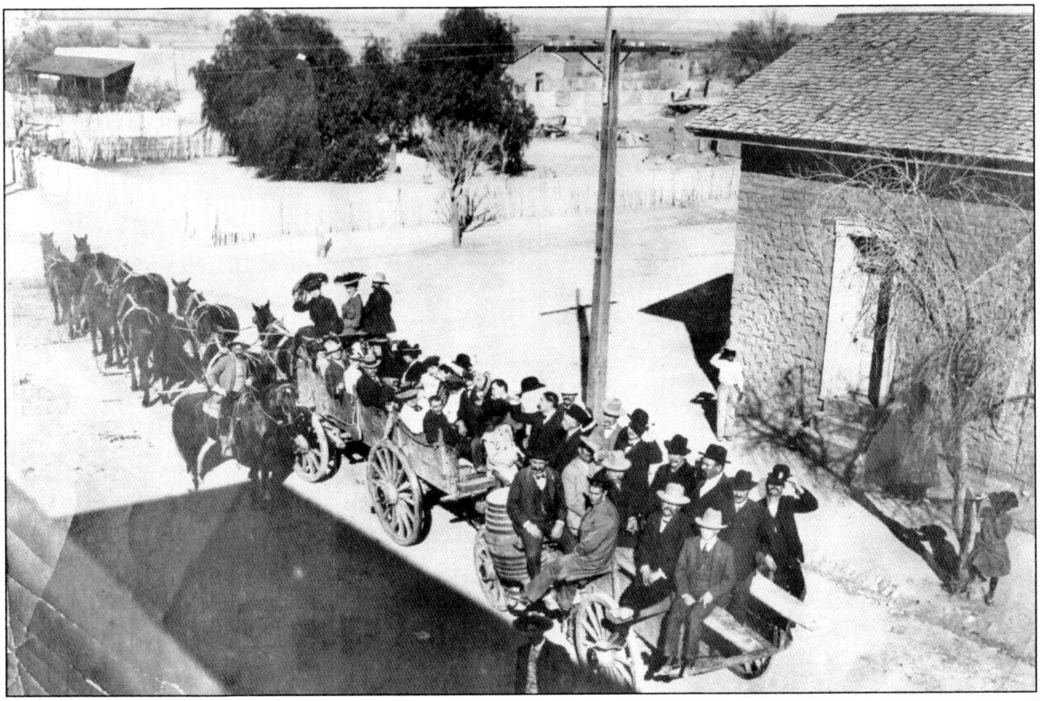

There are twice as many men as women riding on this wagon to a Sunday picnic. Attractive and available women in early Florence were a precious commodity. Was this the "drunken" picnic the town gossips buzzed about, where Louise Kibbey and Wood Porter may have exchanged a love note leading to Porter's murder by Louise's husband, Frank? The alleged affair and subsequent murder shook the town in 1892.

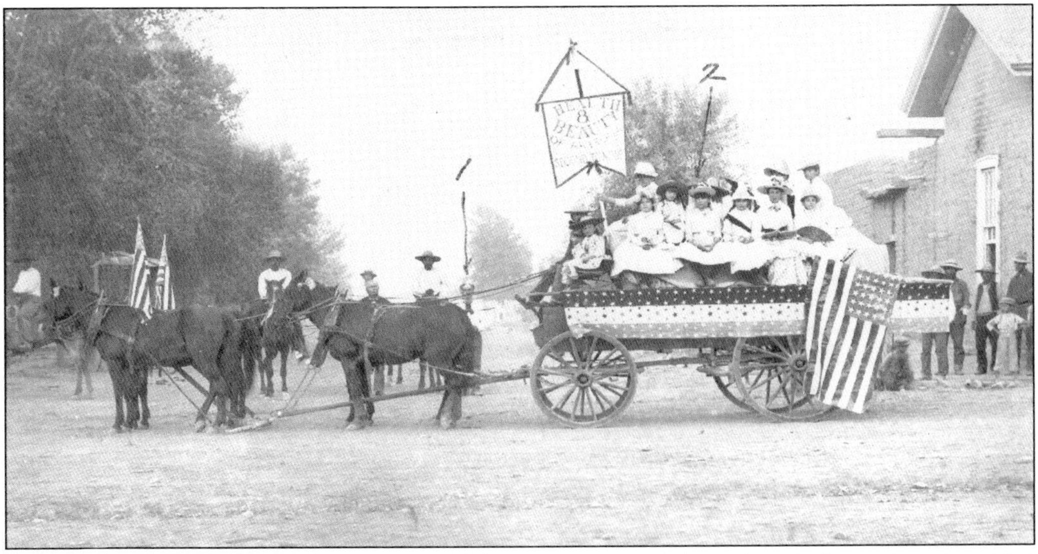

Independence Days, both American and Mexican, were celebrated with festivities. An 1894 Fourth of July parade float touts the charms of local ladies with a banner reading "Health and Beauty of Arizona—Second to None." District attorney and judge Hiram Summers (1) stands near his granddaughter Joy Biery (2). Of the 26 people seen, Summers is one of only two who are hatless, unprotected from the July sun.

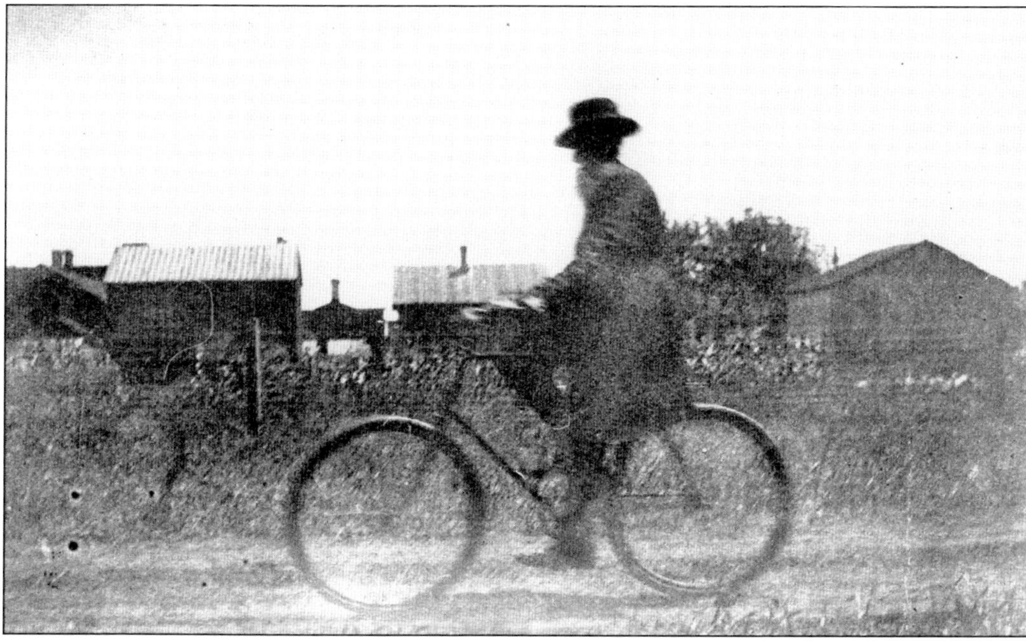

Rev. Isaac Whittemore was 63 years old when he arrived in Florence to start the Presbyterian church. Despite his advanced years, he rode a bicycle around town. Affectionately known as "the little parson," he served until retiring in 1899. In Pasadena, California, Whittemore was killed when his bicycle collided with a trolley while on his way to visit a sick friend in 1904.

The First Presbyterian Church of Florence, organized in 1888 under the leadership of Rev. Isaac Whittemore, met at the county courthouse. Whittemore wrote, "I saw more drinking and gambling and Sabbath-breaking . . . that [*sic*] I had ever known before. I came trembling, but the Lord had sent me." This brick church was built in 1891. Hon. Richard Sloan and Hon. Joseph Kibbey both served on the building committee before becoming Arizona governors.

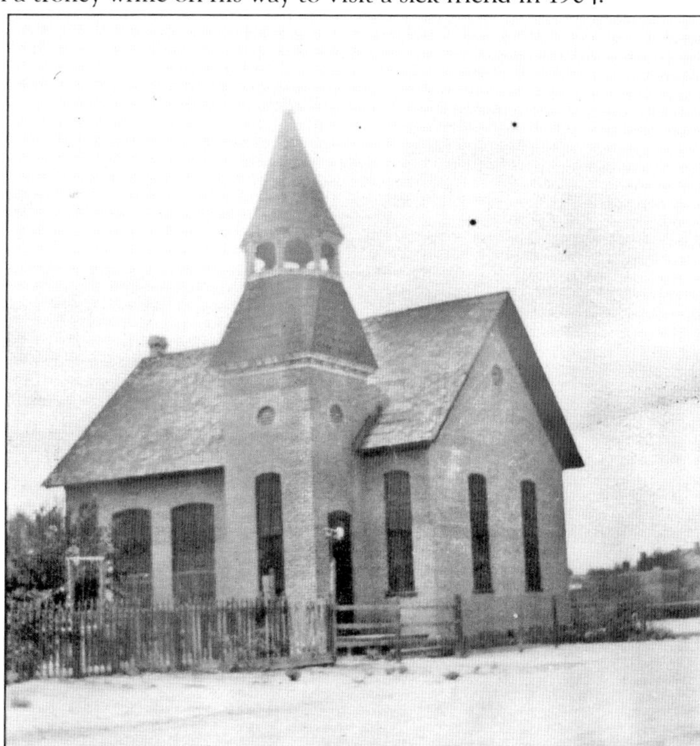

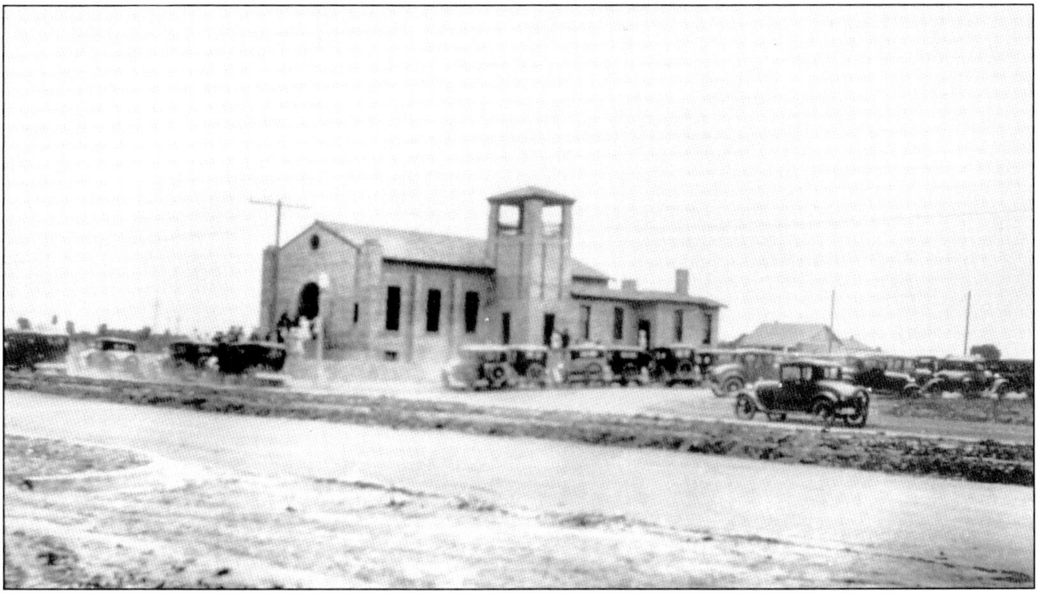

On May 17, 1931, the new First Presbyterian Church of Florence was dedicated. Butte Avenue was not yet paved at the time. The first service had been held on Easter Sunday with Rev. Samuel Hannah officiating. Bricks for the building were sold for 25¢ to finance the project. The building was constructed with prison labor, men Hannah knew from his work there. They were known as "the preacher's gang."

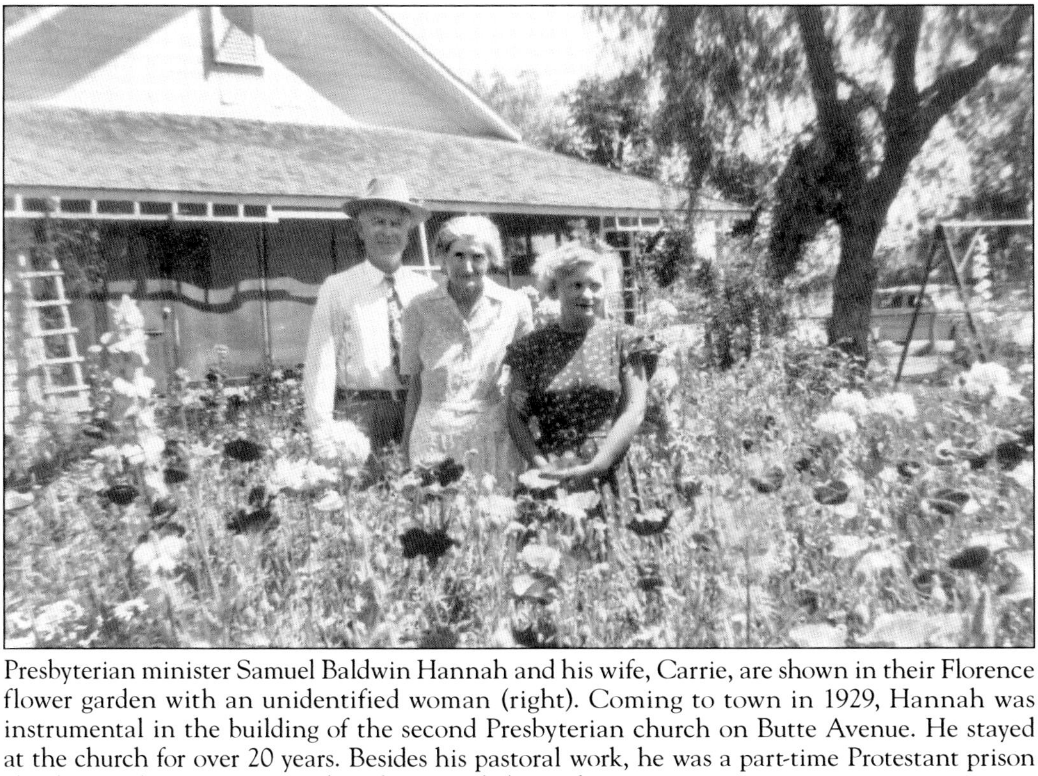

Presbyterian minister Samuel Baldwin Hannah and his wife, Carrie, are shown in their Florence flower garden with an unidentified woman (right). Coming to town in 1929, Hannah was instrumental in the building of the second Presbyterian church on Butte Avenue. He stayed at the church for over 20 years. Besides his pastoral work, he was a part-time Protestant prison chaplain at the state prison, where he started classes for inmates.

Fr. Henri Heitz, the last of the French priests serving Florence's Catholic church, led the effort to build the new brick mission revival–style Assumption Catholic Church, which was dedicated in 1912. An adobe church built in 1882 had stood on the site until it was destroyed by fire in 1893. The architectural style was meant to reflect a new era for Florence and to celebrate Arizona's new statehood.

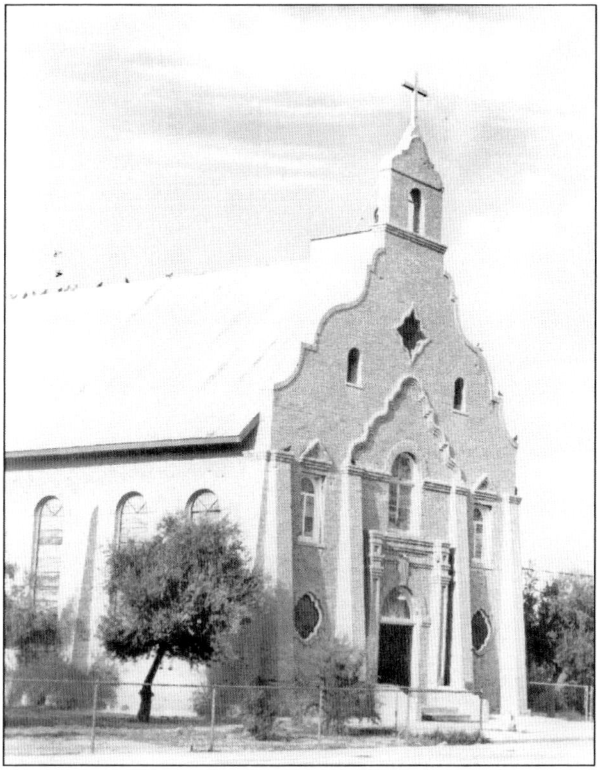

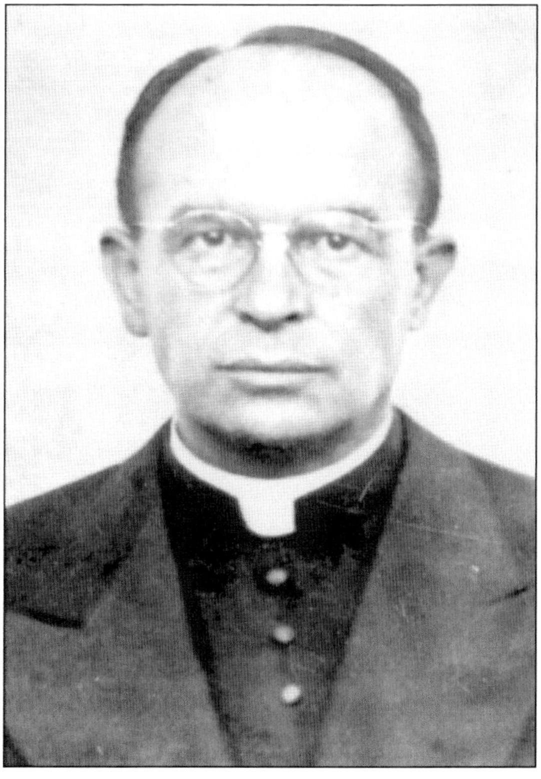

Carmelite priest Fr. Joseph Dominic Jaques served Assumption Catholic Church for nearly 16 years. Wearing his monk's robe and sandals, he often worked 80 hours a week. He learned German and Italian in order to speak to the prisoners at the POW camp north of Florence. He died in 1964 and was buried in Barcelona, Spain. Florence's Jaques Square is named for him.

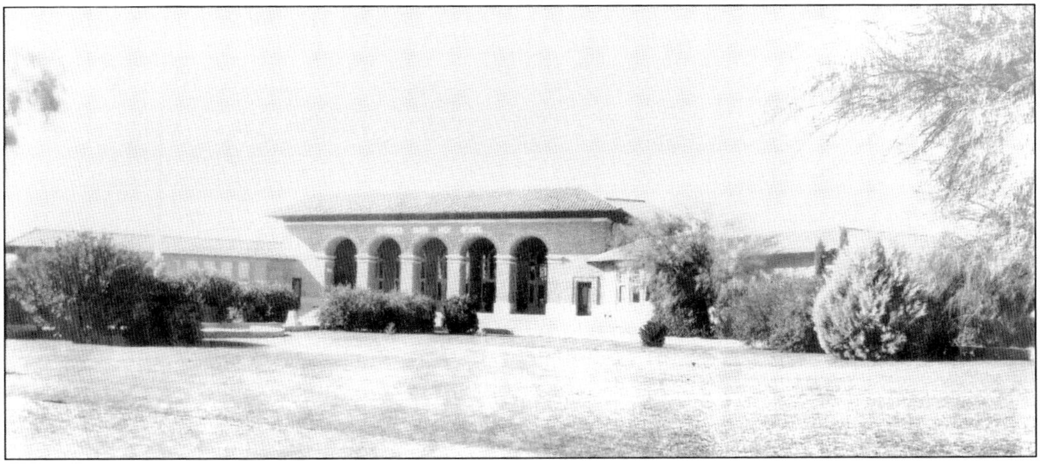

The Florence Union High School was designed by architects Royal Lescher and John R. Kibbey in 1916. The original doors and windows under the arches in the front and back of the auditorium opened to create a cooling cross breeze. Students from Eloy, Picacho, Mammoth, Coolidge, and Red Rock also attended here.

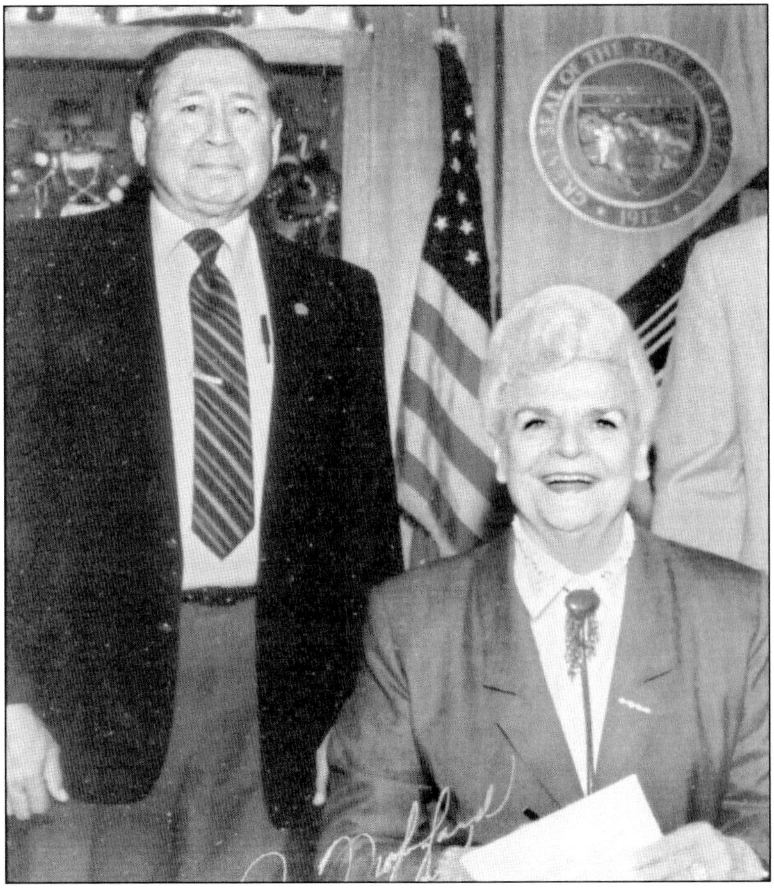

Frank "Art" Celaya has been a mentor to the youth of Florence for much of his life. After college, he returned to teach and became principal and superintendent of the school district. He was elected to the state legislature but kept education on his mind. Celaya has a tradition of funding a scholarship for a local high school graduate. Here he is seen with Gov. Rose Mofford c. 1988.

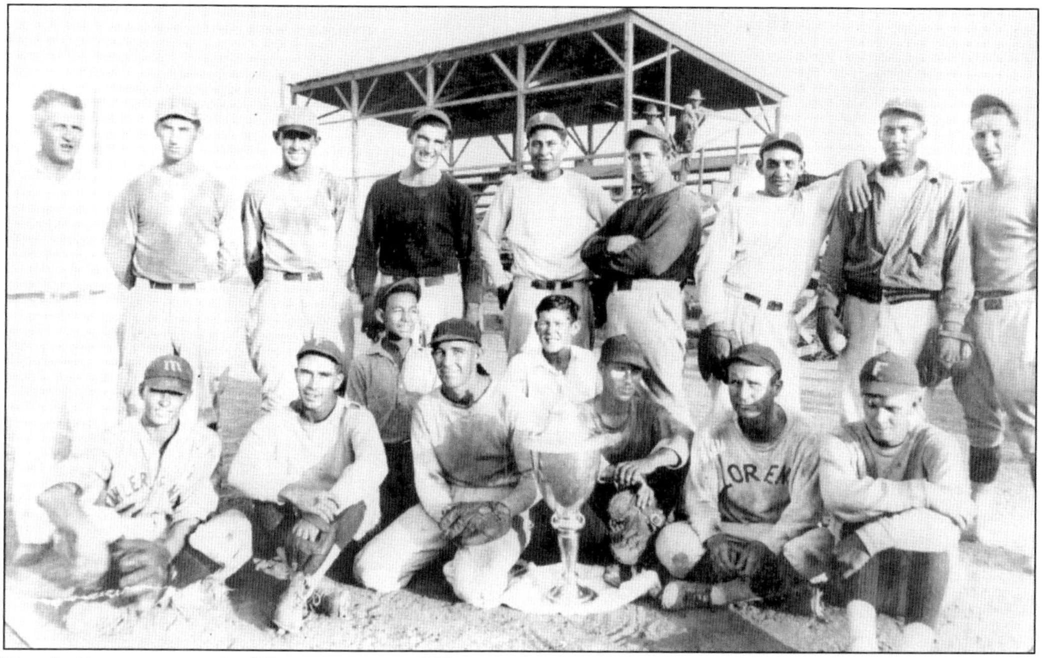

Baseball was a popular Florence sport. The Florence Reds were an early Gila League team. Series competitions were held between neighboring towns. The 1904 *Arizona Blade and Florence Tribune* bragged that the Mesa team playing Florence "will know they have been in a game when it was over." That same year, a special Phoenix and Eastern Railroad excursion took fans to watch a game against Phoenix. Boasting aside, Florence lost.

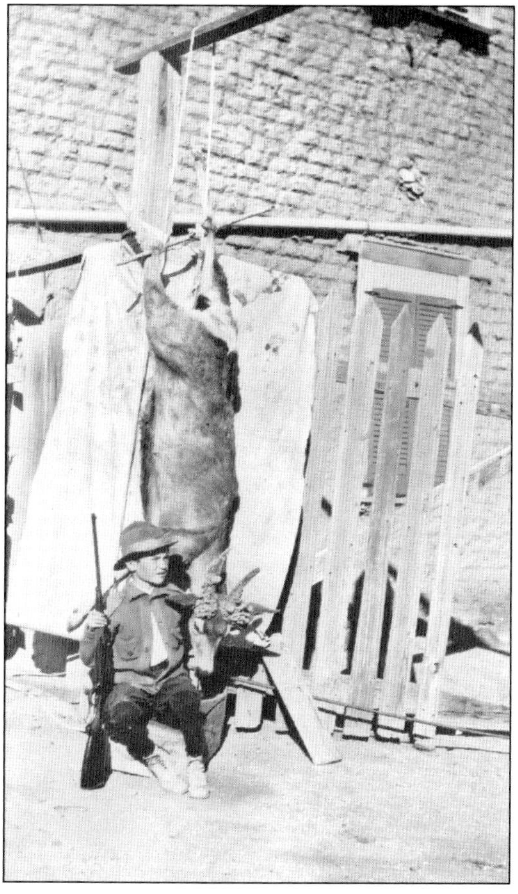

Young John Carroll "Jack" Truman, born in Florence in 1909, poses proudly with the deer he shot. Wildlife was abundant around Florence, situated on the bank of the once-mighty Gila River. Jack is at the home of his maternal grandmother, Doña Elena Barragán Collingwood Bamrick de Stevens. Built in 1877, the two-story adobe boasted a wood floor and lavish furnishings and was long the town's showplace.

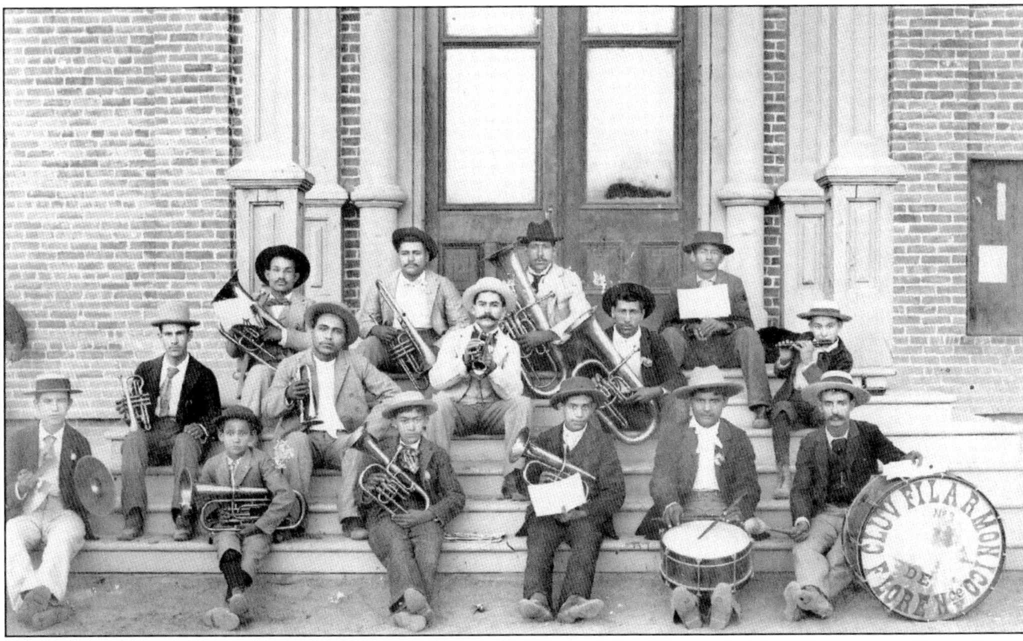

In this 1894 photograph, the Cluv Filarmonic de Florence rests on the Pinal County Courthouse steps. "Florence" did not quite fit on the bass drum, so the sign painter had to improvise.

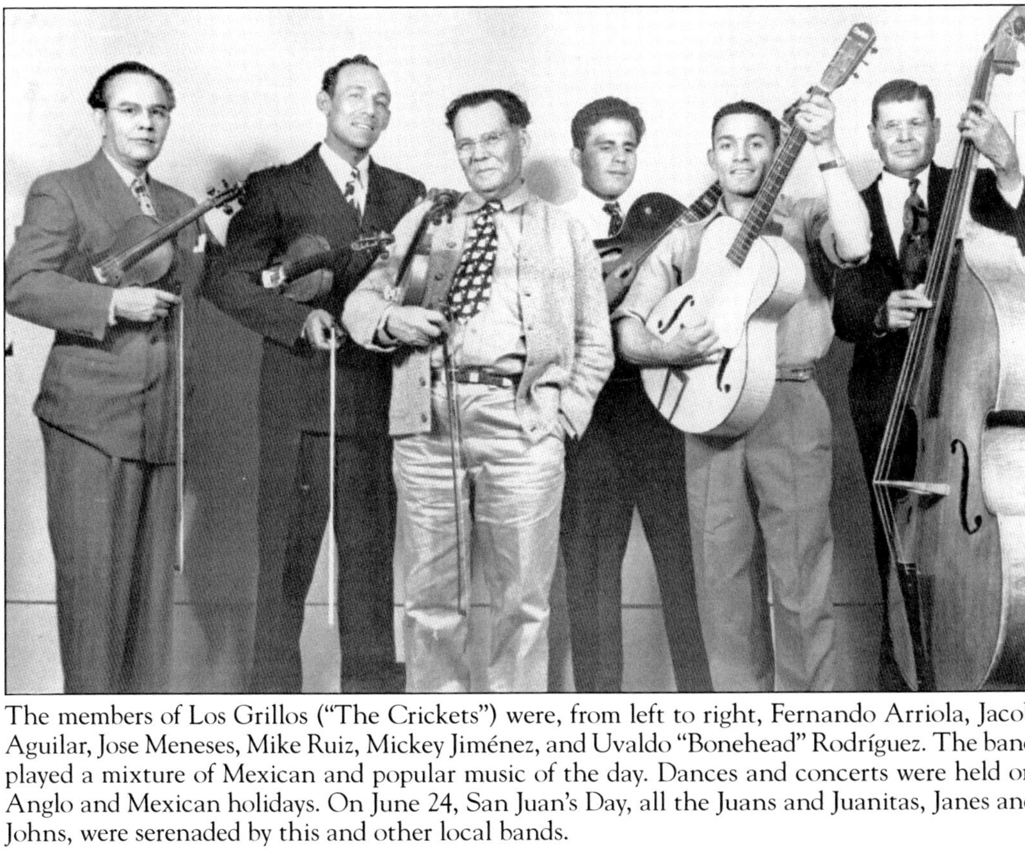

The members of Los Grillos ("The Crickets") were, from left to right, Fernando Arriola, Jacob Aguilar, Jose Meneses, Mike Ruiz, Mickey Jiménez, and Uvaldo "Bonehead" Rodríguez. The band played a mixture of Mexican and popular music of the day. Dances and concerts were held on Anglo and Mexican holidays. On June 24, San Juan's Day, all the Juans and Juanitas, Janes and Johns, were serenaded by this and other local bands.

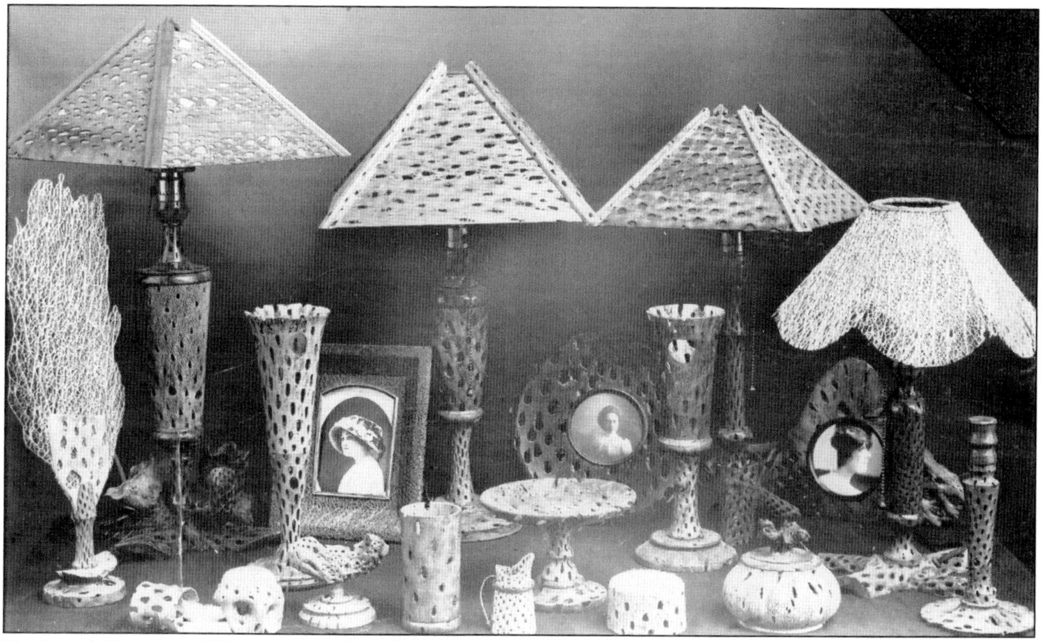

Frederick Emerson White arrived in Florence from California in the 1870s. In 1901, he incorporated his Arizona Cactus Company. This postcard advertisement displays samples of cactus wood furniture and novelties produced by the firm. Stockholders included D. C. Stevens, George Brockway, A. F. Barker, Thomas Peyton, and Ramón Arballo.

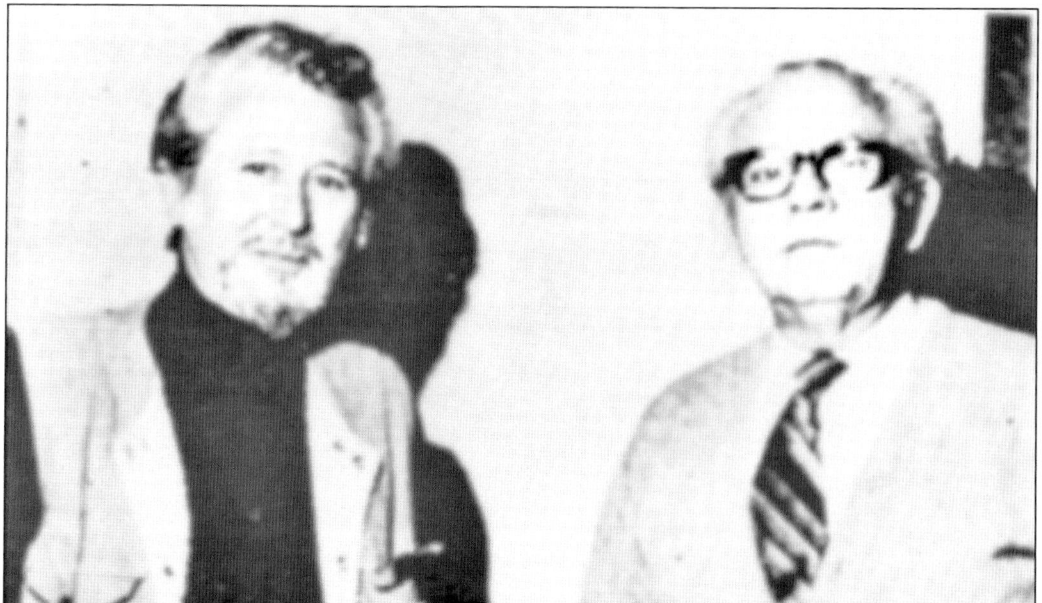

Gustavo "Gus" Arriola (left) took the childhood memories of his large family and turned them into the delightful comic strip *Gordo* for 40 years. With his brother Fernando, he enjoyed a visit to his old hometown in 1970. Although Fernando stayed in Florence and worked at Mandell's Store, he was a talented artist as well.

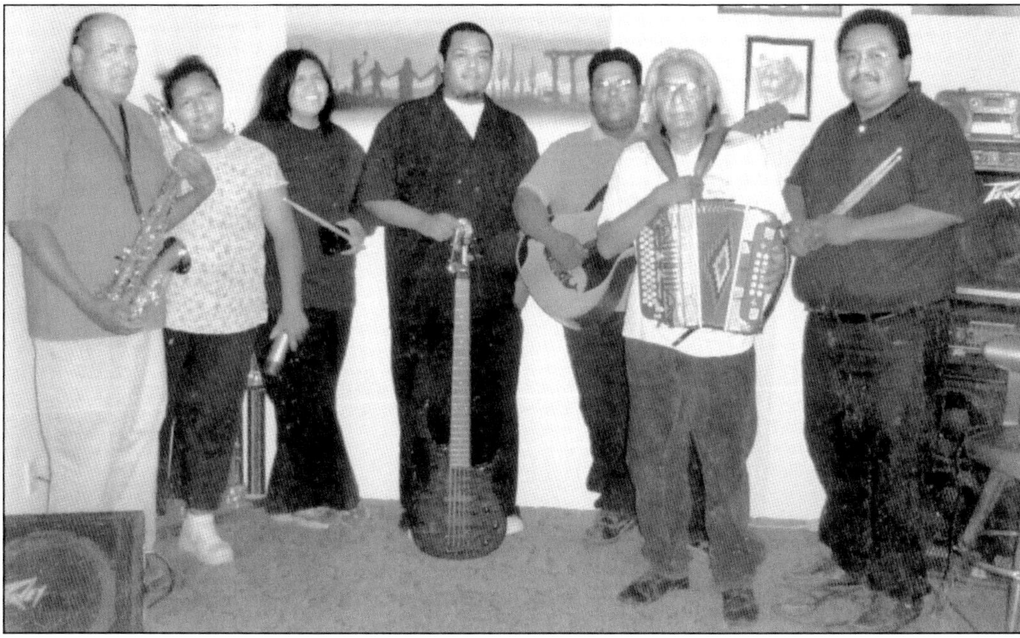

Waila music, begun in the 1860s as a part of O'odham culture, is a combination of European rhythms and instruments and Native American and Mexican influences. Also called "chicken scratch" after the vigorous stepping and scratching on the floor by dancers, waila is passed from generation to generation on the reservations, where waltzes, polkas, two-steps, and mazurkas are played. Ron Joaquin's band Southern Scratch is pictured here.

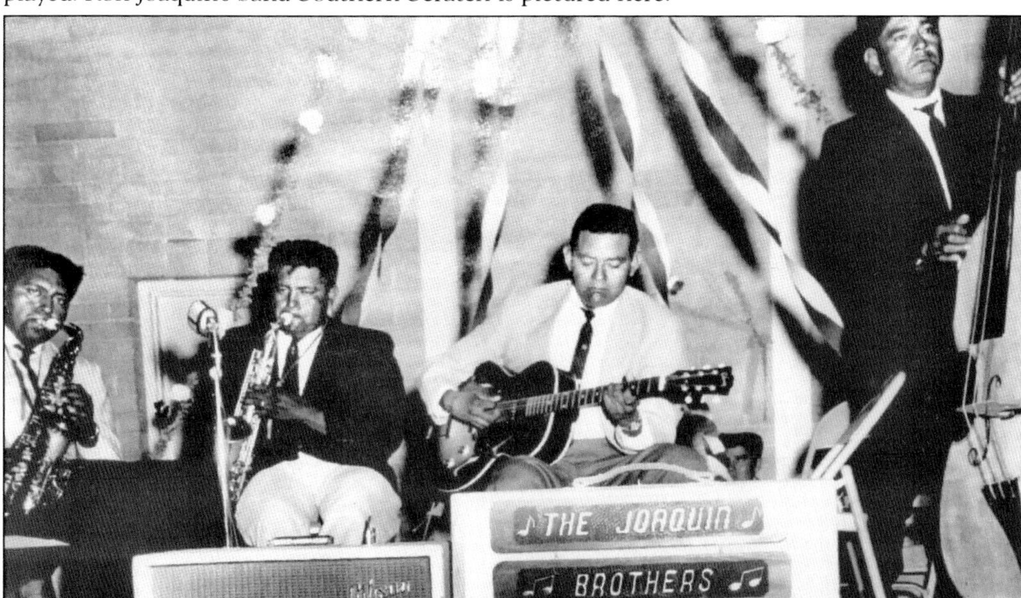

Angelo Joaquin Sr. began the Joaquin Brothers Band in 1957 with his brother Fernando and cousins Frank and Joe Celestine. His brother Daniel joined the waila group later. Angelo recalled that as a boy the typical waila group consisted of two fiddles, a guitar, a snare drum, and a bass drum. Accordions and electrical instruments were added as the genre evolved. The Joaquin Brothers Band performed at Carnegie Hall and at the Smithsonian Institution.

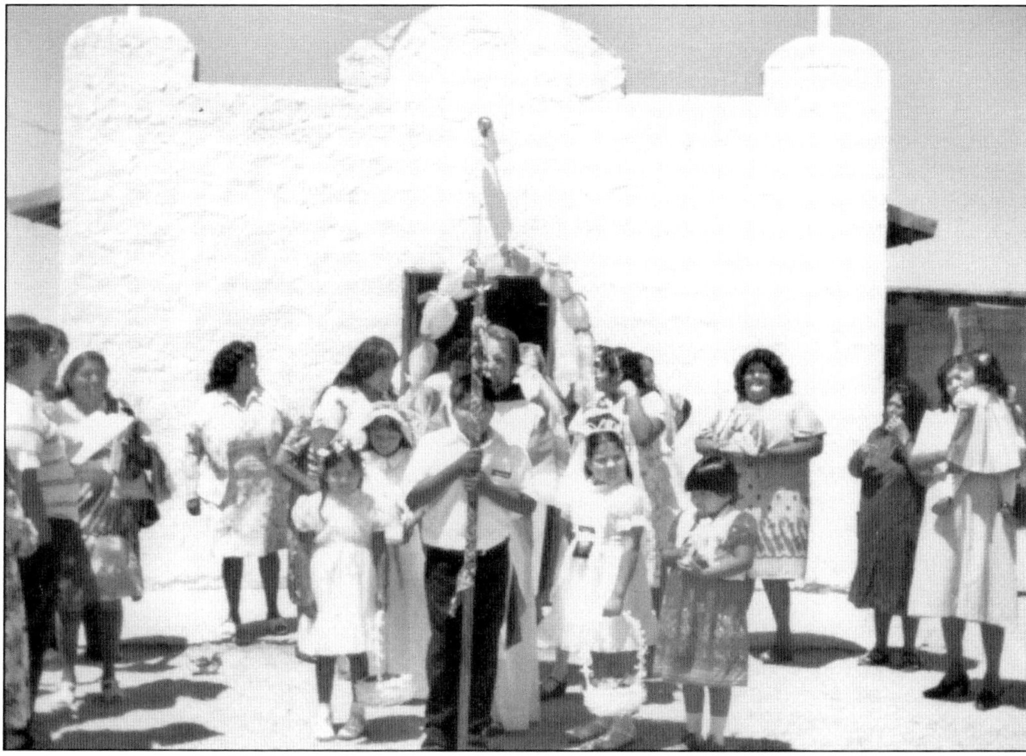

The Florence Indian Village west of town retains many early O'odham traditions while combining outside influences. Seen here is a procession out of the St. Elizabeth Church. Villagers to this day refer not to going to Florence but to "the place of the cottonwoods," thus keeping alive the memory of Florence's tree-lined streets and cottonwood-lined Gila River.

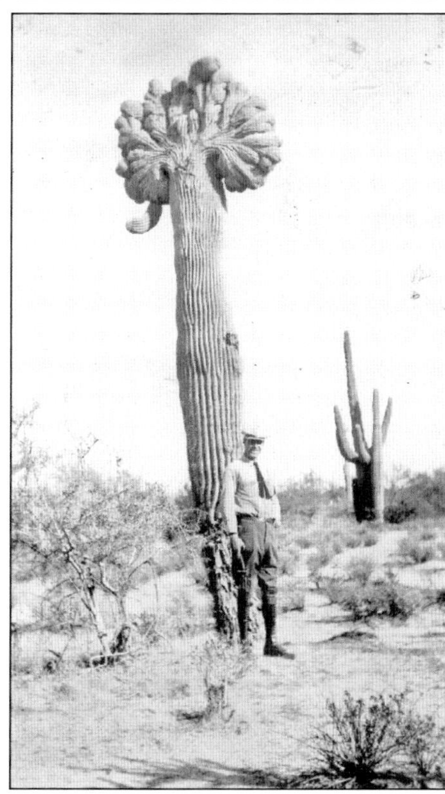

Florence historian and author Albert W. Gressinger poses with a rare crested saguaro. Beginning in the 1930s, Gressinger interviewed and photographed many Florence founders. A past president of the Pinal County Historical Society, he housed his archives there as a valuable resource. His book *Charles D. Poston—Sunland Seer*, the definitive work on Father of Arizona Charles Poston, was published in 1961.

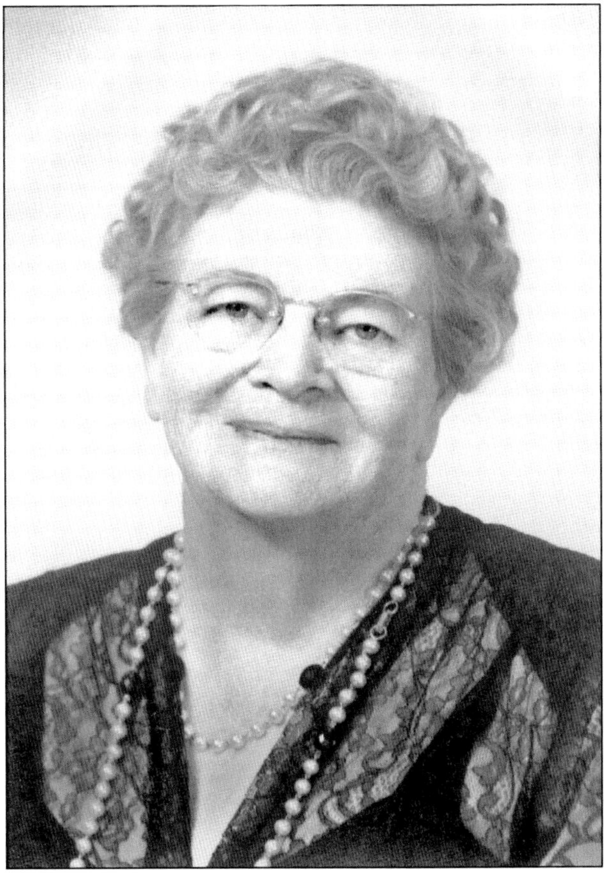

Charlotte "Lottie" Colton was born in Florence in 1889. As a little girl, she remembered peeking at bandit Pearl Hart. She was delighted that Pearl smiled and waved back. When Lottie's husband, Edwin Devine, died in 1944, she was appointed to fill his seats as justice of the peace and town magistrate. Lottie was very civic minded, and her soft-spoken demeanor balanced her firm but fair administration of justice.

The Town of Florence, the Presbyterian church, and the Pinal County Historical Society benefitted from the time and dedication of Della Arcadia Redondo Meadows. Raised on the A Diamond Ranch, Della began working at the Arizona State Prison in 1948 as the warden's secretary. She gained the respect of inmates and staff alike. After her retirement in 1983, a prison unit was named for her.

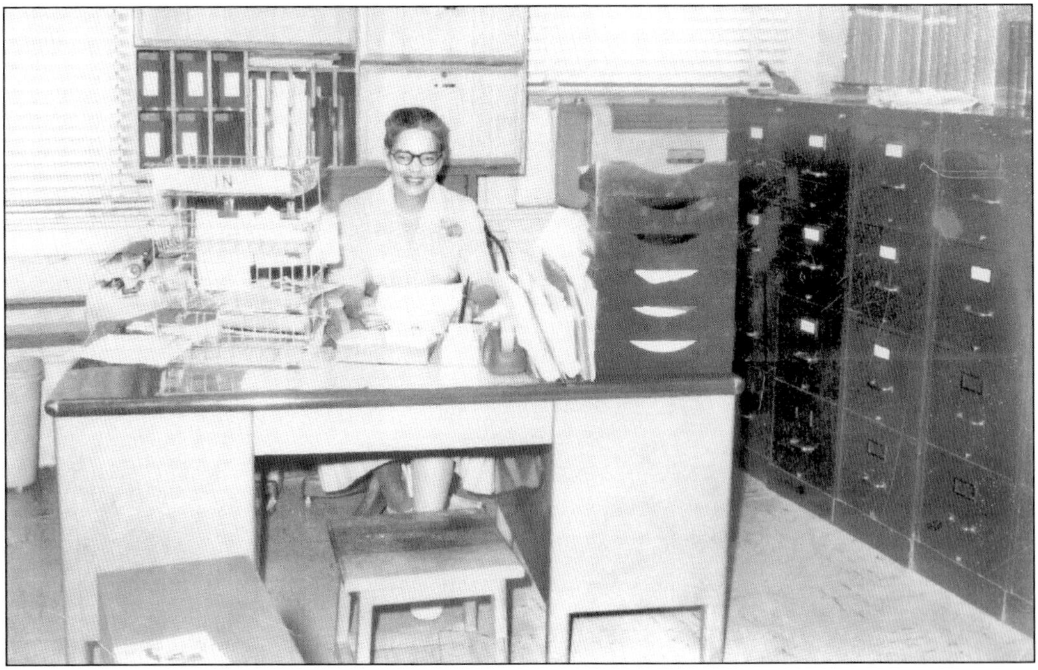

Five

Dreams Meet Reality

Florence prospered. Mines were operating nearby, and as the county seat, Florence was a draw for people. The Silver King Hotel, later called the Florence Hotel, catered to newcomers as well as those on their way to somewhere else. General merchandise stores and other businesses served mainly townspeople.

People had to come to Florence to record documents and serve on juries, so government was an important part of the life of the town. County business soon outgrew the original courthouse. Prominent architect James M. Creighton was hired to design the new brick Victorian-style second Pinal County Courthouse. The ambitious project was meant to reflect Florence's coming of age and readiness for Arizona statehood. Budget shortfalls caused some cutbacks on the construction. Instead of a working clock in the tower, false faces were painted on, reading a perpetual 11:44. The project was completed in 1891. Many individuals started their governmental careers here. Four Arizona governors—Joseph Kibbey, Richard E. Sloan, Robert T. Jones, and Ernest W. McFarland—spent at least part of their careers in Florence.

The Pinal County Sheriff's Posse used horses to perform its duty of capturing criminals and jail escapees for many years into the 20th century. The desert and the mountains were so rough that in many cases automotive power was not an option. With the coming of the automobile in the early 1900s, however, livery stables slowly gave way to service stations and garages.

After the Silver King Mine played out, Florence became more agricultural. Although other crops were grown, cotton was planted acre upon acre. New technology helped make the usually labor-intensive crop more profitable.

Always of concern was water. Upstream diversion of the Gila River had affected Florence-area farmers as well as the Pima Indians. In 1930, Coolidge Dam was built on the Gila River east of Florence. Its purpose was to bring more water to the Pima Indians and to the farmers farther west, who needed large amounts of irrigation to grow cotton.

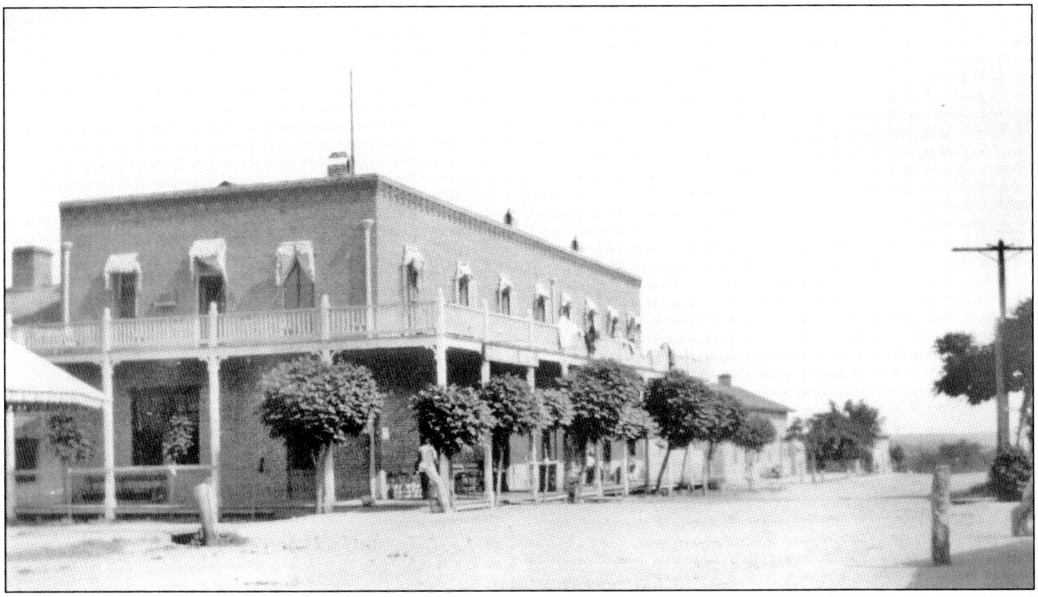

William H. Long, one of the Silver King Mine's discoverers, built the adobe Silver King Hotel and opened for business in late December 1876. The main structure burned in 1893 and was replaced with the two-story brick building that stands on Main Street today. By 1916, the hotel's name had been changed to the Florence Hotel. Once one of the most important hostelries in the Southwest, the hotel is scheduled for restoration. (Courtesy Arizona Historical Society, No. 19164.)

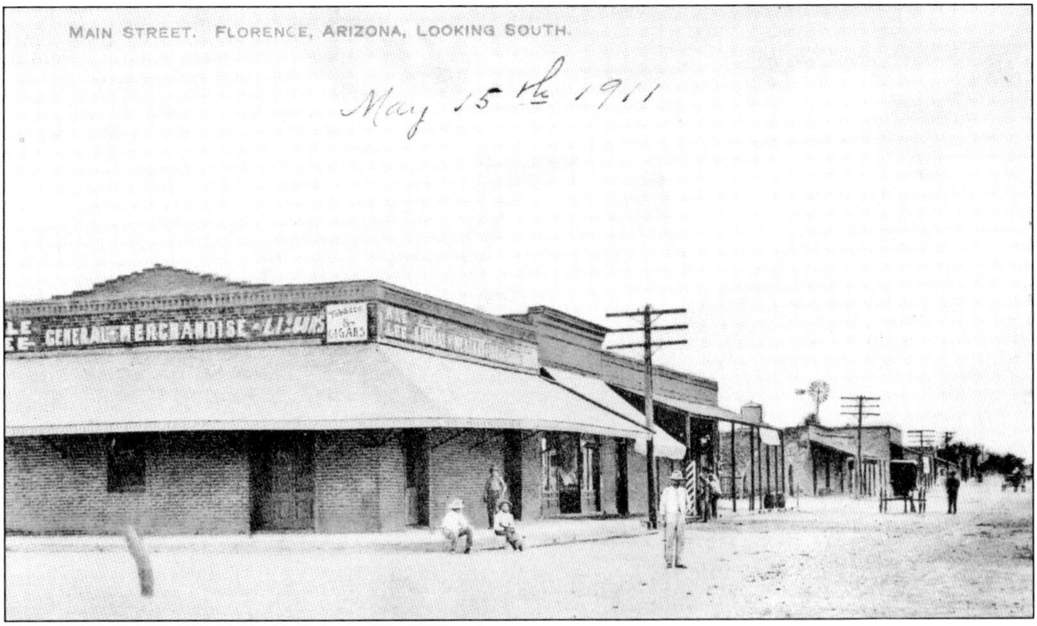

This postcard depicts Ah Lee's store despite the different spelling on the sign. Lee's 1908 newspaper advertisement boasted "nice fresh groceries, . . . cold bottled beer always on hand, right off the ice." Chum Kin, Lee Sin Kee, Jim Sam, Antonio the Chinaman (as he was known), and other Chinese businessmen prospered in Florence. Grocer Lem Wing Ching advertised Chinese handkerchiefs and genuine Chinese tea and novelties in 1892. Sing Lee's bakery and restaurant served regular meals for 25¢ in 1898.

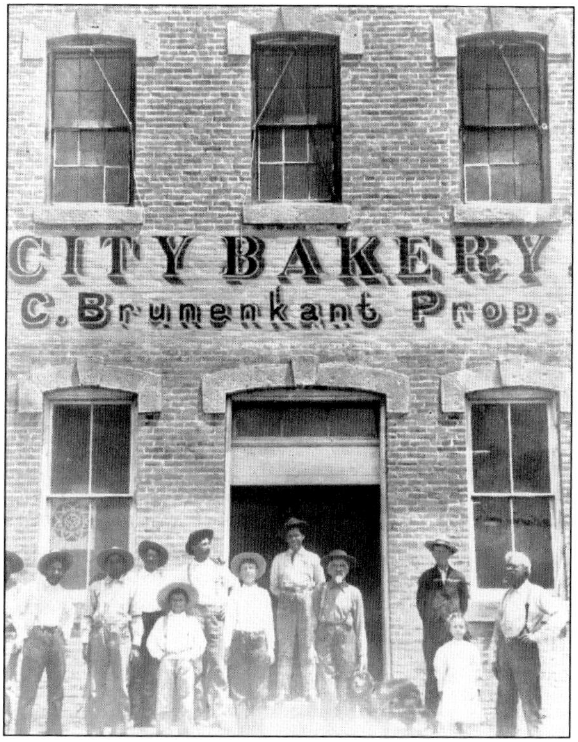

The three people at far right are members of the Brunenkant family. Along with workers and other townspeople, Alvin (left), Wilhelmina Caroline (center), and their father, Conrad, pose in front of Conrad's City Bakery. After the Great Depression, Alvin started the AB Grocery Store in his father's building. He served as mayor of Florence for six terms and as interpreter for the superior court, as he spoke five languages.

The Bank of Florence, pictured in 1908, was one of the businesses that sprang up to serve the region as the town prospered. In addition to Florence, the bank served the communities of Casa Grande, Kelvin, Superior, and Ray. Its authorized capitalization was $50,000. Energetic businessman D. C. Stevens held the office of president, with F. A. Chamberlain as vice-president and T. C. Eagin as cashier. Those seen here are unidentified.

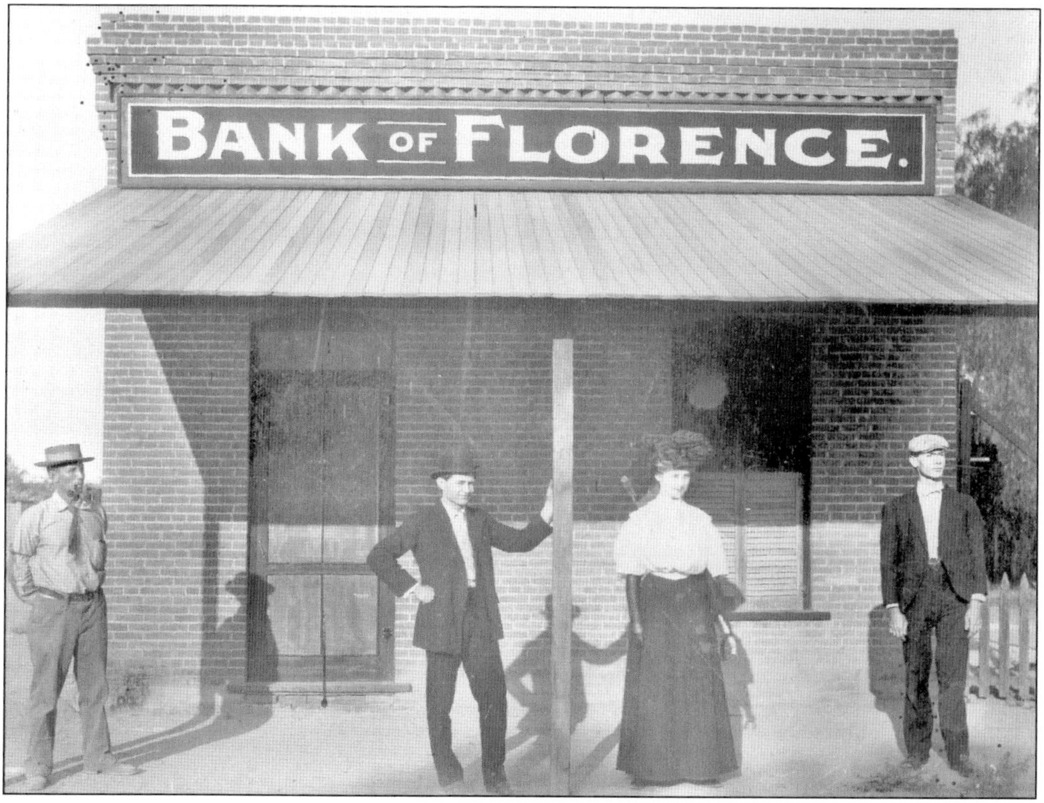

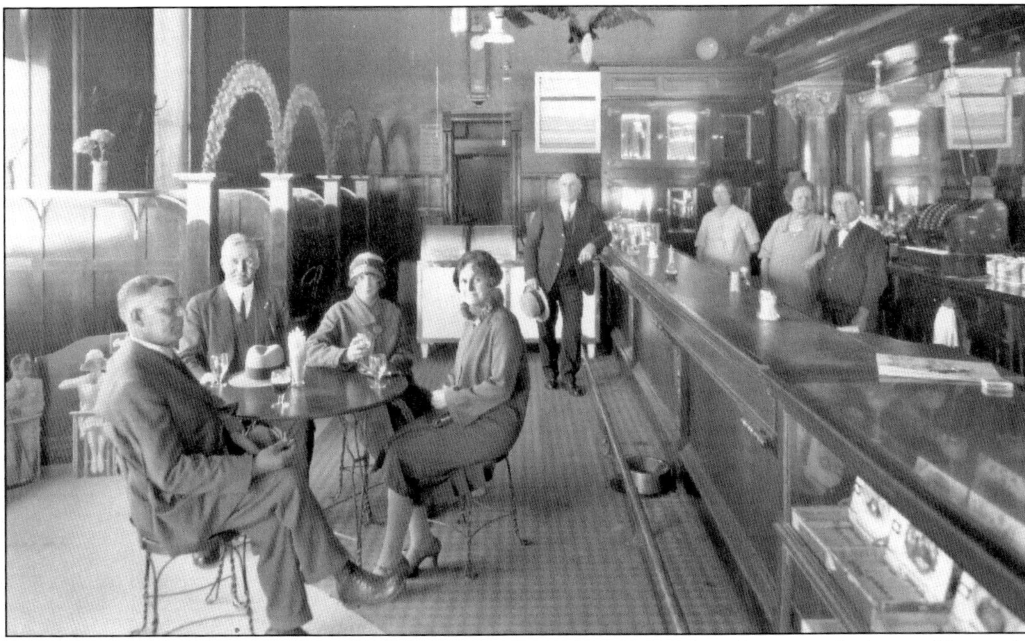

Ed Devine built a confectionery and drugstore around 1914. In this photograph, he and his wife, Lottie, stand behind the counter. Superior court judge E. L. Green (left foreground) sits with some friends. Notice the private booths and Coca-Cola advertisements. Lottie's family came to the town in the 1890s. Her memoir, *Es Verdad*, captures a child's view of early Florence. She became the first female justice of the peace in the county.

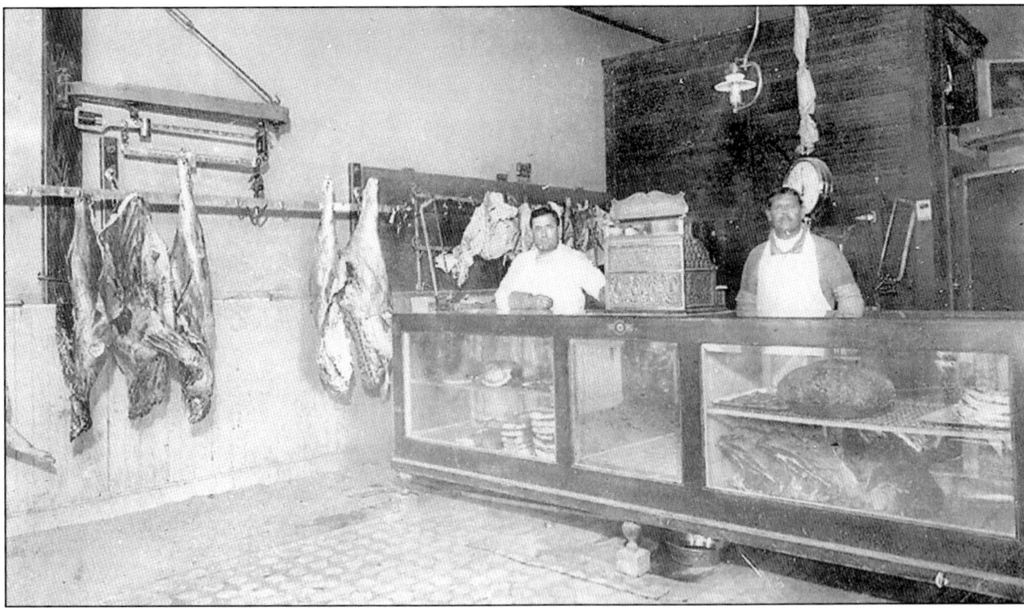

In 1915, the Nicholas Meat Market was a popular butcher shop. Phil Nicholas bought the shop from Gabriel Angulo. In this photograph of Francisco Andrade (left) and ? Rodríguez (right), notice the long scale hanging from the ceiling. Meat was not refrigerated, so once bought it was cooked immediately. Delicate pieces like heart, liver, and brains were in the counter case. "Chi-chi-ronies," pork cracklings, were a favorite treat.

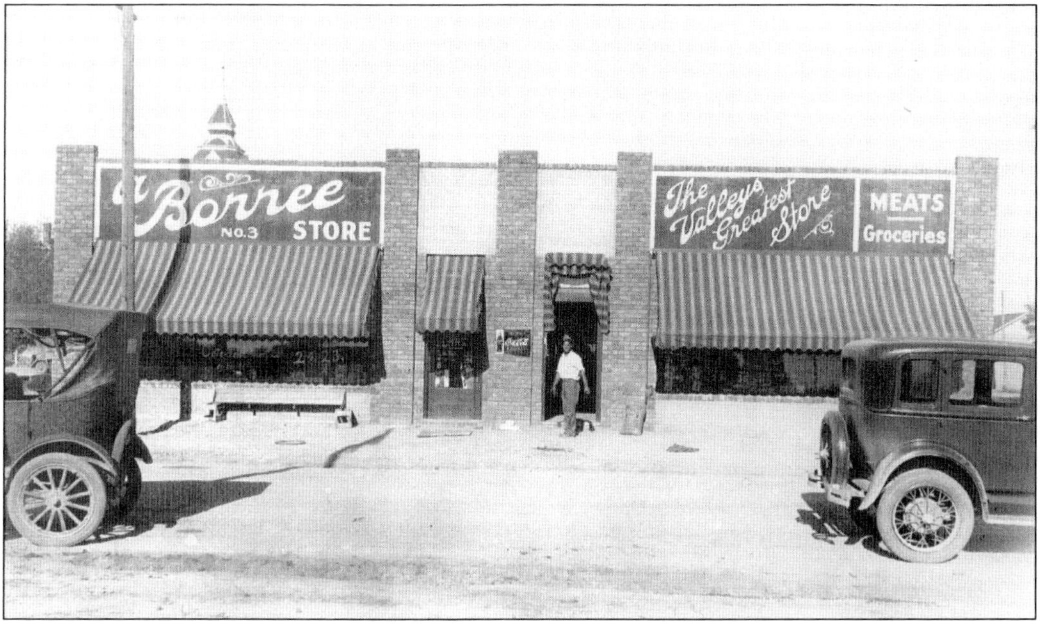

Nelson Borree stands in front of his market on Bailey Street. Built in 1928 of locally fired brick, this was an addition to his other stores at Borree's Corner and Casa Grande. After his death in 1946, his son James and his wife, Dorothy, ran the store. They worked six days a week, 10 hours a day, for the next 47 years. The store finally closed in 1992.

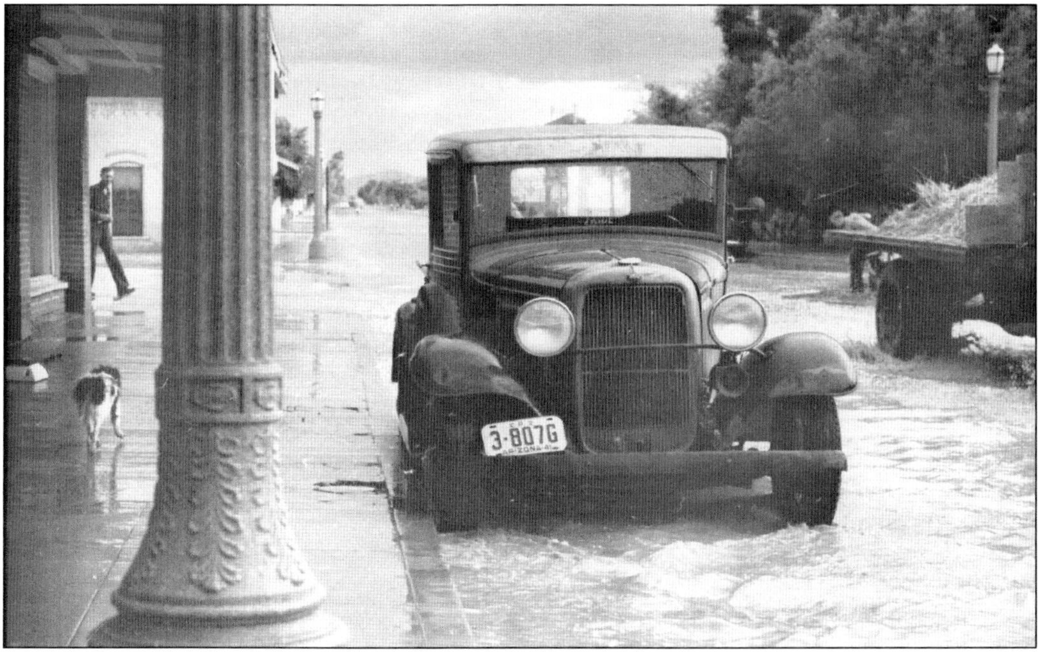

Built near the banks of the Gila River, Florence often flooded from the river or drainage from higher ground to the south. Seasonal monsoon rains created havoc until recent construction diverted runoff. Main Street sloped toward the river to the north. Sidewalks and curbs were built level, and many are unusually high. Passengers in today's lower-built cars must take care to avoid hitting car doors on Florence's high curbs.

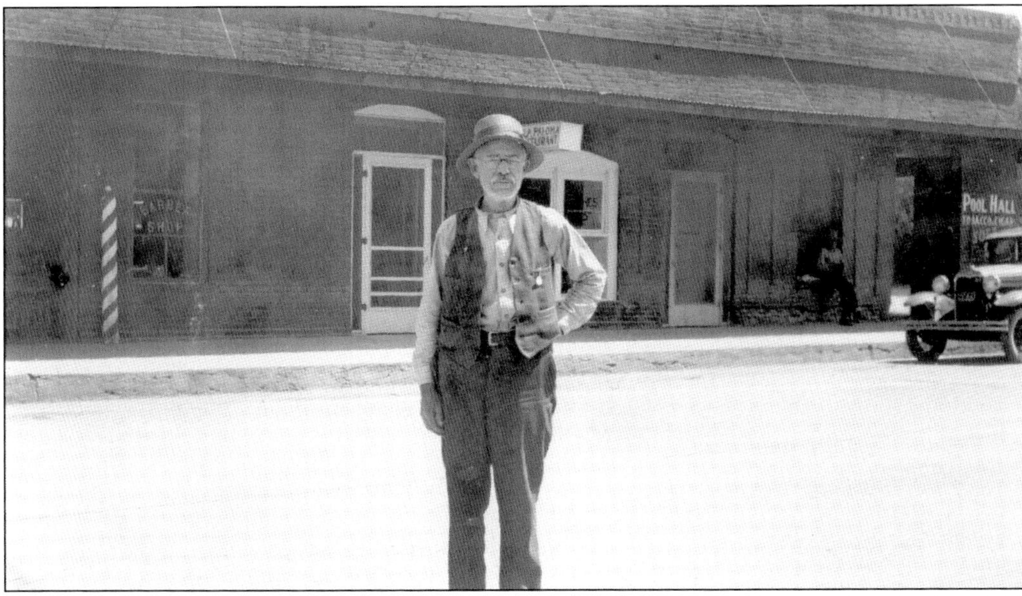

Guy S. Herr was an old-time journeyman printer back when everything was done by hand. He started his apprenticeship on the *Florence Enterprise* in 1888 and for many years worked in the composing room of the *Blade-Tribune*. The assertive Thomas Weedin had consolidated the *Florence Tribune* and *Arizona Blade* under the name *Arizona Blade and Florence Tribune* in 1902.

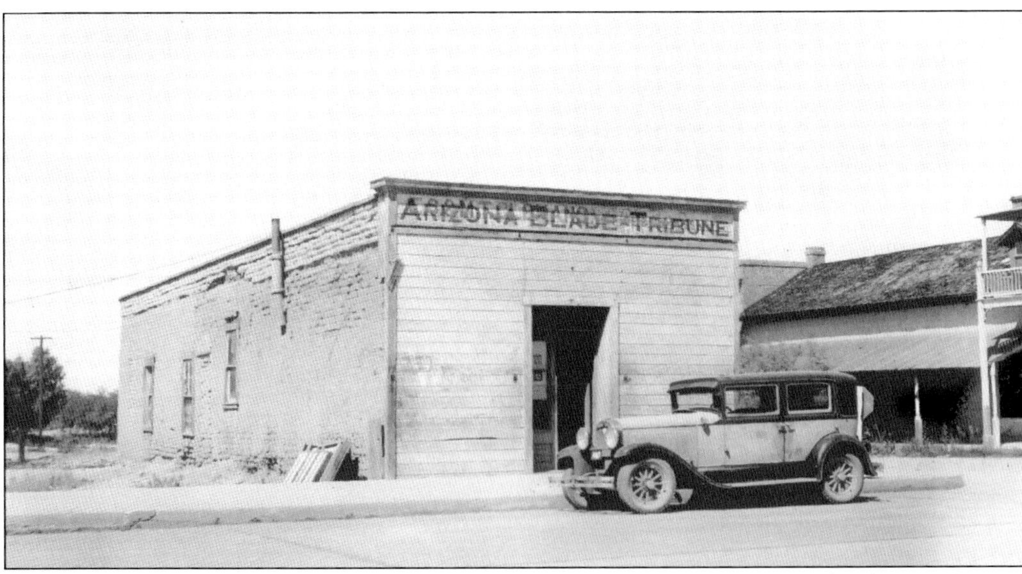

When Arizona gained statehood in 1912, Thomas Weedin ran for governor but lost to G. W. P. Hunt. He then sold his newspaper to A. C. Wrenn. Pictured around 1929, this small adobe building still stands alone on Main Street across from the Silver King Hotel. In 1957, Jack Purves established and began editing the *Florence Reminder*. Eventually all three would combine under the banner *Florence Reminder and Blade-Tribune*, owned by publisher Donovan Cramer.

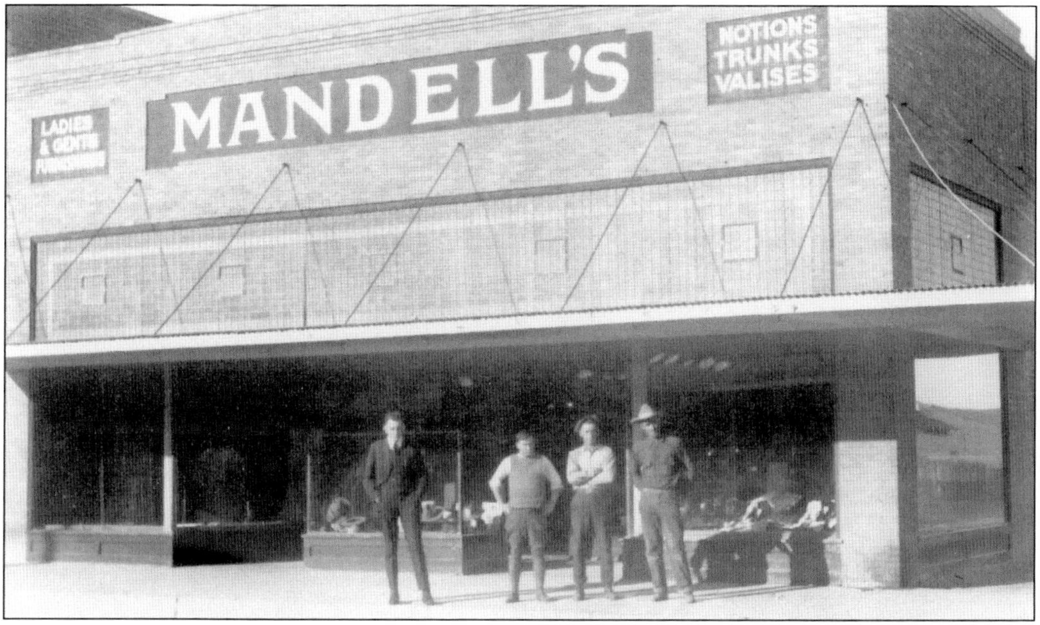

Shown soon after Kaufman Mandell Sr. established his department store on Main Street are, from left to right, Leo Bloch, Ramón Sesma, Pablo Loroña, and Antonio Ruiz. Bloch managed the store while Mandell opened others in small Arizona towns. Eventually Kaufman "Kay" Mandell Jr. would operate the business. By that time, "Ladies and Gents Furnishings, Notions, Trunks, Valises" had given way to "Men's Wear and Ladies' Wear."

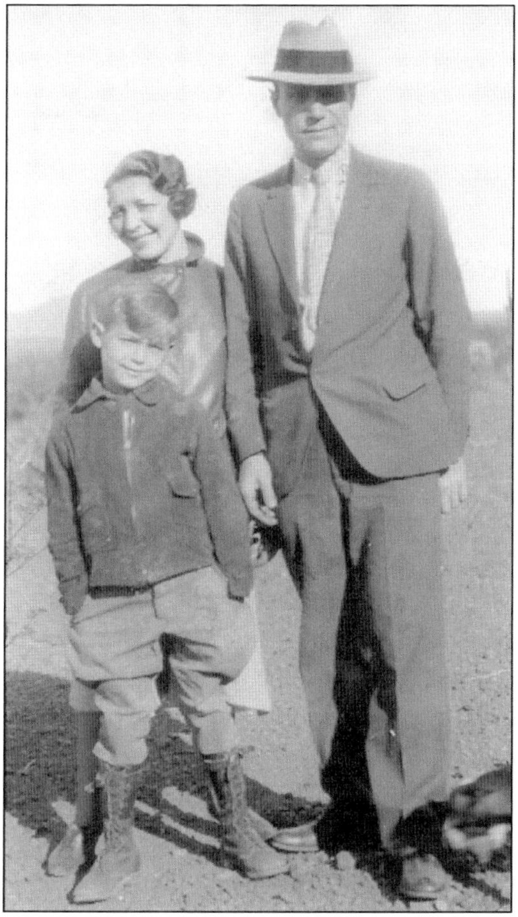

Kaufman Mandell Sr. and his wife, Marjorie, are pictured with their young son Kay about 1935. Born in France, Kaufman Sr. followed his brothers to this country at age 16. In 1919, he bought C. G. Powell's People's Store building and renamed it Mandell's. On his 80th birthday, he was honored for his 50 years as a Florence merchant.

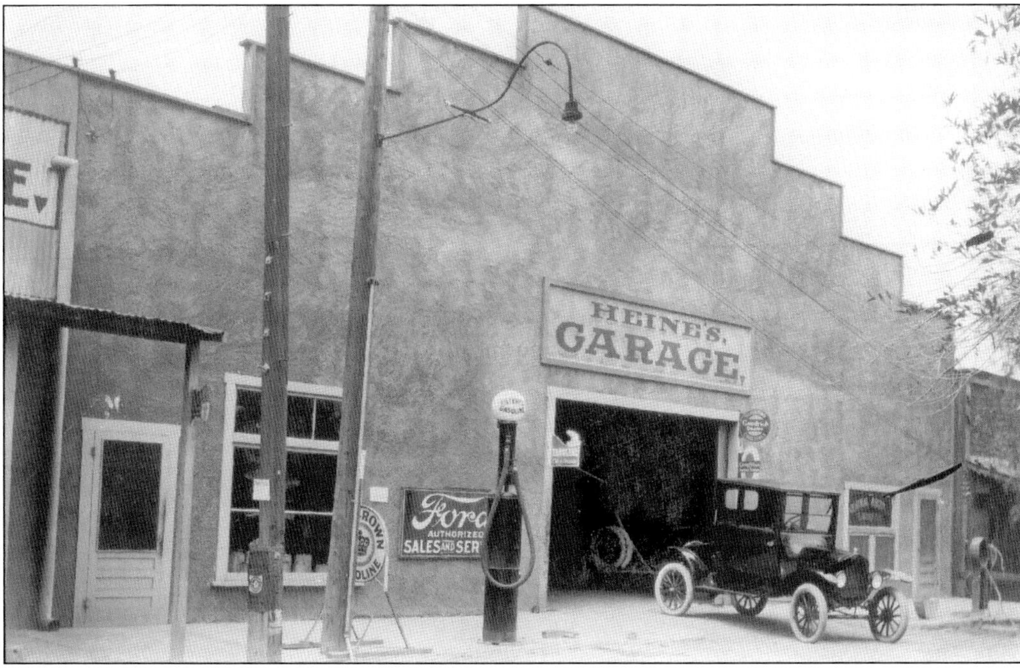

Heine's Garage dates from the early 20th century. Hendrik Schewel's business began as a Ford dealership on the corner of Sixth and Main Streets. His May 1918 newspaper advertisement warned, "The manufacture of all cars will be cut 75 per cent. How much of a chance will you have to get one this summer unless you order now?" World War I was still raging.

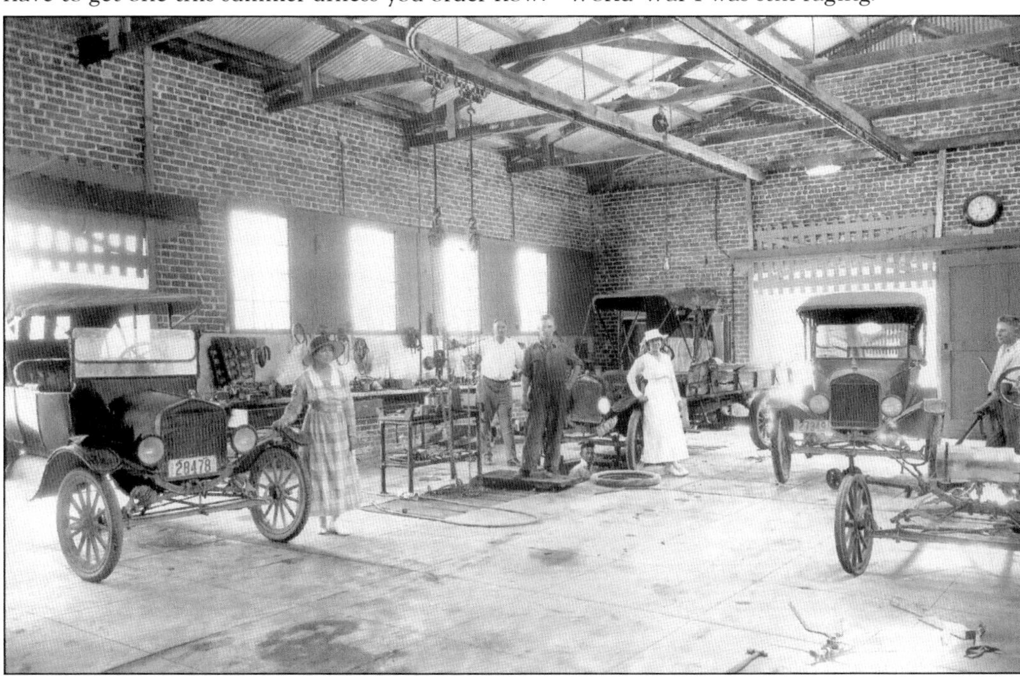

The interior of the service department is proudly displayed in this photograph of Schewel's mechanics and perhaps he and his wife, Flossie. The automobile license plates date the image to 1920. A mechanic peers out of a hole in the floor used for undercarriage work.

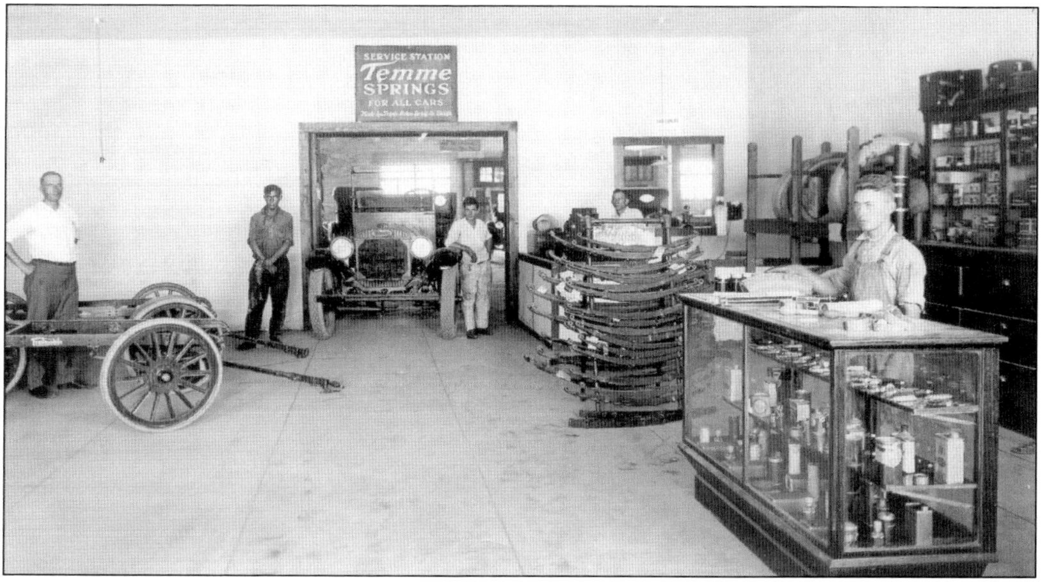

The parts department of Heine's Garage had a large selection of automobile springs. Early automobile owners found they got damaged on the bumpy Arizona roads. In June 1929, Heine's Garage is advertising the Chevrolet Six: "Learn what a marvelous performance you get in a low price car of $595."

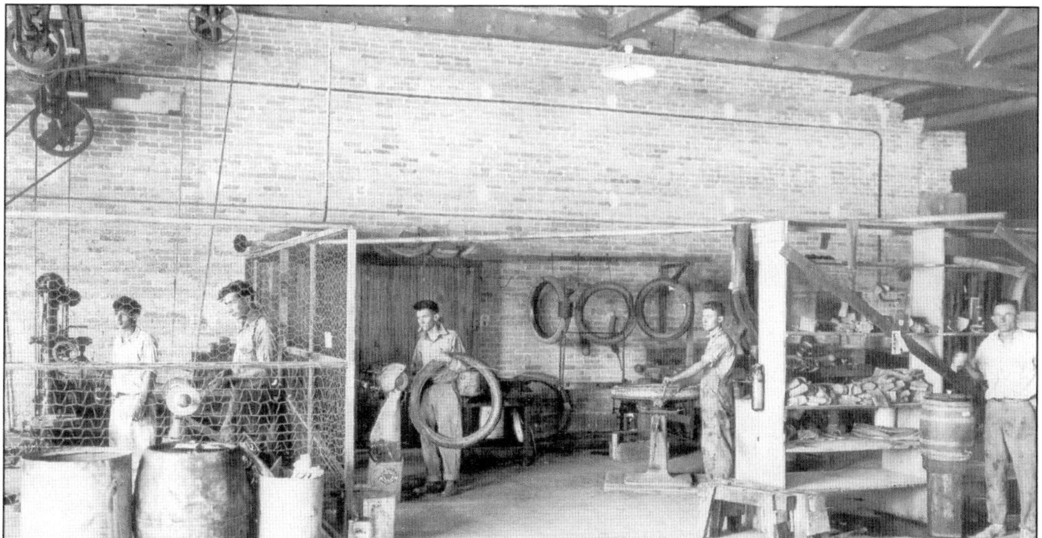

The tire department of Heine's Garage was an active part of Schewel's business. With few paved roads and the threat of cactus and mesquite thorns, Arizona's early drivers always carried spare tires. The machine shop was operated by one electric motor that could power many individual machines with a system of belts and pulleys.

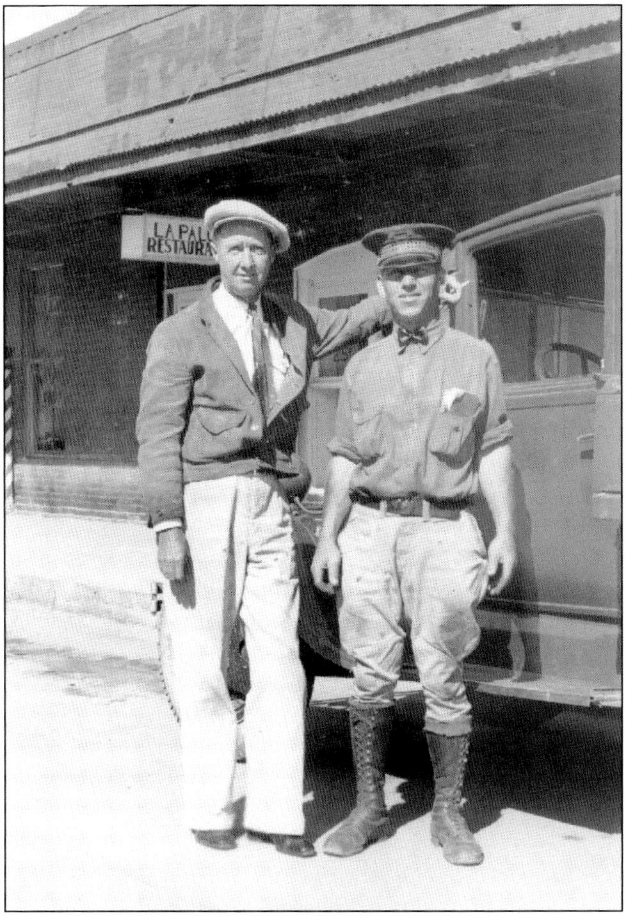

Lee Brown (left) and Louis E. Diehl stand in front of La Paloma Bar and Restaurant in 1933. Brown was a surveyor for the U.S. Indian Service and president of the local Arizona Game Protection Association. Diehl, a veteran of World War I, worked as a Standard Oil wholesale distributor. He was also a charter member and commander of the McLellan-Parsons Legion Post in Florence.

W. J. "Bill" Bley (left), a Silver King miner in his much younger days, a young Charles A. Whitlow (center), and Roy Guild are pictured in front of the Florence justice of the peace office in 1933. Whitlow, a rancher and cowboy, was at one time town marshal. Guild, who lost his leg in an accident, served as justice of the peace.

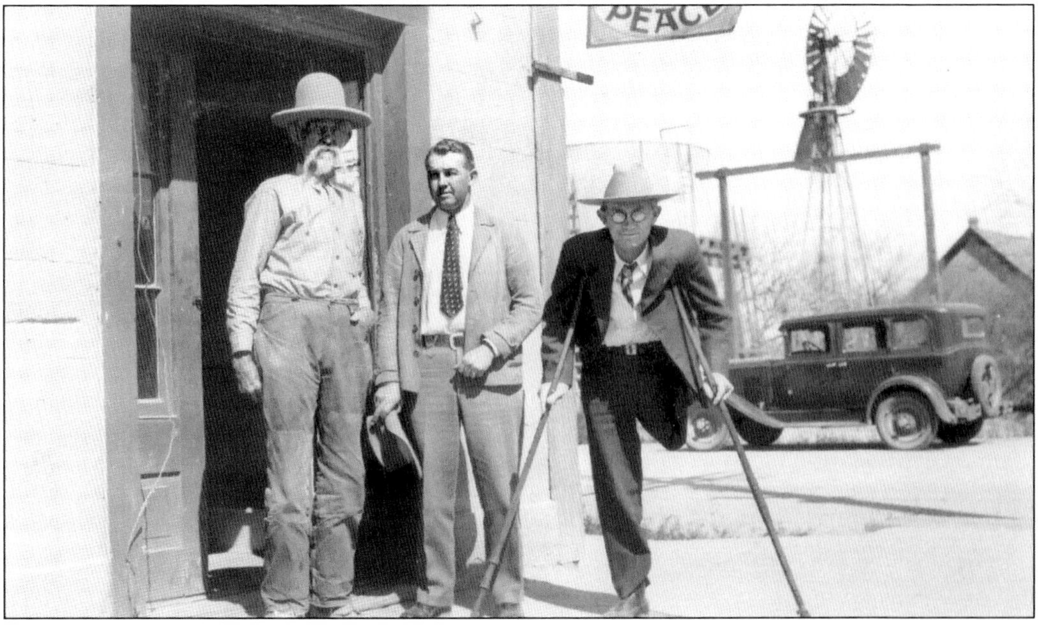

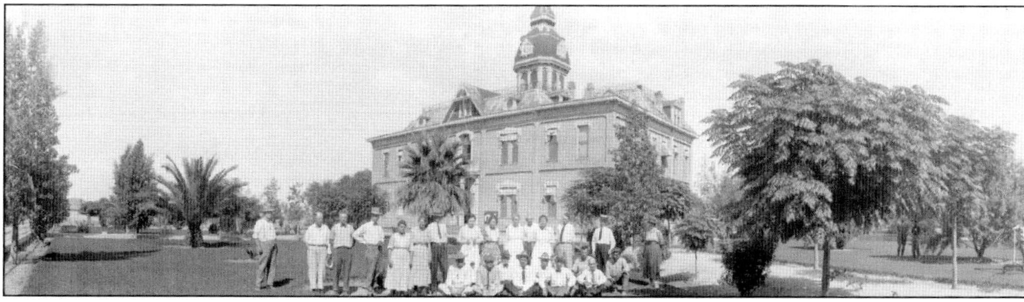

Pinal County officers and employees pose in front of the 1891 courthouse (the second courthouse) in 1930. Included here are individuals whose names are prominent in Florence history: Charles Mason (first row, left); chief deputy sheriff and son of Florence pioneer Charles G. Mason; Charles Niemeyer (first row, third from left), clerk of the board of supervisors; and John Keating (second row, left), highway commissioner.

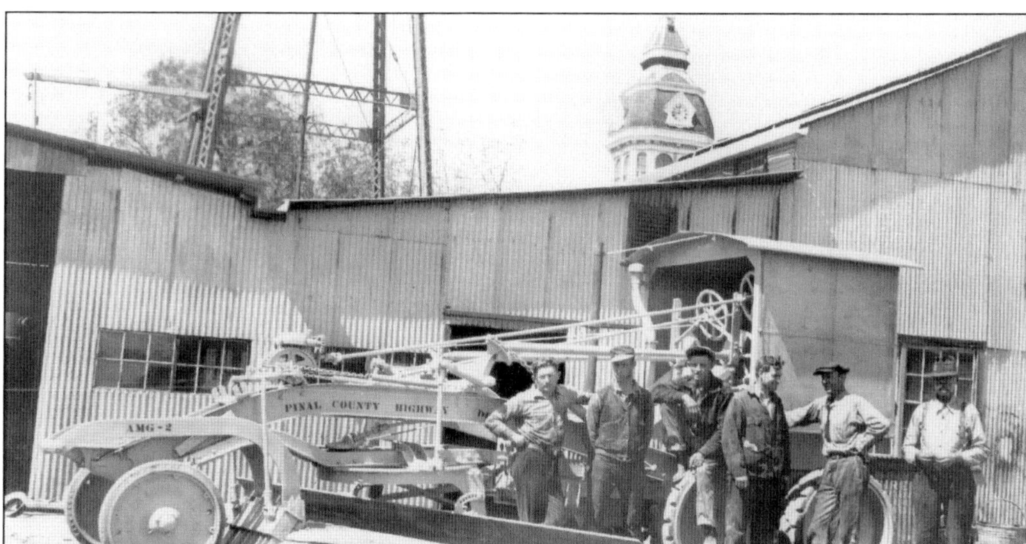

Shown in 1916 is the Pinal County Highway Department's White truck, nicknamed "the Boss of the Road." With rear wheels measuring 22 inches wide and front wheels measuring 11 inches, the truck could go only three miles an hour. The highway department was building the road from Kelvin to Florence to provide a shorter route to the county seat.

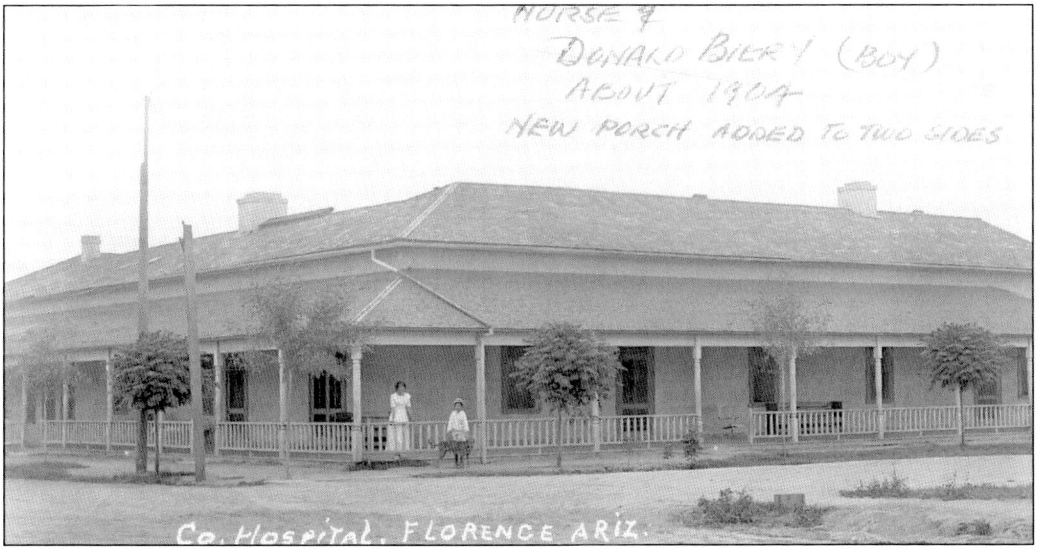

A nurse stands in front of the old adobe courthouse, which became the county hospital when a new courthouse opened in 1891. The *Arizona Blade and Tribune* reported in 1903 that the exceptionally pure, dry atmosphere and lack of stagnant water made Florence the healthiest town in Arizona, although a hospital was needed for those injured in the mines.

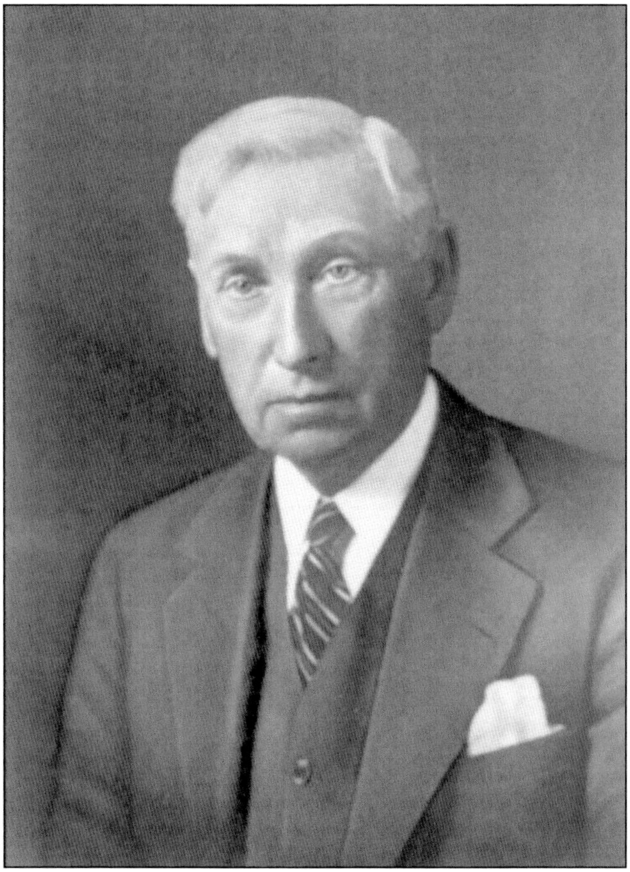

In 1886, Ohio-born Richard Elihu Sloan was elected district attorney in Florence. After holding other government offices, he was appointed territorial governor in 1909 and served until Arizona gained statehood on February 14, 1912. In his book *Memories of an Arizona Judge*, he related stories of life in Florence. He died in 1933.

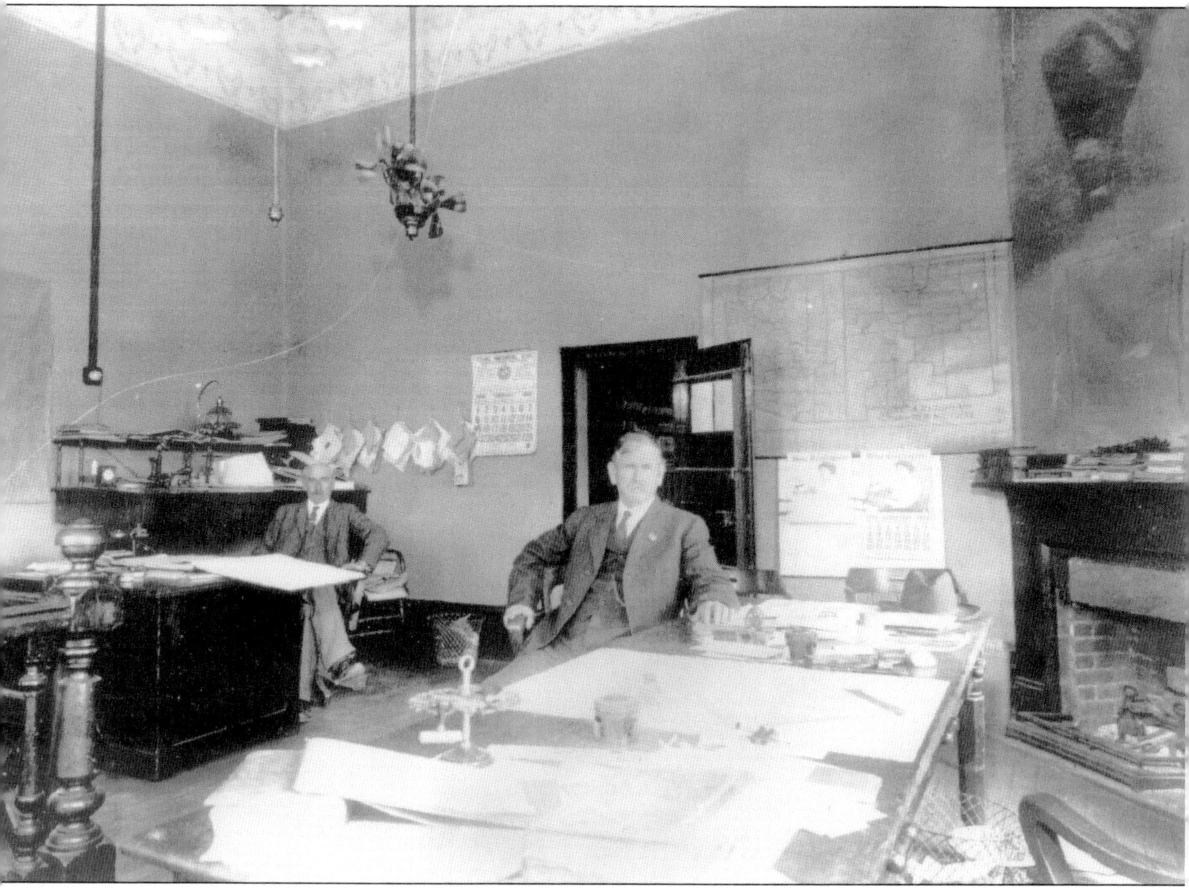

Two Florence boosters who devoted time to public service were Charles H. Niemeyer (left) and John Keating, shown in the second courthouse. Early in his life, Niemeyer worked at the 700-foot level of the Silver King Mine. He was also clerk of the county board of supervisors. A stage driver, Keating owned the downtown block including the Tunnel Saloon. He served as a legislator in the 23rd Legislature, where he wrote House Bill 149 to fund the bridge over the Gila River. He was a mayor, treasurer, chairman of the county board of supervisors, and a major in the Arizona National Guard. (Courtesy Arizona Historical Society, No. 765A.)

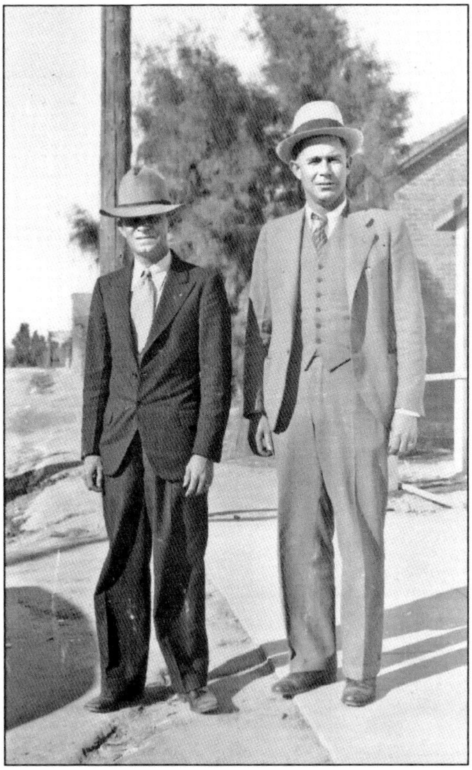

Tom Fulbright (left) appears with his law partner, Ernest W. McFarland. After Fulbright became an attorney through a correspondence course, he served for the prosecution as the first full-time deputy under McFarland and then as a defense attorney. According to the writer of the preface to Fulbright's book *Cow-Country Counselor*, he "has knowledge of what makes people tick which is virtually limitless."

The courtroom is seen on the last day Ernest W. McFarland presided as Pinal County Superior Court judge. McFarland had been both a county attorney and a defense attorney. During his career, he served in all three branches of government—as a U.S. senator, where he was majority leader; as governor of the state of Arizona; and as an Arizona Supreme Court chief justice.

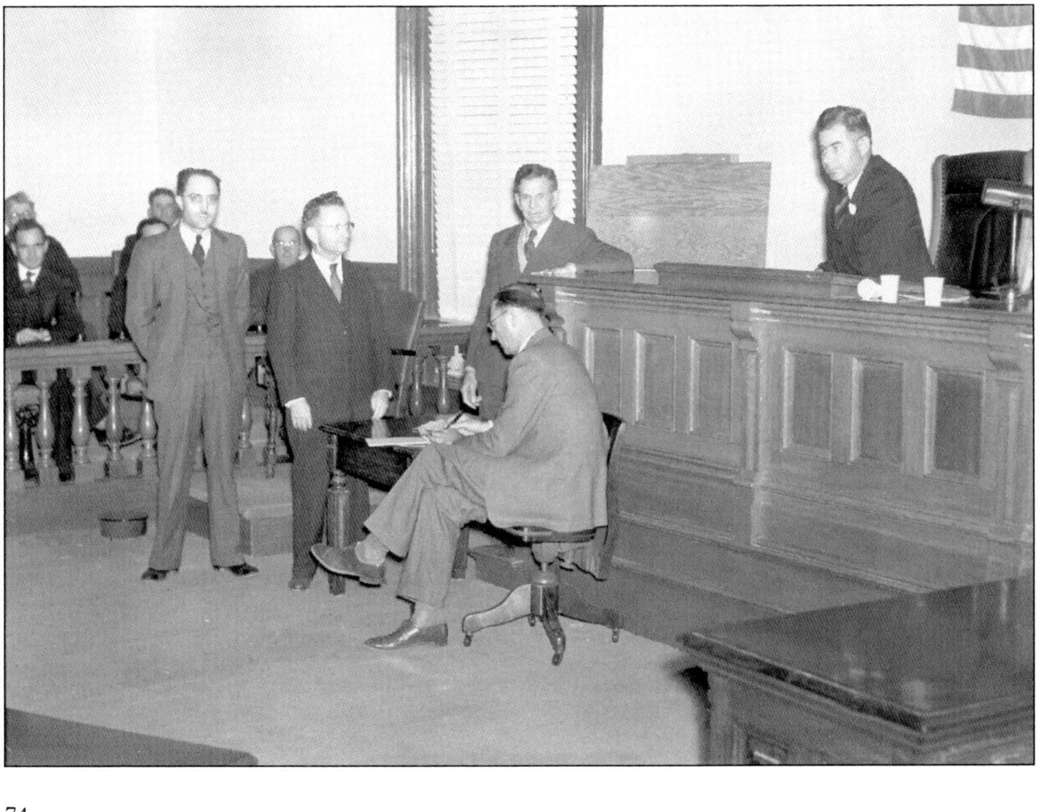

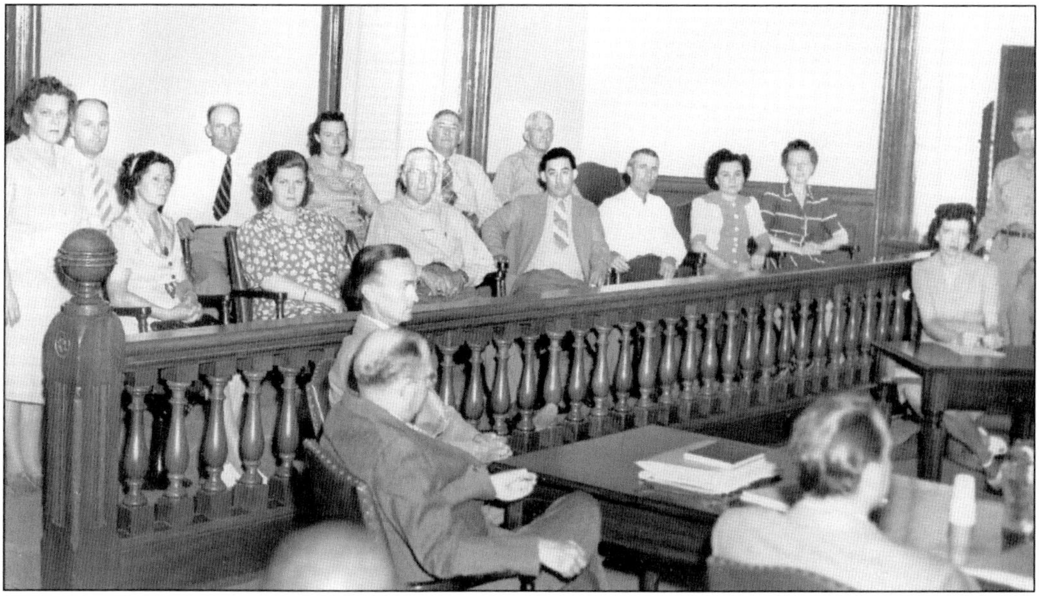

The first official jury session in Pinal County including women occurred on May 22, 1945. Seated in the foreground and seen from the back are county attorneys J. Johnson (left) and T. Fulbright (center) and deputy county attorney F. Preston Sult. Pictured in the jury box, from left to right, are the following: (first row) N. Beesley, R. Fowler, C. Harrison, ? Sáinz, W. Sims, M. Espinoza, and V. Louks; (second row) bailiff S. Smith, Louis ?, unidentified, E. Sherrill, P. Felix, and A. E. Humphries. In the right background are deputy clerk M. Freeman (left) and bailiff H. A. Trammel.

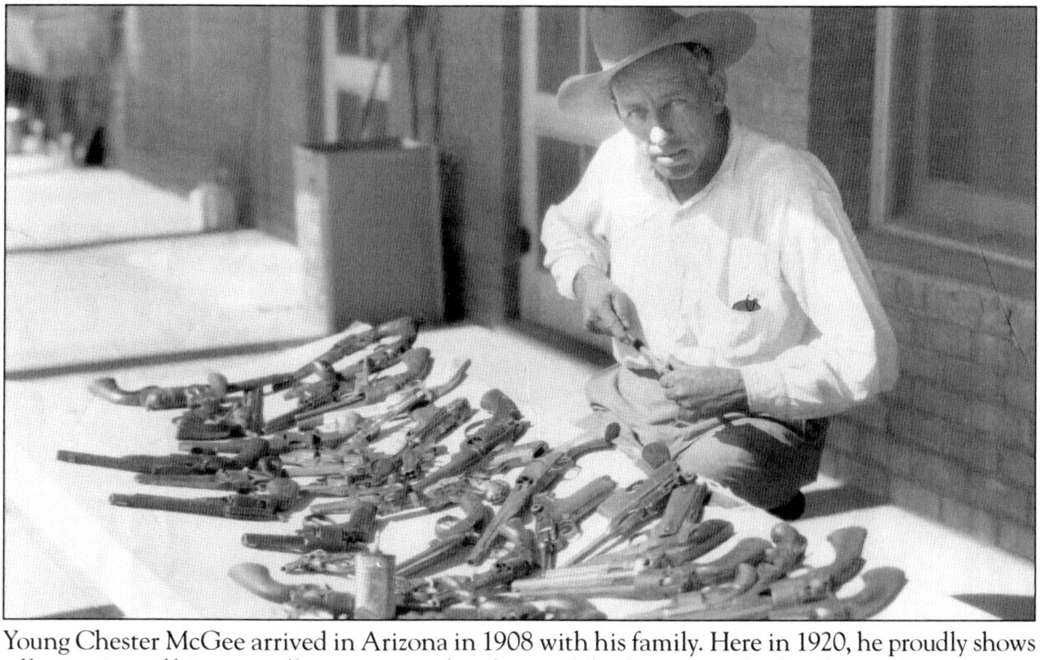

Young Chester McGee arrived in Arizona in 1908 with his family. Here in 1920, he proudly shows off a portion of his gun collection, considered one of the largest in the Southwest. He served as a Pinal County deputy sheriff for 14 years. His father, James McGee, worked as a Pinal County sheriff and Arizona Ranger.

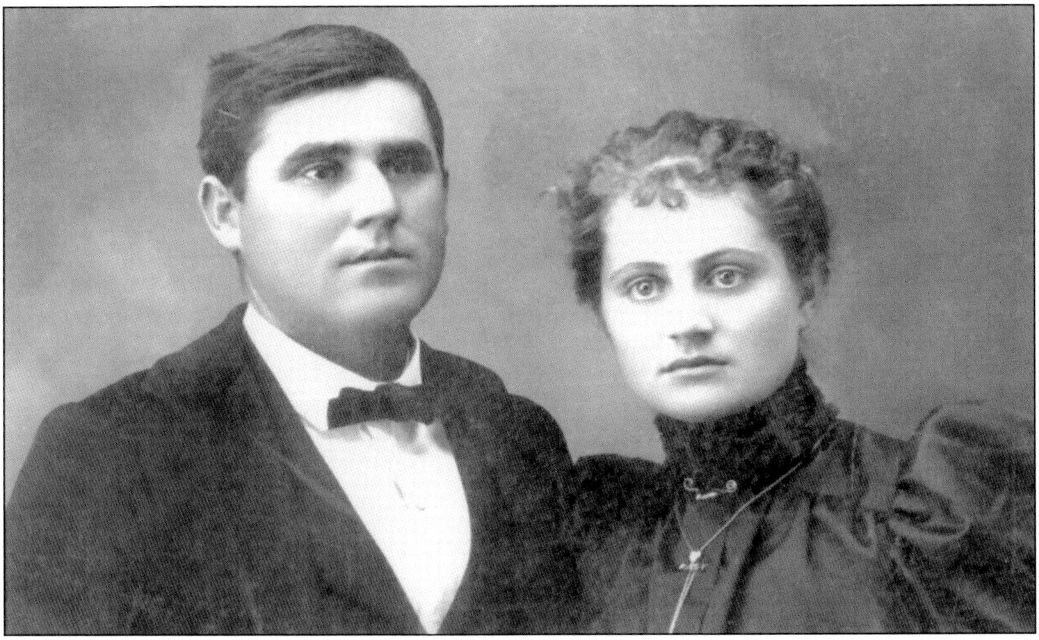

Henry David Hall, pictured with his wife, Martha "Mattie," became sheriff after the untimely death of Sheriff McGee. County supervisors were deadlocked over their pet choices. Finally names were tossed into a hat, and ex-sheriff William C. Truman turned his head and pulled Hall's name. The *Arizona Blade-Tribune* reported, "His family with seven daughters would be some addition to Florence's population and incidentally the school census." A son later joined his sisters.

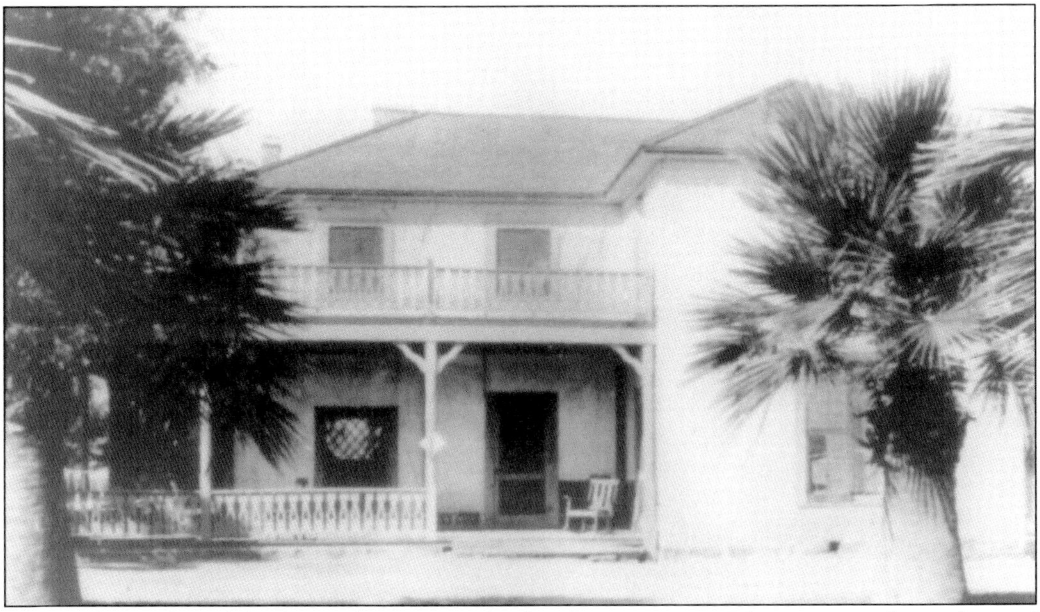

The Halls purchased this home from Hon. Fletcher Doan in 1919. The two-story home burned to the ground in 1929 as Mattie, the county recorder, was busy with elections. Her daughter Cynthia "Baby Lou" had lit a fire against the fall chill, unaware the flue had not been cleaned for winter. The family and the boarders (who were schoolteachers and the movie theater manager) lost almost everything.

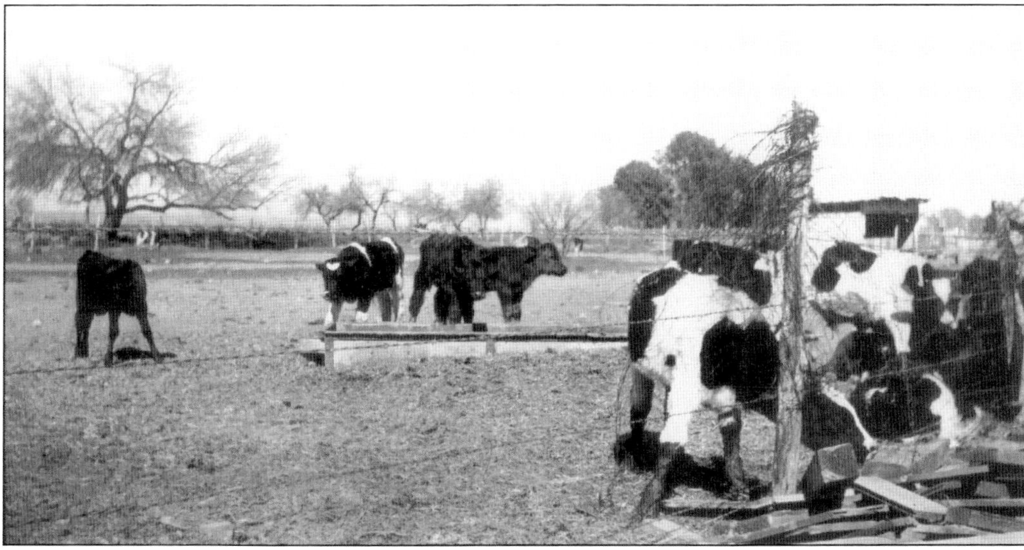

Raleigh H. Moorhouse ran the dairy pictured here outside of Florence. John Swearengin wrote in his book *Good Times Bad Times*, "Never was there a finer man than 'Pappy' Moorhouse." The town could depend on his help during the hard years of the Depression.

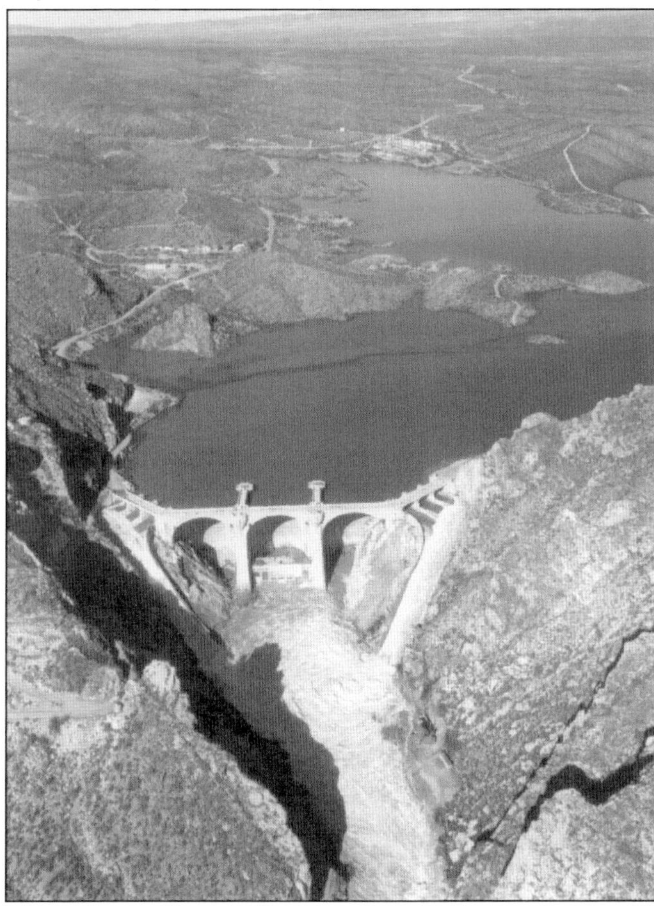

In 1929, the Coolidge Dam was completed on the Gila River. The Pima Indians and the farmers in the Florence–Casa Grande region were hoping that the reservoir behind the dam would provide water for their crops. On March 4, 1930, a huge banquet and dedication ceremony was held on top of the dam. Guests of honor included the dam's namesake, Pres. Calvin Coolidge, and humorist Will Rogers.

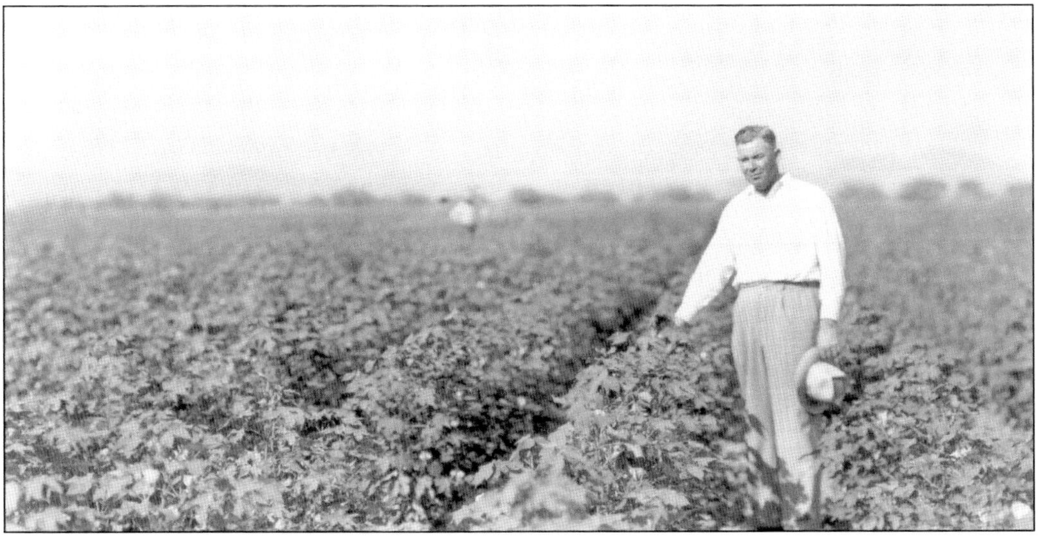

Although he lived in Phoenix and Washington, D.C., Ernest W. McFarland did not forget his Florence roots. Here he stands in front of his acres of farmland planted in cotton. After years of public service, McFarland returned to Florence weekly to administer the farm payroll and to oversee farming operations.

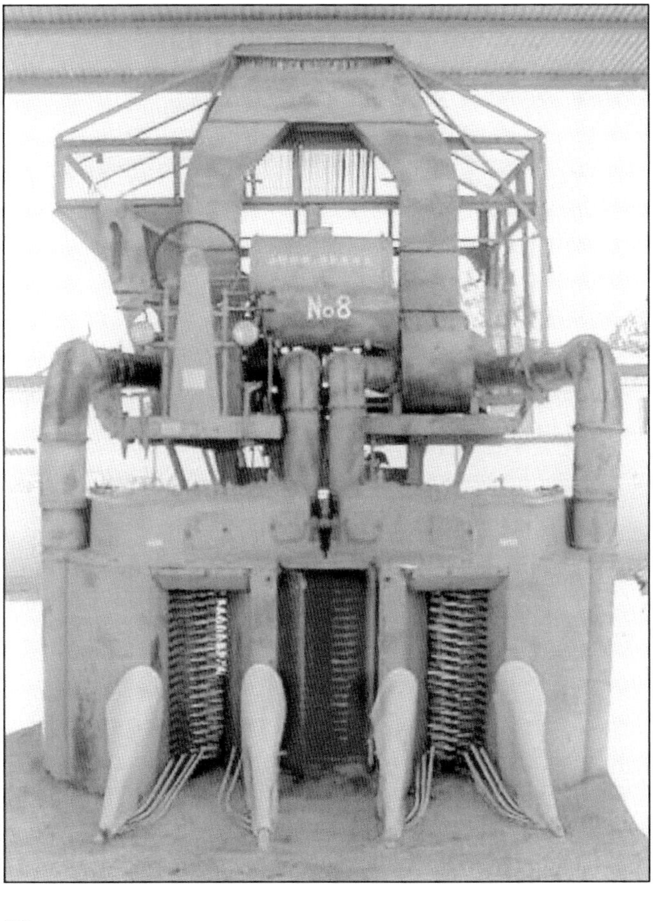

"Cotton was king" in Arizona in the 1950s. Both short-staple and long-staple cotton were cultivated, but mostly short-staple cotton is grown today. Shown here is a 1948 John Deere two-row cotton picker. The No. 8 picked 17 acres a day; recent models can pick as many as 75 acres. Before the invention of the mechanical picker, cotton was picked by hand and labor camps dotted the landscape of south-central Arizona.

Six

Rodeo and Cowboy Celebrities

With the many ranches around town, horseback riding was simply part of growing up. Young people showing off their horse-riding, roping, and cattle-wrangling skills became a town activity. Soon more organized activities came on the scene. At the end of World War I, the cattle industry was in decline, so the Pinal County Cattle Growers Association thought that a way to emphasize the skills and sports associated with cattle ranching was to hold a rodeo. In response, the Pinal Punchers Parada was held from 1919 to 1930. This adults' rodeo occurred behind the high school and included activities not usually considered part of the rodeo such as baseball games and boxing matches.

In 1932, Charles A. Whitlow Sr. started a youth rodeo to raise money for the children's milk fund. This event, now grown into an important Arizona rodeo called the Junior Parada, still raises money for children's causes. The Parada is held during the weekend following Thanksgiving and includes a parade and junior rodeo for youth ages 5 to 18. In the 1960s, photographer Louise L. Serpa regularly captured the action at the Junior Parada. She was the first female photographer allowed to take photographs inside the National Professional Rodeo's arenas, leading to her election to the Cowgirl Hall of Fame. As owners of the World's Championship Rodeo Corporation, the Clemans family of Florence produced championship rodeos in Madison Square Garden, New York City, during the late 1930s.

The western environment of Florence drew those interested in ranching and the rodeo. Well-known individuals such as Rex Allen, Ken Curtis (Festus in *Gunsmoke*), and Gene Autry have been supporters of the Parada. Tragically, cowboy movie star Tom Mix lost his life in a car crash just south of Florence.

Today Florence still bills itself as the "Cowboy Cradle of the Great Southwest."

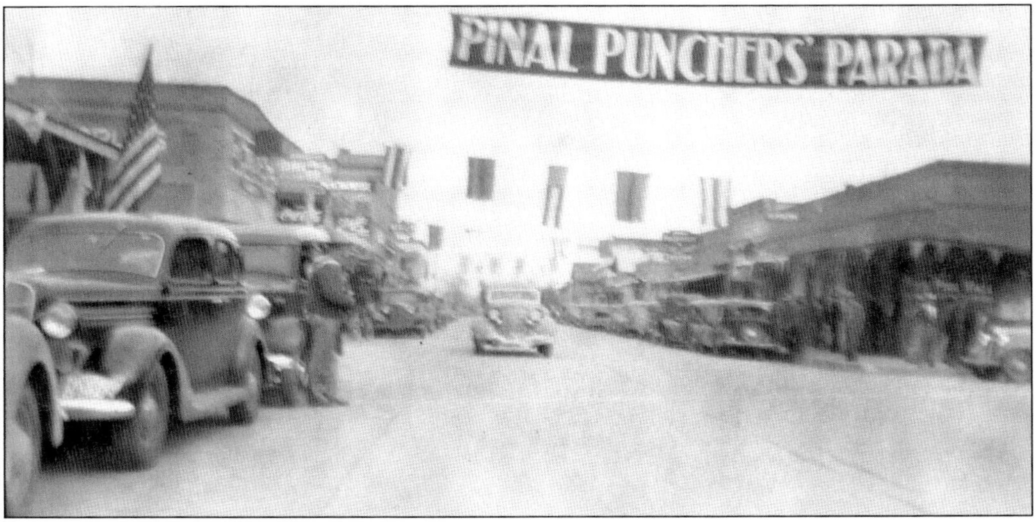

A banner proclaims an early Florence Pinal Punchers Parada. For the first Parada, M. Twain Clemans, as president of the Pinal County Cattle Growers Association, appointed committees to handle the challenges of the undertaking. The organization budgeted $900 to fund the event. Cash prizes were given and bronze medals awarded.

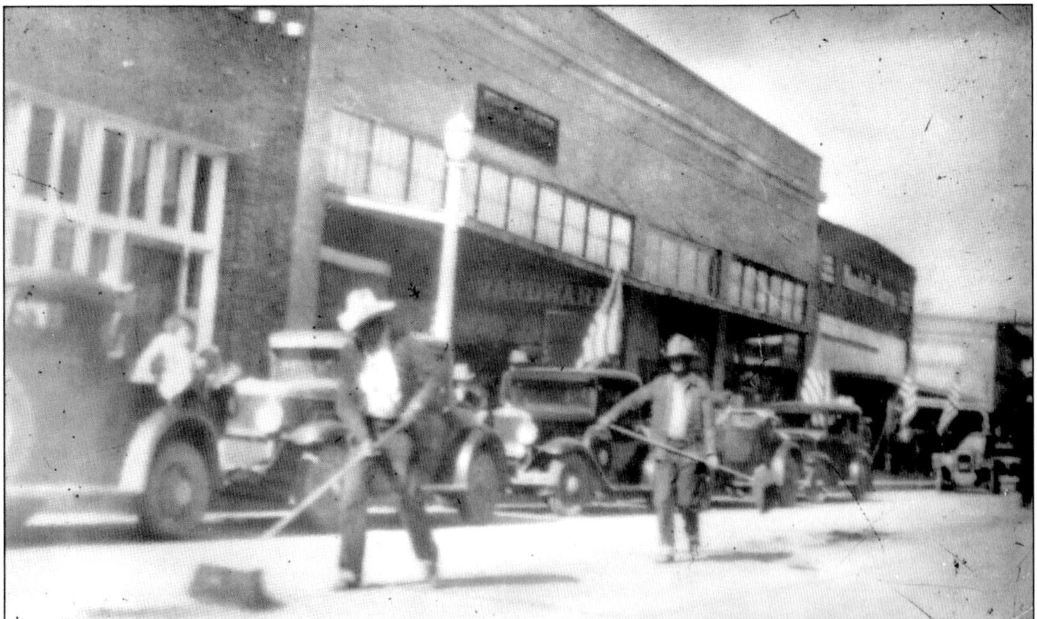

In this photograph, the parade for the Pinal Punchers Parada has just ended. As with every parade that includes horses, a clean-up crew follows. Crowds have likely already gathered at the rodeo grounds created behind the high school, where cars could pull up to the fence for a good view.

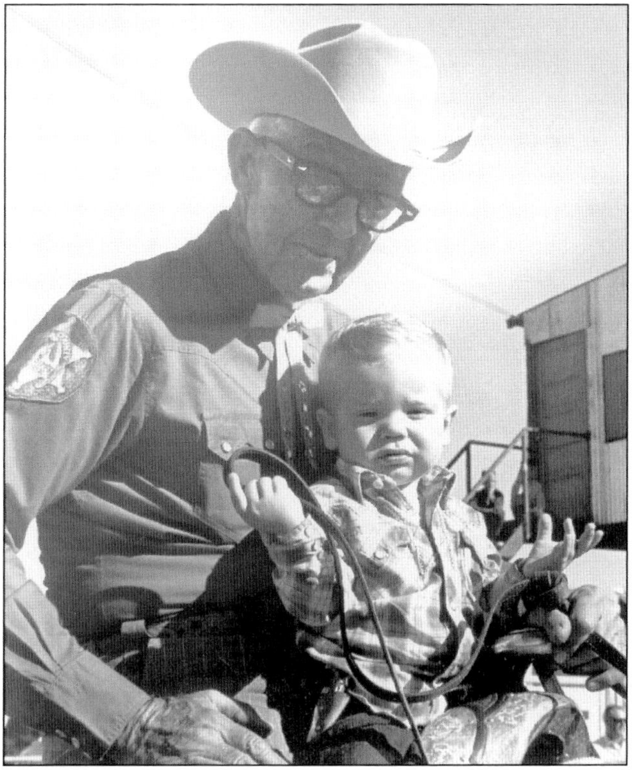

Charles A. Whitlow Sr. proudly leads the parade of the 1967 Junior Parada with great-grandson Charles A. Whitlow IV snug in front of him on his saddle. Known as the father of the junior rodeo, Whitlow went on to manage and direct the event for 37 years. He won the Rodeo Cowboys Association World Championship in Team Roping with Pete Grubb in 1940. (Courtesy L. L. Serpa.)

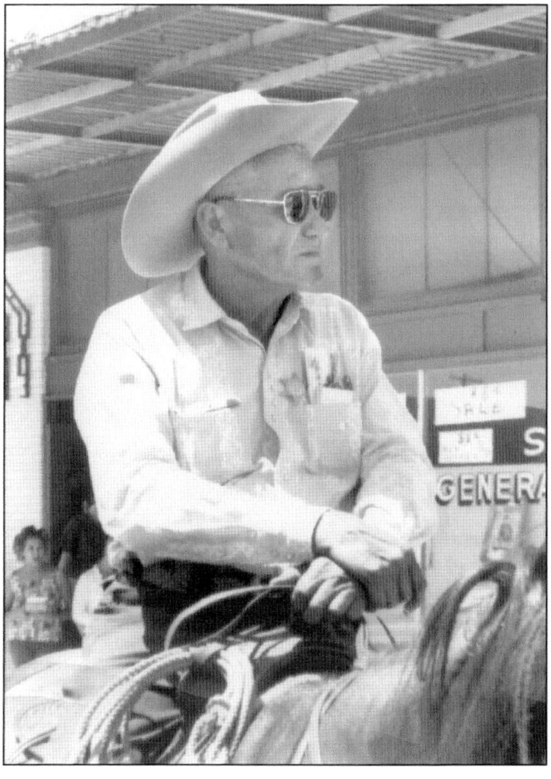

Pete Van Haren sits on his horse in the Junior Parada. Although town marshal from 1946 to 1977, he refused to wear a police uniform, dressing in his cowboy shirt, freshly pressed Levis, and cowboy hat instead. Van Haren was a charter member of the Pinal County Sheriff's Posse. A lover of horses, he broke and trained them for his friends and family.

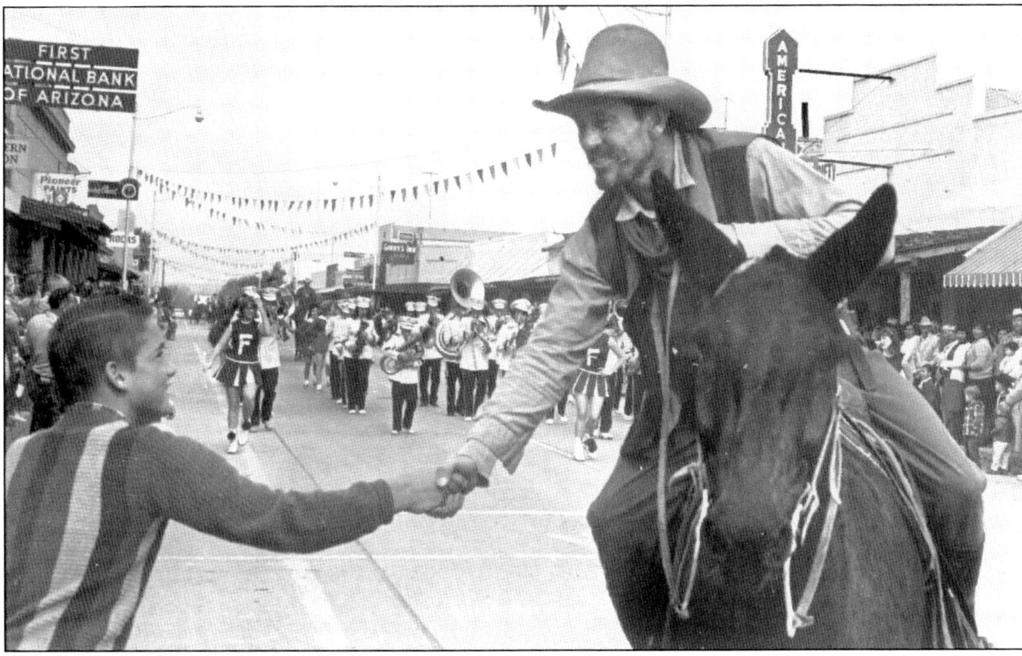

Ken Curtis, popular as Festus Haggen, the lovable sidekick on the television series *Gunsmoke*, was a special attraction in 1965 and 1968. Children flocked around him. Here he greets a bystander as the parade moves down Main Street. Behind him marches the Florence High School band. (Courtesy L. L. Serpa.)

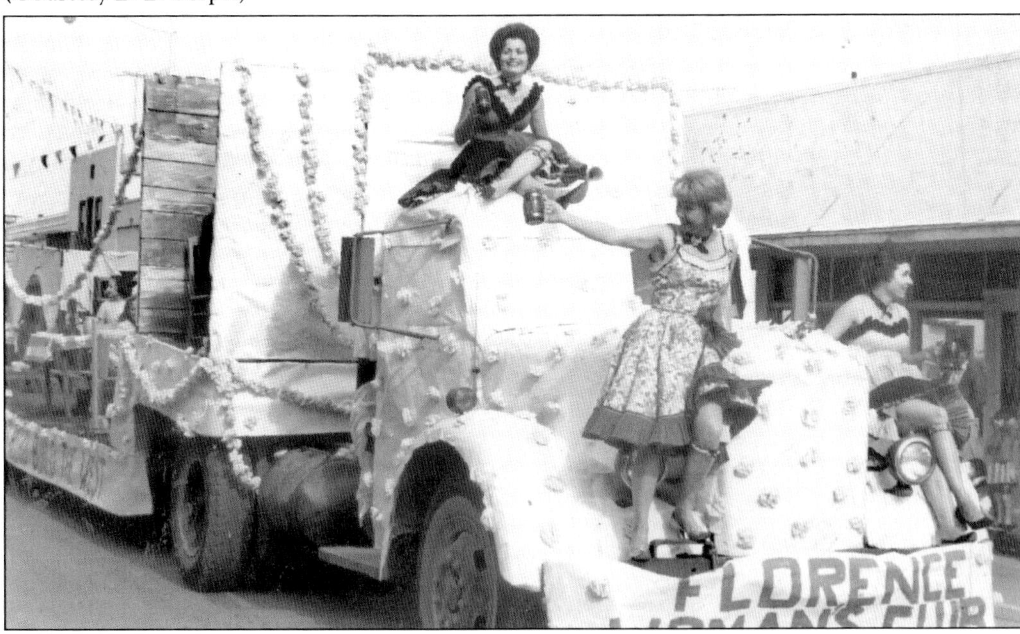

Unidentified members of the Florence Woman's Club adorn their parade float as 1890s dance hall girls. The group grew out of the Florence Village Improvement Club and, in 1901, became an early part of the Arizona Federation of Woman's Clubs. Members raised money through fund-raisers, loans, and public subscriptions in order to build their clubhouse in 1929. For three years during World War II, the clubhouse was rented to the USO for $75 a month.

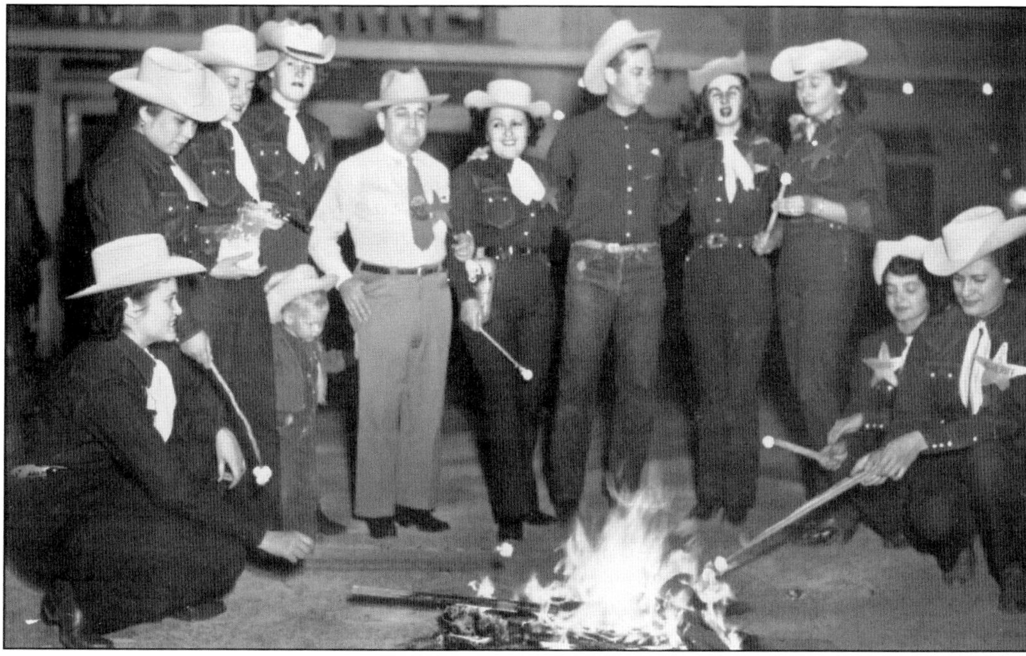

The Sheriffettes gather for a marshmallow roast in 1948 after a day of "arresting" citizens who were not wearing Western clothes for Parada week. Seen here from left to right are Juanita Avenenti, Adeline Sepulveda, Helen Malloque, Jackie Hawkins, Howard Peters (judge of the Kangaroo Court), Dora Brash, Ernest Buyas, Penny Schewel, Emeline Van Haren, Rosemary Cathemer, and Mary Arvizu.

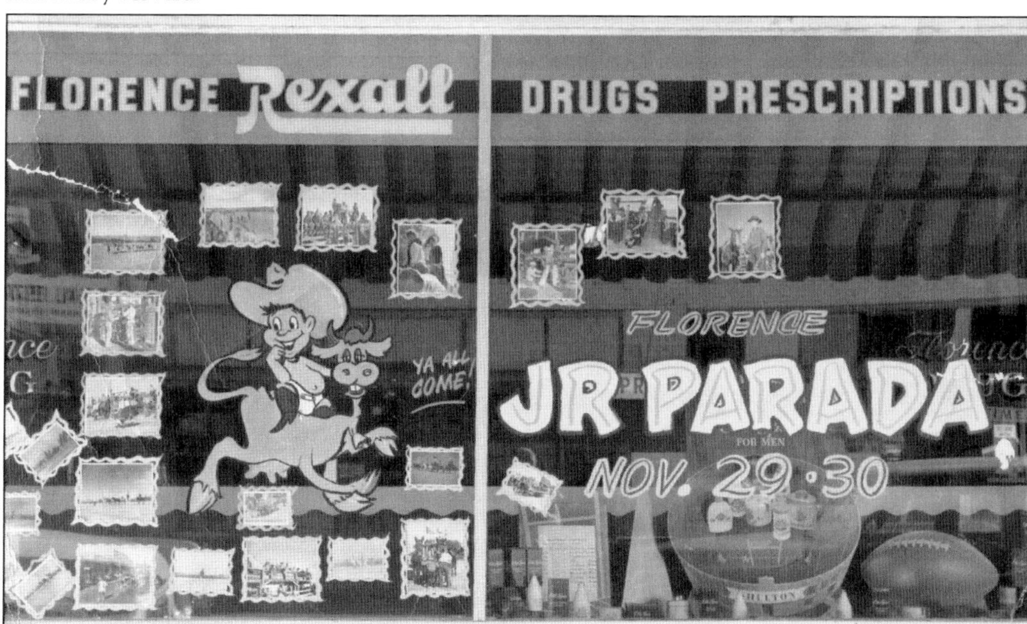

The town has always gone all out to celebrate Junior Parada week. Decorated store windows line the parade route, and the street is closed off for Western bands and dancing. Florence High School graduates, no matter where they may have moved, return for Parada weekend reunions.

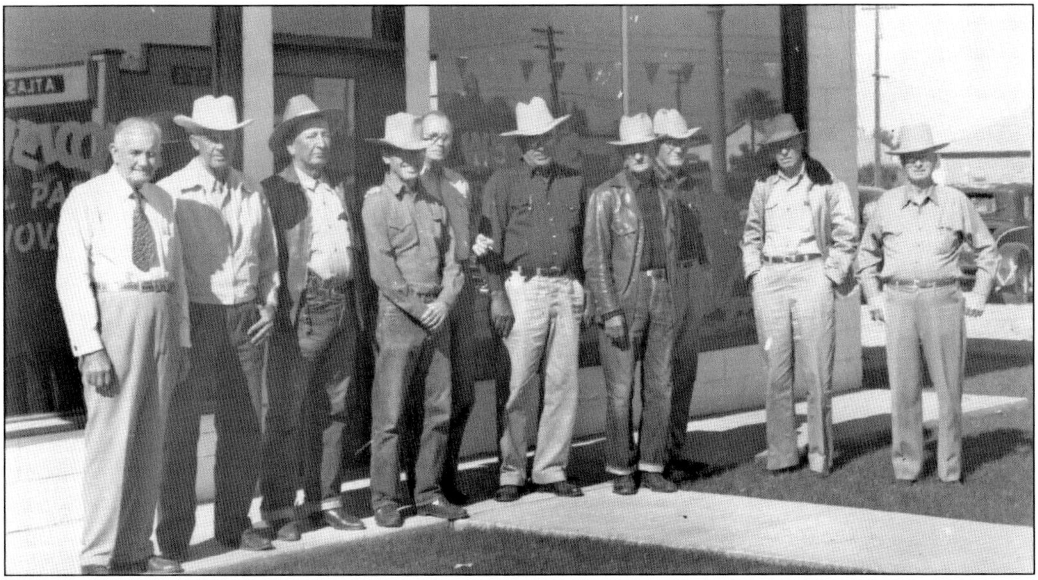

In this 1940s photograph, town elders gather on Parada Day. Pictured here from left to right are Dugald Stewart, Charles A. Whitlow Sr., Thomas H. Bamrick, William Clemans, John Zellweger, Louis Cathemer Sr., George Morrell, M. Twain Clemans, Alfred Gressinger, and Dave Brice.

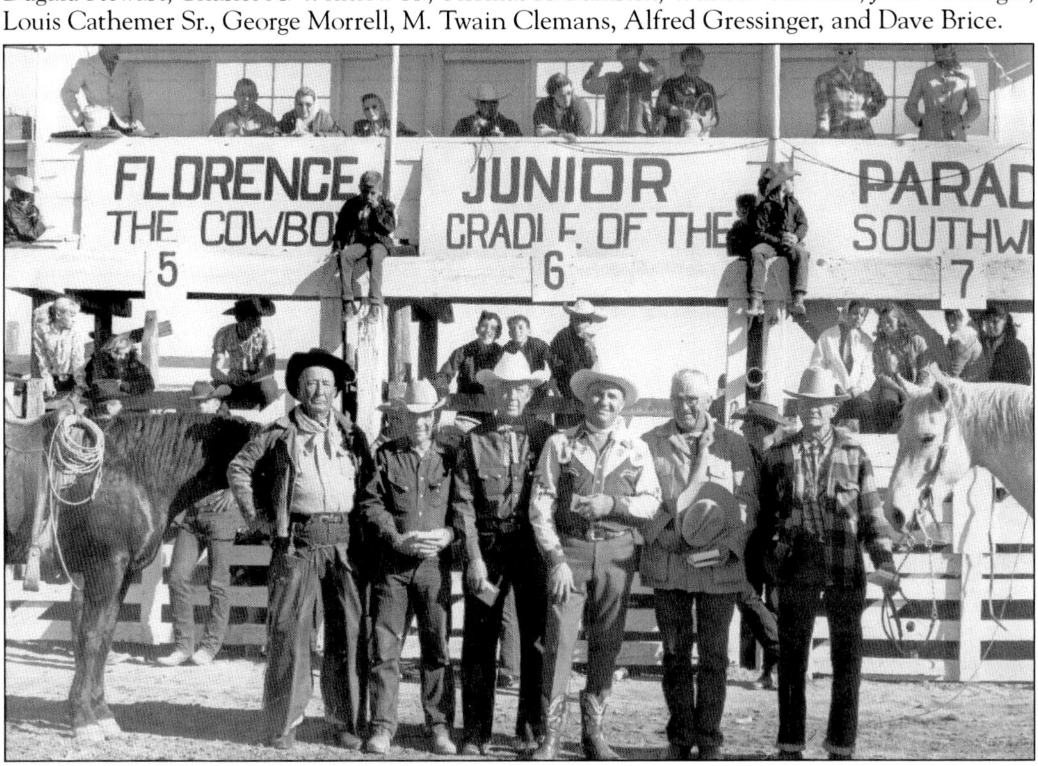

The Florence Junior Parada, the oldest continuing youth rodeo in the country, has been supported by many celebrities over the years. In 1955, Gene Autry poses with some of the local ranchers and rodeo founders. Standing here from left to right are Tom Bamrick, Al Holt, Charlie Whitlow, Gene Autry, M. Twain Clemans, and George Morrell. Many future rodeo stars got started at the Parada.

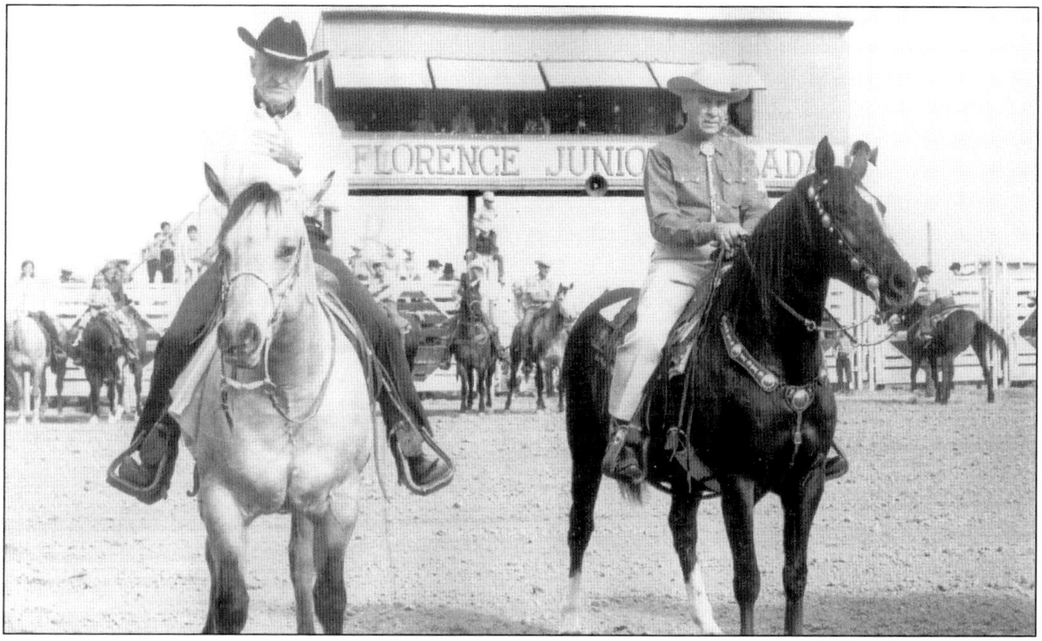

Roy Wales (left) and Frank Eyman ride their horses in the Grand Entry of the Junior Parada Rodeo in 1970. Eyman served as Arizona State Prison warden from 1955 to 1972 and for many years rode in the parade, usually in front of the prison band. In 1979, he was grand marshal. Wales, a rancher and horse breeder, sits atop his horse Driftwood Ike.

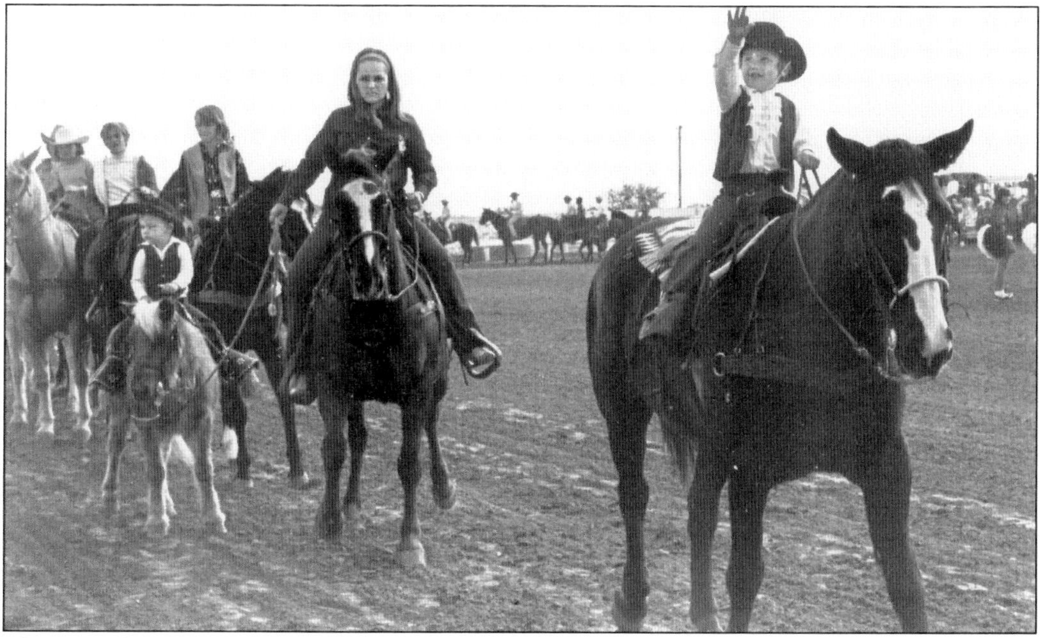

The Grand Entry of the 1967 Junior Parada has Charlie Whitlow's grandchildren on parade. At left is young William Foster on his Shetland pony. Carefully holding the reins of her little brother's pony is Susan Foster, who was at the time running for Miss Pinal County. Leading at right is sister Barbara Jo. They are the children of Cliff Foster and his wife, Rosalie "Posie." (Courtesy L.L. Serpa.)

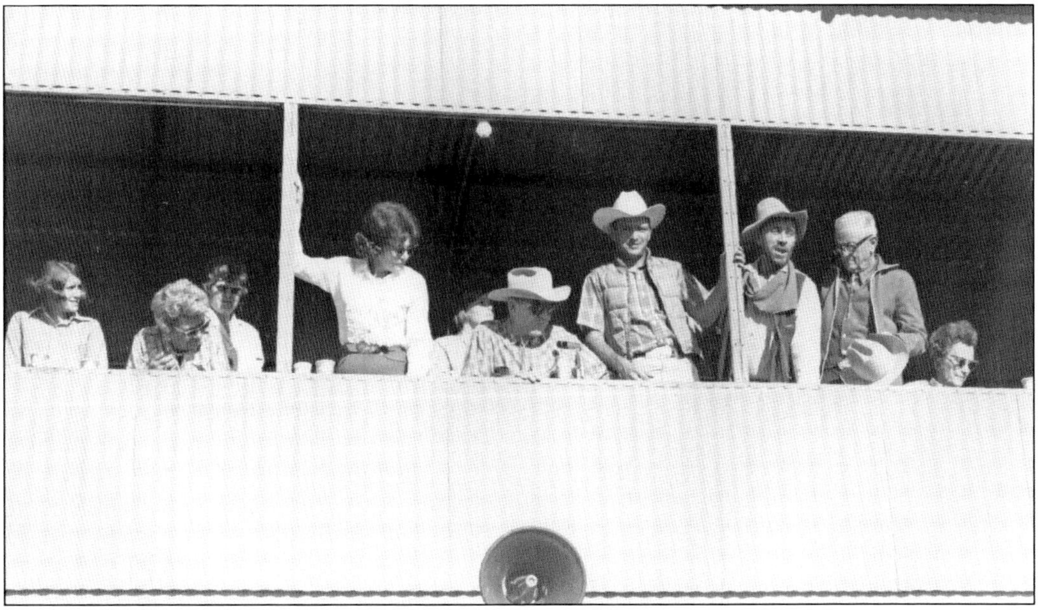

The announcer's booth is filled during the 1968 Junior Parada. Pictured from left to right are Judy Wales, Rose Clemans, Torrie Curtis, Ruth Wales, Chuck Parkinson, Mark Clemans, Ken Curtis, M. Twain Clemans, and India Jo Whitlow. Rose Clemans monitored the timing for years. Chuck Parkinson, who also announced most major rodeos, had started his career as a bareback rider and bull rider. (Courtesy L. L. Serpa.)

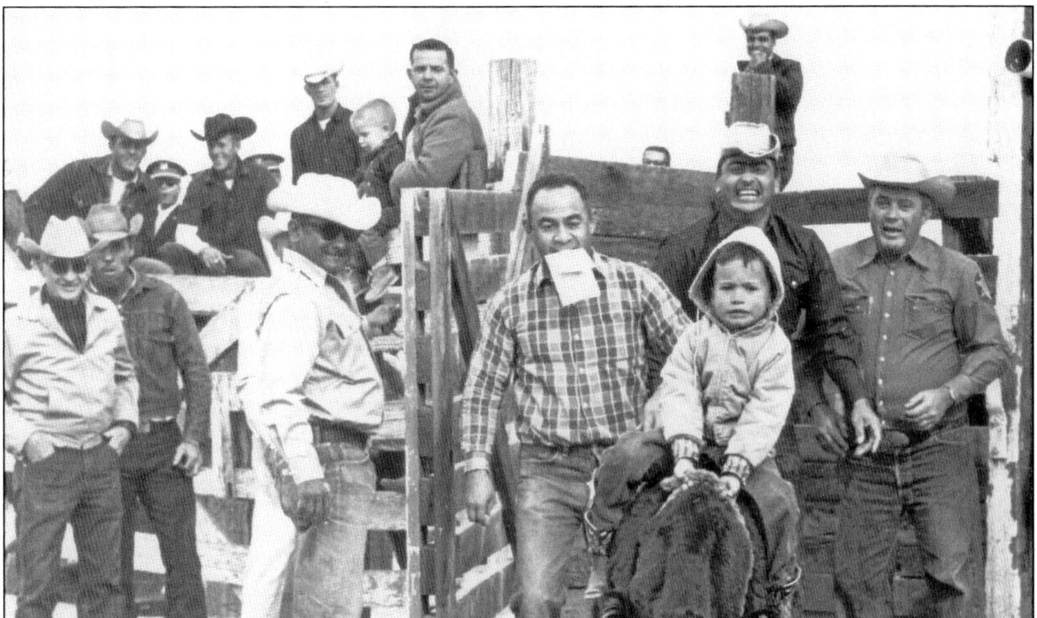

Sporting a determined expression, Matthew Bagnall is perched atop his bucking calf in 1963. At left as bucking chutes gate man is Robert Encinas, in the white hat and white shirt. Wearing a plaid shirt is Andrew Jiménez, and Edward Padilla is behind the little rider. At far right, in his Pinal County Sheriff's Posse shirt with the star on the upper shoulder, is Matthew's watchful father, Harry Bagnall. (Courtesy L. L. Serpa.)

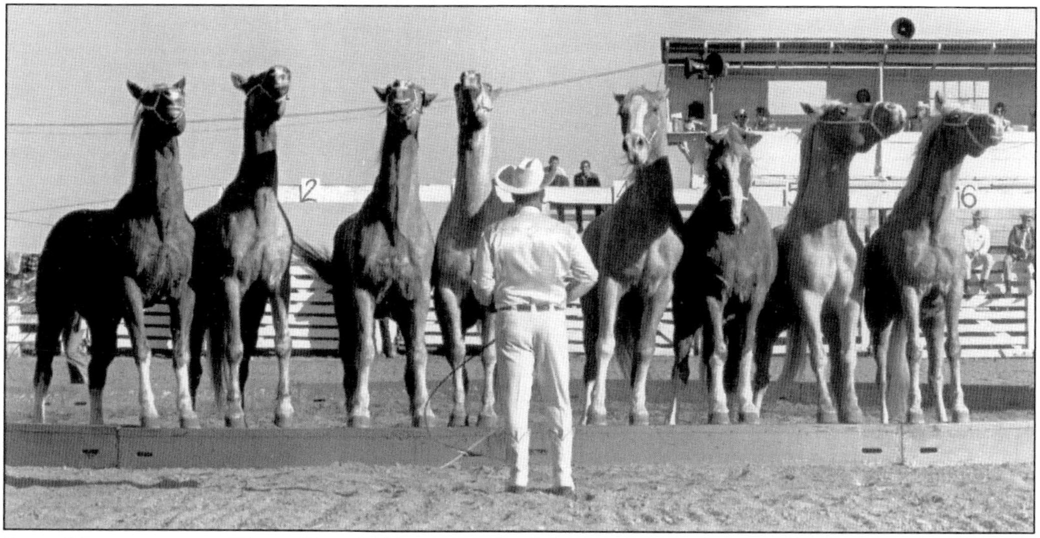

Famed horse trainer Glenn Randall brought the Liberty Horses, beautiful palominos who could perform tricks by vocal command, to the 1964 Parada. Randall trained horses for movies such as *Ben Hur*. In 1960, he actually brought the *Ben Hur* chariot horses. He trained Gene Autry's Champion and Roy Rogers's Trigger. Eventually training Trigger Jr., Randall later sent that horse—to the delight of the children. (Courtesy L. L. Serpa.)

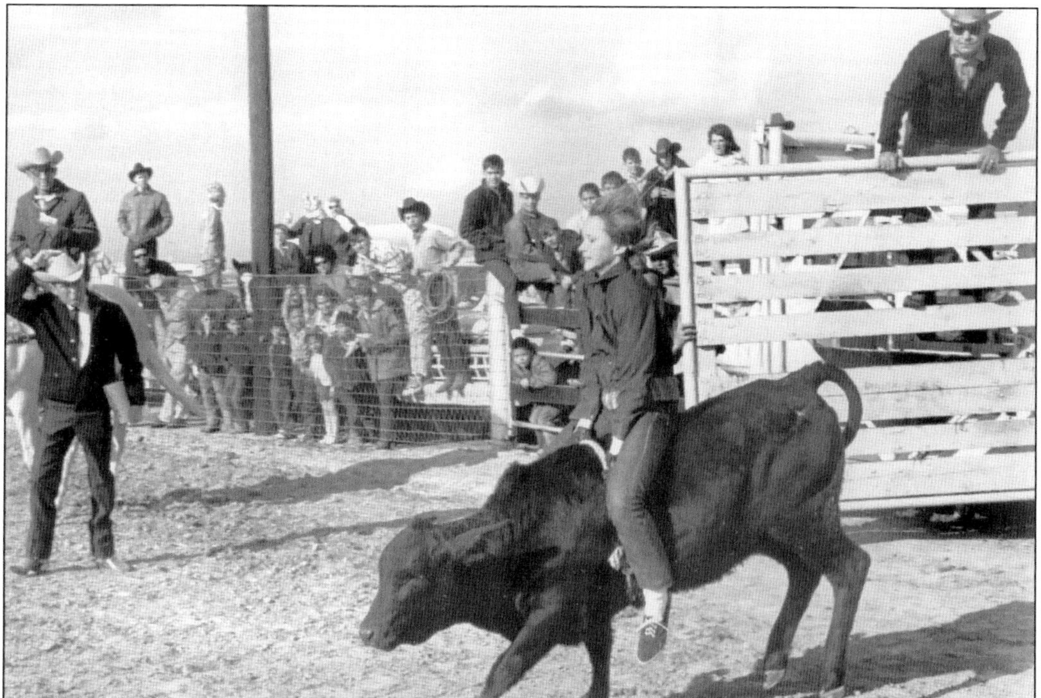

The crowd watches as a young Sharon Borree, her hair blowing, comes out of the bucking chutes in 1968. At the far left, Robert Eidson holds his hat. He was a rodeo cowboy himself, but here at the Junior Parada he is serving as a judge. Behind Eidson, Charles A. Whitlow Sr. sits on his white palomino Heavy Duty. (Courtesy L. L. Serpa.)

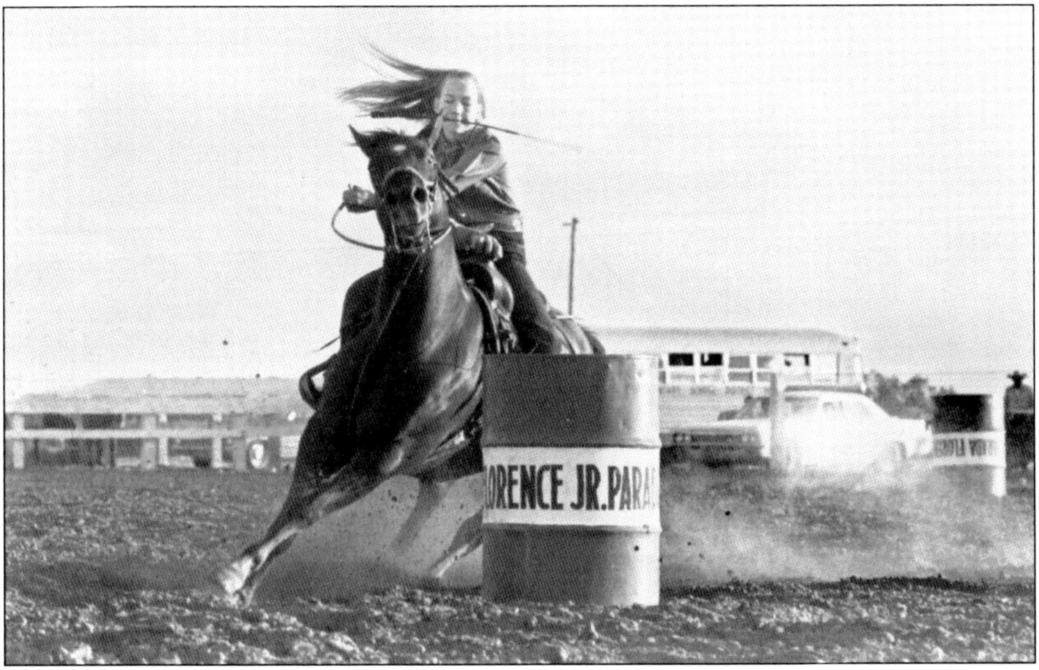

In 1968, an unidentified cowgirl races against time around barrels with her quirt in her mouth, ready to urge her horse on to the next barrel. The girl whose horse can run the fastest and make the tightest turns without hitting the barrels wins. The barrel race originated in Texas in the 1940s. (Courtesy L. L. Serpa.)

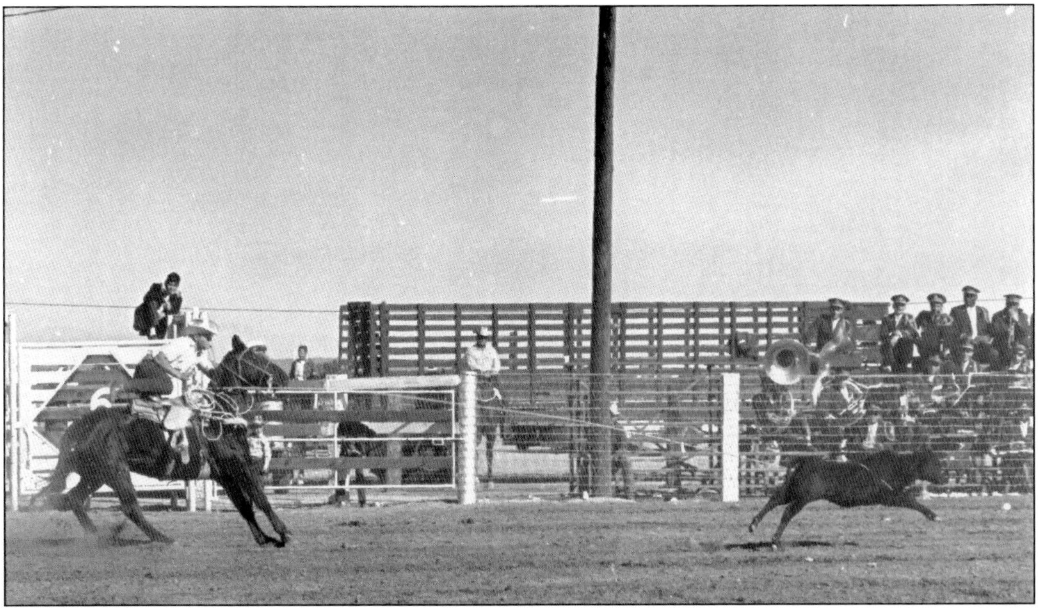

Kenny Melugin is roping during the 1966 Parada. Calf roping is one of the oldest events organized at the Junior Parada. The cowboy and his horse work together to rope and tie the calf in the shortest time. Since 1977, the youth have competed in three categories: ages 5 to 12 years, 13 to 15 years, and 16 to 18 years. Behind the fence, the Arizona State Prison band Stars Behind Bars enjoys the excitement. (Courtesy L. L. Serpa.)

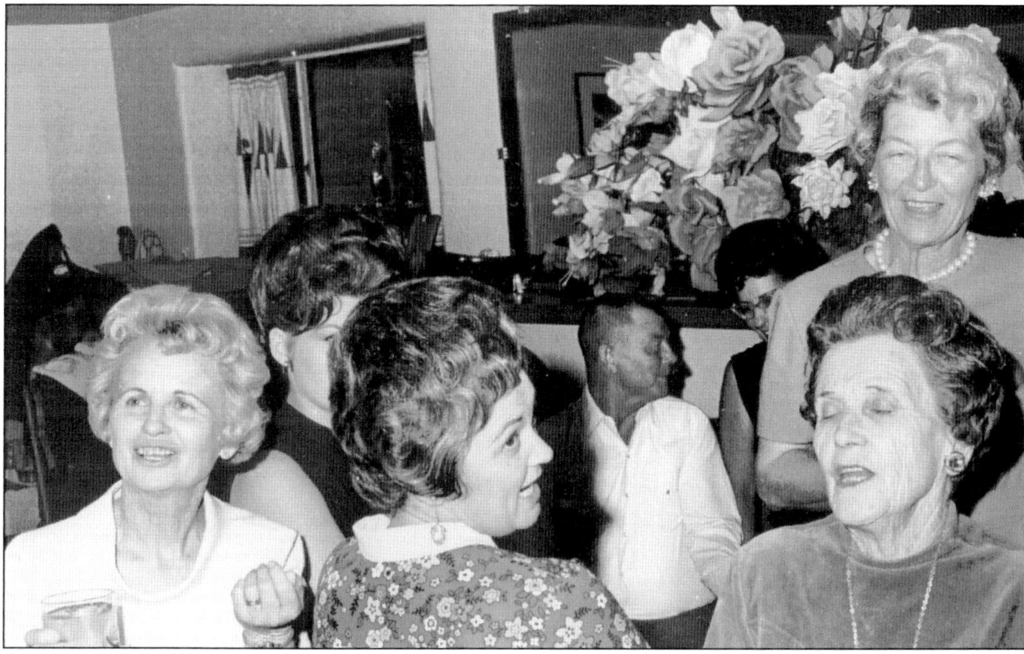

On the Saturday night of Junior Parada weekend, M. Twain Clemans and his wife, Rose, would invite friends and the rodeo's special guests to their ranch home for a party. Charles A. Whitlow Sr.'s wife, India Jo, would play the piano for group singing. Seen here from left to right are the following: (first row) Margaret Sims, Whitlow's daughter Posie Foster, and Whitlow; (second row) Ruth Wales, Charles A. Whitlow Jr., and an unidentified woman. Rose Clemans is standing at right. (Courtesy L. L. Serpa.)

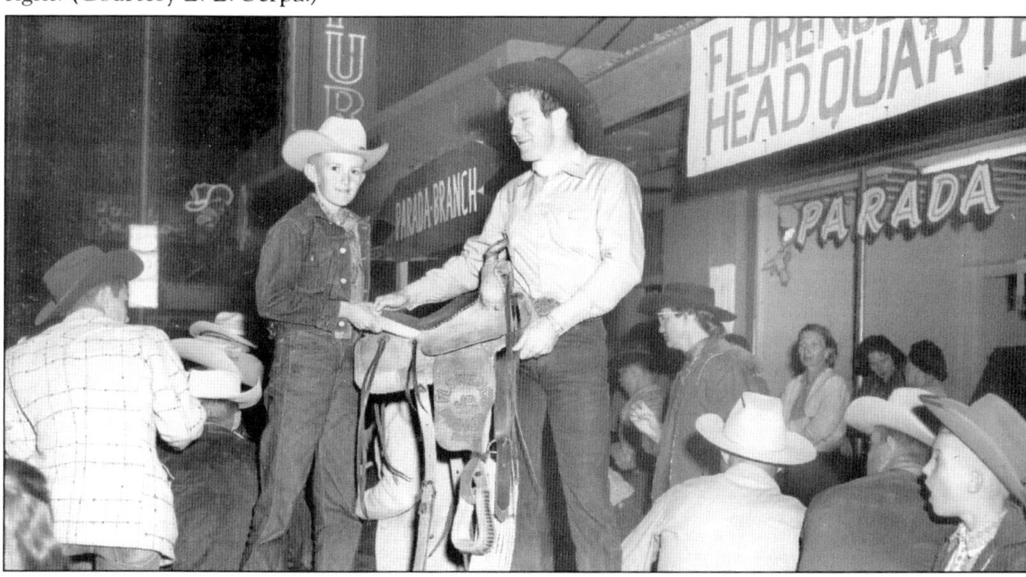

Casey Tibbs, All-Around World's Champion Cowboy and World Champion bronc rider, presents trophies to the Parada winners in front of the Spur Theater in 1959. Joe Clem won Junior All-Around and a youth saddle. In 1961, Tibbs returned for an exhibition of saddle bronc riding at the Sunday afternoon performance. For many years, Gene Autry donated a silver belt buckle for the Senior All-Around winner.

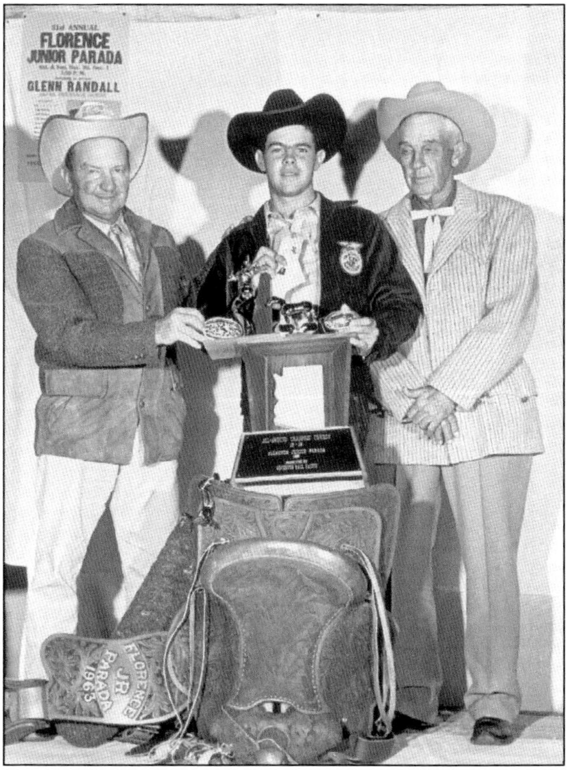

John Graham poses with his trophy saddle and belt buckle after winning Senior All-Around Cowboy at the 1963 Junior Parada. Well-known horse trainer Glenn Randall stands below a poster announcing him as a special attraction. This year, Randall brought his dressage horse, which had been trained in the highest and most exacting form of riding. Parada founder Charles A. Whitlow Sr. stands at right. (Courtesy L. L. Serpa.)

All-Around Cowgirl Debra Earnhardt is awarded her trophies and new saddle after the 1967 Parada. Standing on the stage with Earnhardt are, from left to right, unidentified, general chairman and producer Charles A. Whitlow Sr., judge Robert Eidson, and announcer Chuck Parkinson. Now youth even travel from neighboring states to participate. They camp beside the Charles Whitlow Arena with their horses, trailers, and recreational vehicles. (Courtesy L. L. Serpa.)

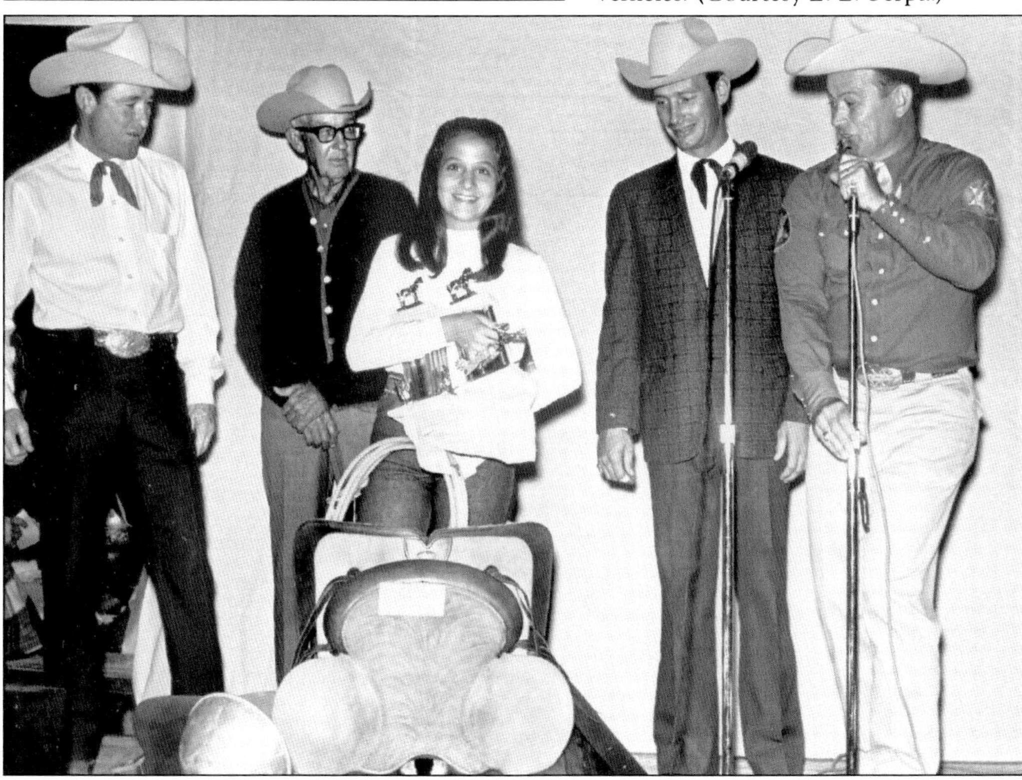

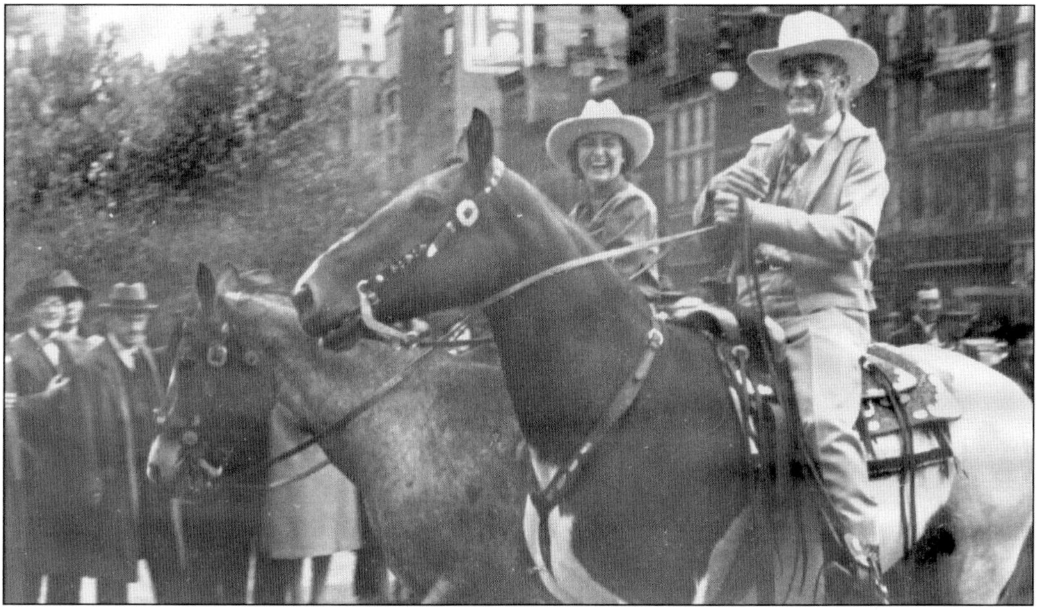

M. Twain Clemans and his wife, Rose, parade with their horses in New York City around 1938. Clemans and his brother William were executive officers of the World's Championship Rodeo Corporation, producers of the Madison Square Garden rodeos. Cowboys and cowgirls, with stock from their Lightning C Ranches of Dublin, Texas, and Florence, traveled by private train. The corporation put on the world championship rodeos of the day.

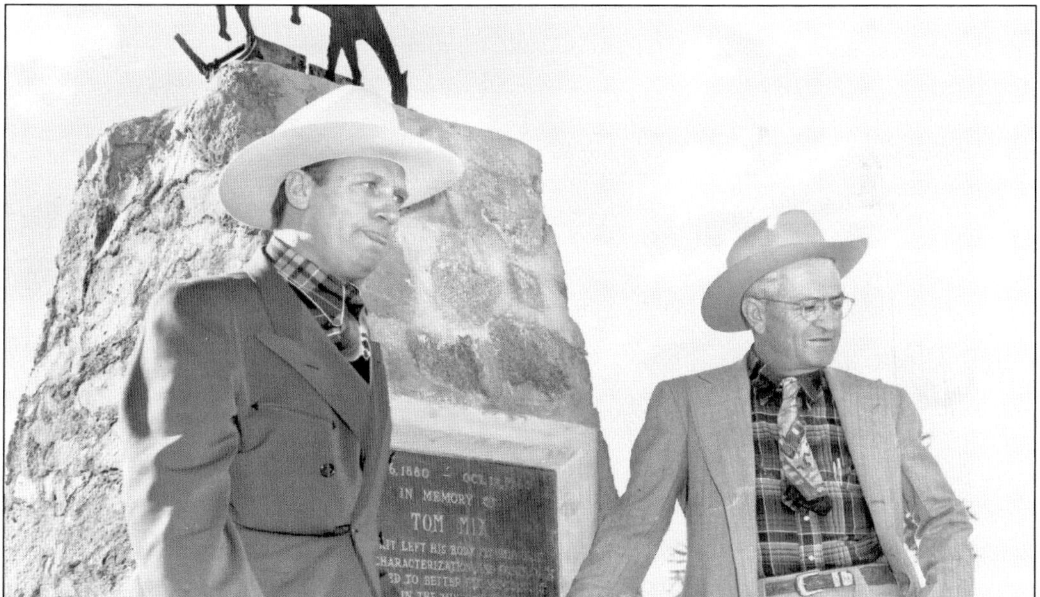

Gene Autry (left), a popular star of many Westerns, and Florence cattleman M. T. Clemans stand beside the monument erected in memory of international cowboy movie star Tom Mix. The site is near the scene of his death in an automobile accident south of town in 1940. Mix's daughter had been married to a local rancher and rodeo cowboy. Fernando Arriola designed a sculpture of Tom Mix's horse Tony that sits atop the 7-foot pillar.

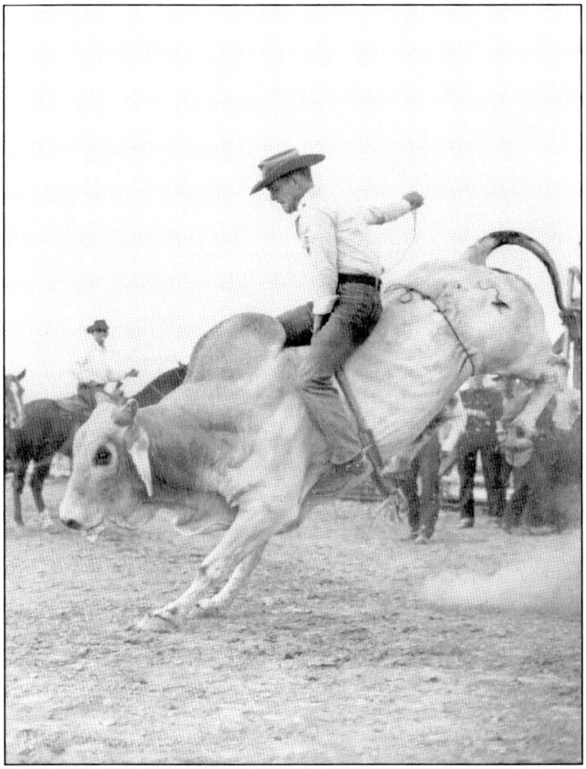

Rodeos were popular all over Arizona. Stella Redondo Glenn, who grew up on a ranch near Florence, was Phoenix Rodeo Queen in 1946. Enthusiastic Florence-area youth who were bareback, bronco, and bull riders participated in rodeos in neighboring towns. Here Amos Hawkins Jr. competes as a bull rider in nearby Coolidge about 1953.

For several years in the 1980s, the Arizona State Prison held the Outlaw Rodeo at their arena. Almost 100 inmates tested their skills against bucking broncs and bulls. Larry Mahan, All-Around Champion and professional cowboy, taught the inmates skills. A special attraction called Money Earned the Hard Way involved 75 prisoners trying to remove a tobacco sack filled with money that was tied between the horns of a bull, loose in the arena.

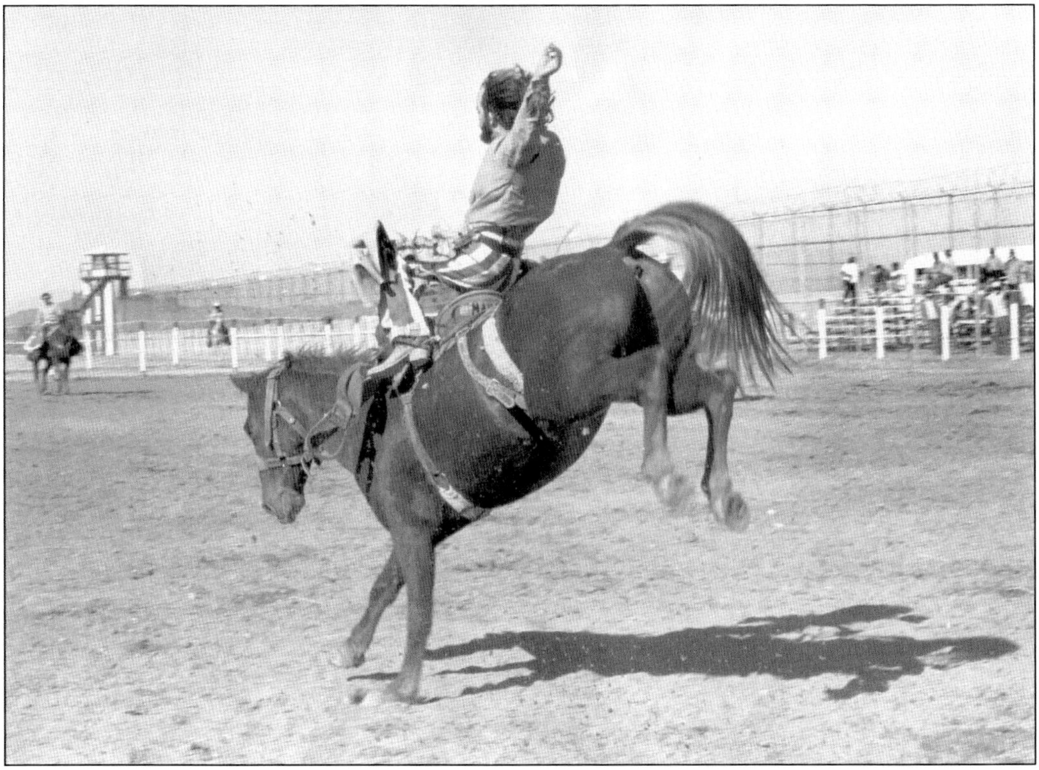

Seven

PRISON
A NEW DIRECTION

In 1908, eighteen inmates in the company of two or three guards got off a train at the Florence depot north of town and walked across the desert and the Gila River to the site of what was to become the new territorial prison. The inmates cleared the land and built footings for the prison wall and for buildings that they would later construct. With the coming of the territorial prison, a new direction was taken by the town of Florence. Money was available for material but not for labor. Warden Thomas Rynning established a practice called two-for-one in which an inmate worked for two days building the prison and then received time off his sentence. Although the first inmate was assigned to the Florence prison in 1908, the move was not completed until 1912.

During the middle decades of the 20th century, many new buildings were constructed at the prison. Besides the acreage planted in crops, livestock was raised, and there were workshops for learning such skills as carpentry, welding, and auto mechanics. Administrators believed in prison self-sufficiency and in prisoner rehabilitation. Many photographs in this chapter were taken during these decades.

Often prisoners attempted to escape, and some succeeded. Up until recently, mounted guards and expert trackers with bloodhounds hunted through cholla, rocks, and dry riverbeds to chase down escapees. The prison at Florence held many dangerous men and, until the 1980s, women. Early on in its statehood, Arizona had no death penalty, but after a gunfight in which law officers were killed, the punishment was reestablished. Thereafter many convicted murderers were executed at the prison. Some were notorious to the degree that their exploits were known nationwide.

Today the Florence complex of the Arizona State Prison is just one of several prisons in town, including private prisons and homeland security. The prison industry benefits Florence with jobs for its citizens even when times are difficult.

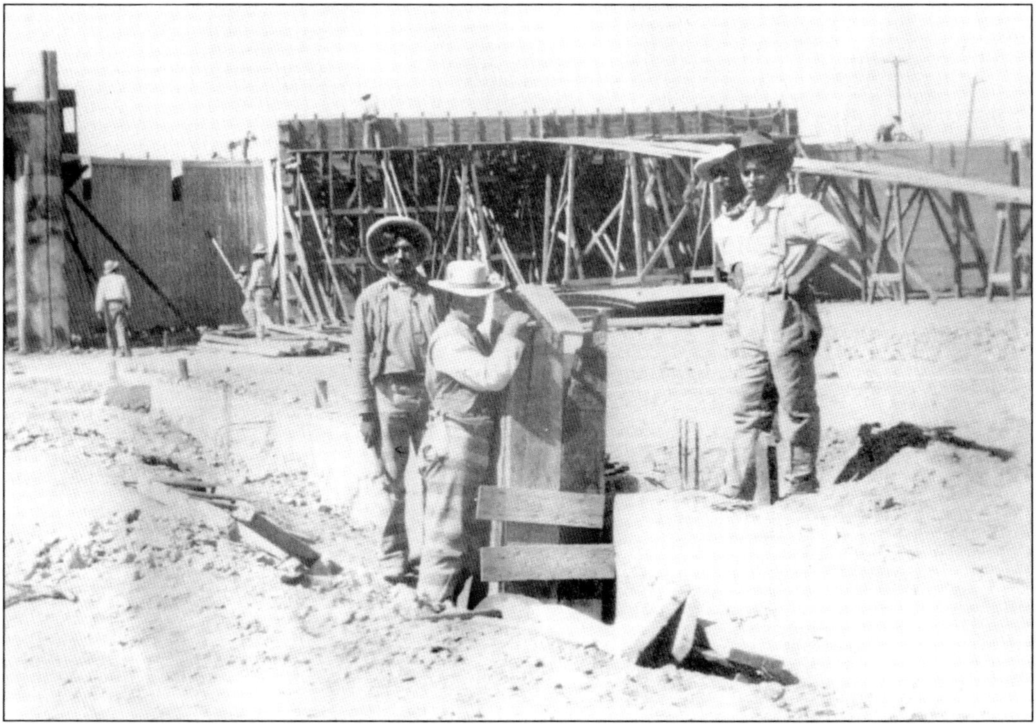

Here the walls of the first prison building are being created. The five buildings, part of the first construction, would house the cell block and facilities such as a dormitory, chapel, kitchen, mess hall, and hospital. Materials were brought by railroad to the Florence station and carted to the site by local residents.

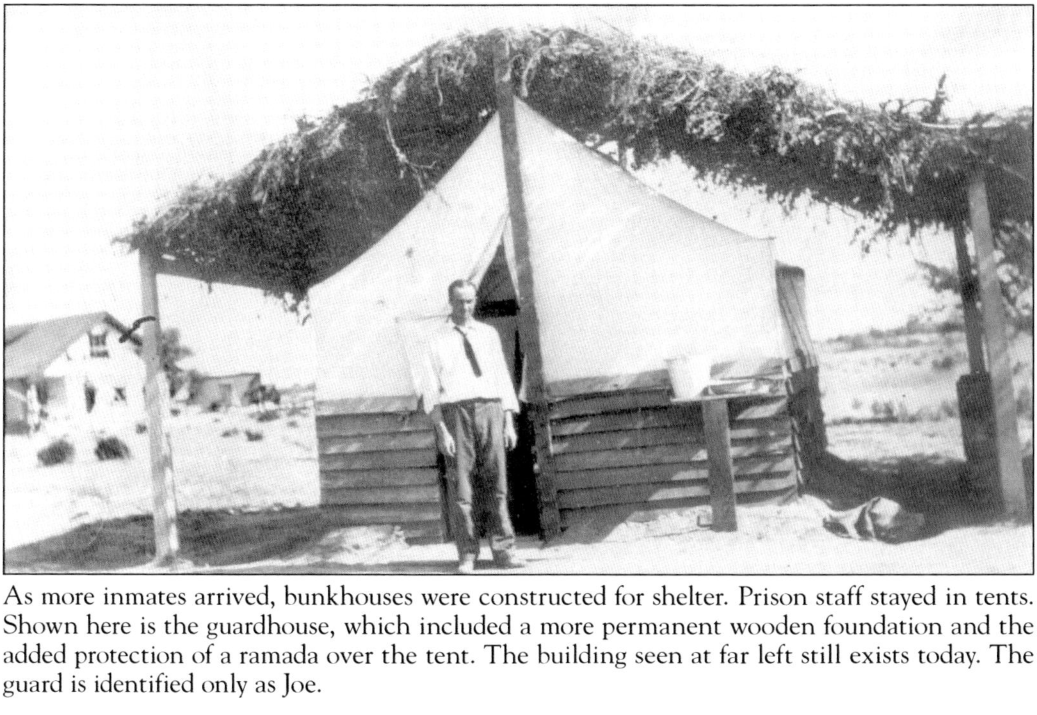

As more inmates arrived, bunkhouses were constructed for shelter. Prison staff stayed in tents. Shown here is the guardhouse, which included a more permanent wooden foundation and the added protection of a ramada over the tent. The building seen at far left still exists today. The guard is identified only as Joe.

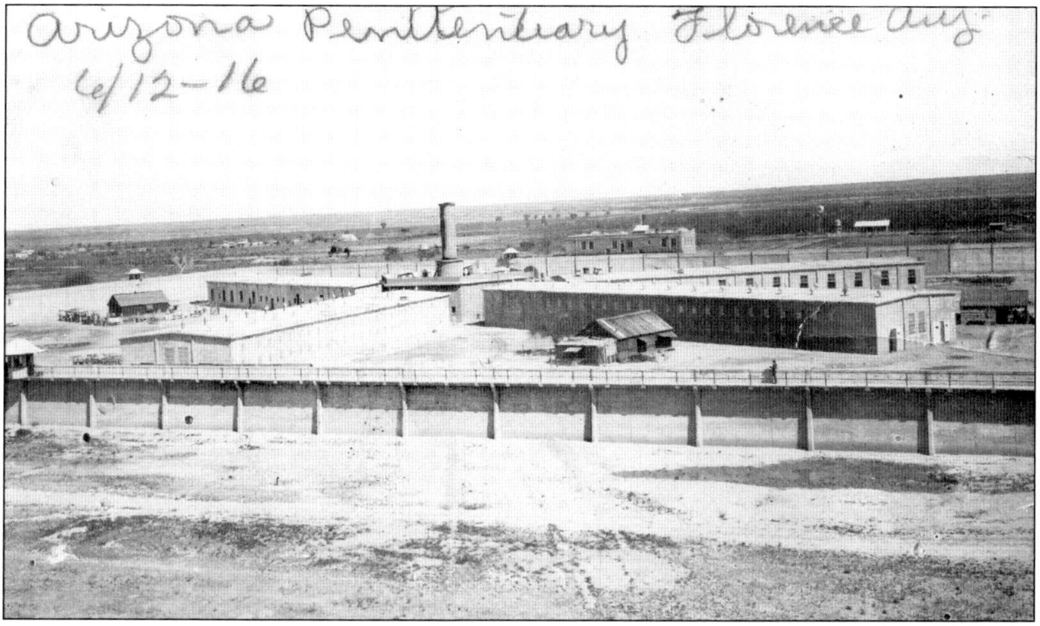

In this postcard, postmarked 1916, the prison wall and the first cell block can be seen. The cell block had small four-man cells on two levels. The cell block and the service buildings were constructed as spokes on a wheel from a six-sided central building hub, the powerhouse. Note the smokestack. The powerhouse contained boilers to heat water for the prison's use.

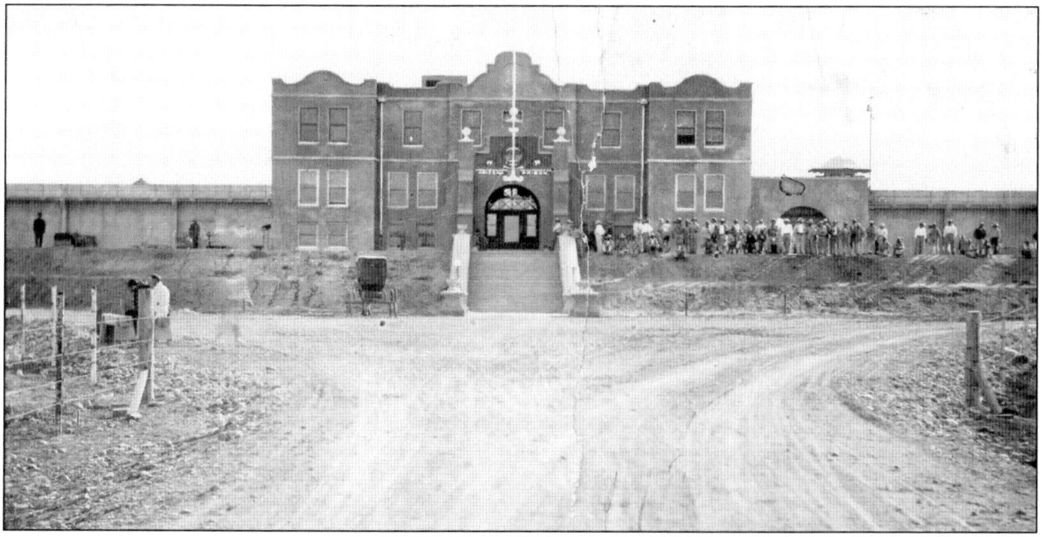

Construction of the administration building, seen here in an early view, was started in the summer of 1909. It was built of reinforced concrete with wall thicknesses of between 8 and 10 inches. The stone steps were constructed on the slope that led up to the building. Architect Thornton Fitzhugh designed it in the mission revival style.

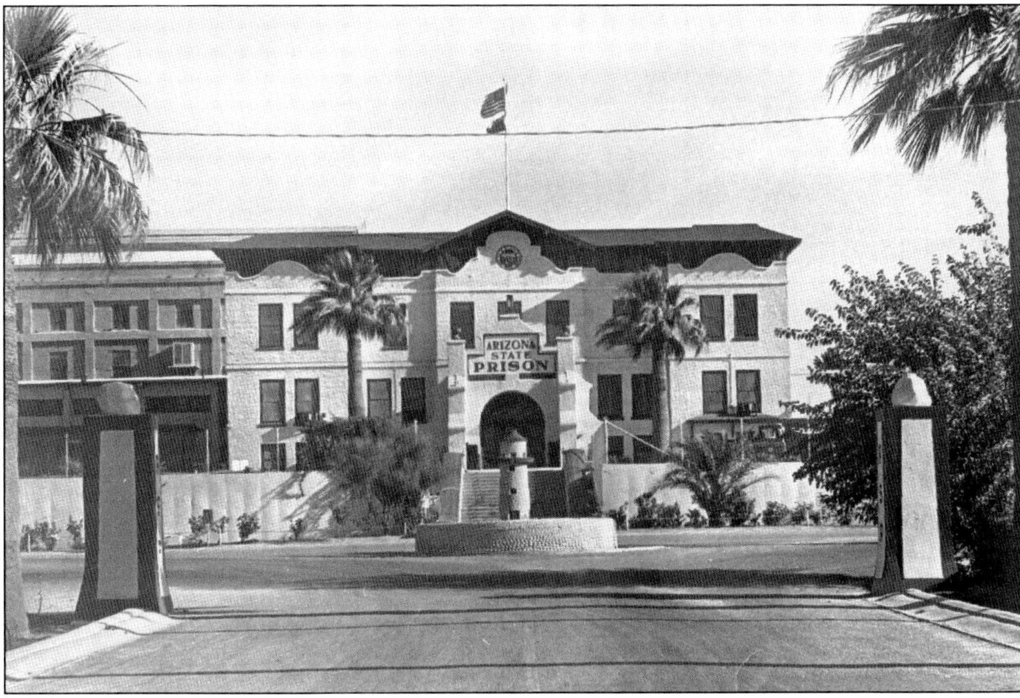

In the early 1920s, the fountain in front of the administration building was built to commemorate the installation of electricity to the prison. Goldfish were kept in this fountain for many years, and it was also used for baptisms. The baptisms were discontinued because of the possibility of escape. The fountain was removed during major renovations in the 1970s.

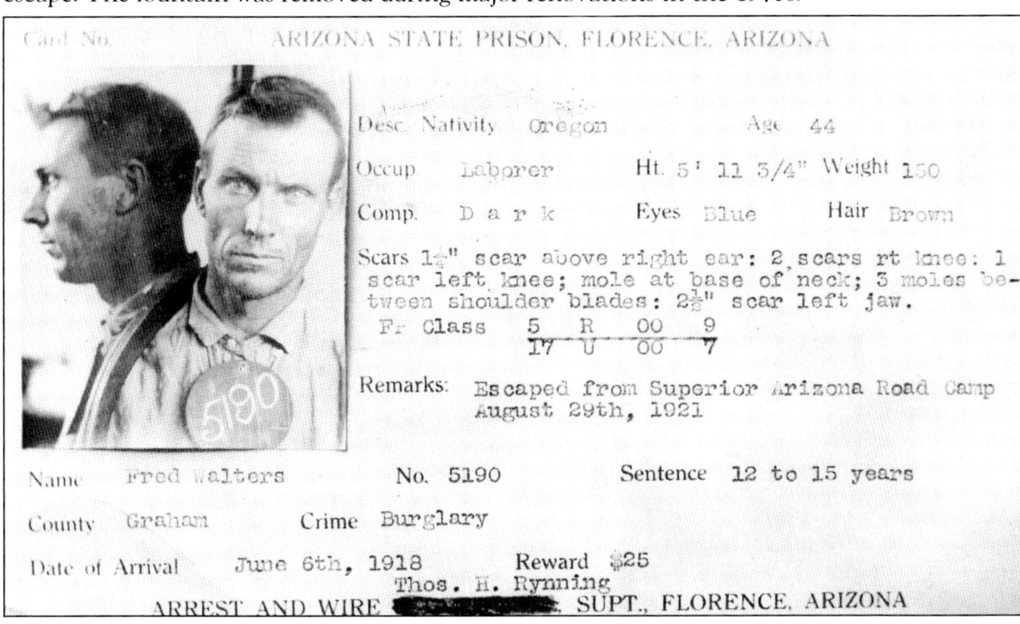

Card No. ARIZONA STATE PRISON, FLORENCE, ARIZONA

Desc. Nativity Oregon Age 44

Occup. Laborer Ht. 5' 11 3/4" Weight 150

Comp. D a r k Eyes Blue Hair Brown

Scars 1½" scar above right ear: 2 scars rt knee: 1 scar left knee; mole at base of neck; 3 moles between shoulder blades: 2½" scar left jaw.

Fr Class 5 R 00 9 / 17 U 00 7

Remarks: Escaped from Superior Arizona Road Camp August 29th, 1921

Name Fred Walters No. 5190 Sentence 12 to 15 years

County Graham Crime Burglary

Date of Arrival June 6th, 1918 Reward $25

Thos. H. Rynning

ARREST AND WIRE [redacted] SUPT., FLORENCE, ARIZONA

Of constant concern to the prison administration were prisoners' escapes. This postcard was sent to the chief of police of San Francisco from warden Thomas Rynning, former Arizona Ranger captain (and the warden that had brought the prison from Yuma to Florence). Rynning inquires as to whether a prisoner who escaped from a highway construction detail has been sighted or not.

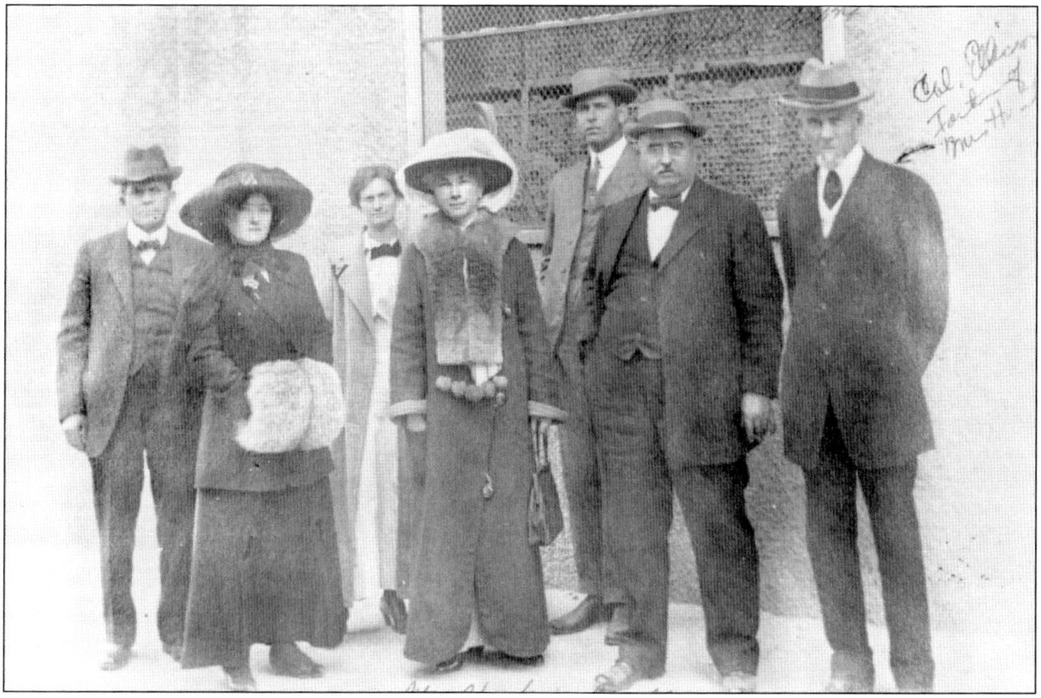

Gov. George Wylie Paul Hunt (second from right) is shown at the prison standing beside his wife, Helen. An advocate of prison reform, Hunt often made weekend trips to the prison, spending Saturday night in the spare room at the warden's home. His interest in prison reform came after reading Victor Hugo's *Les Miserables*. Opposed to the death penalty, he served as president of the Anti-Capital Punishment Society of America in 1914.

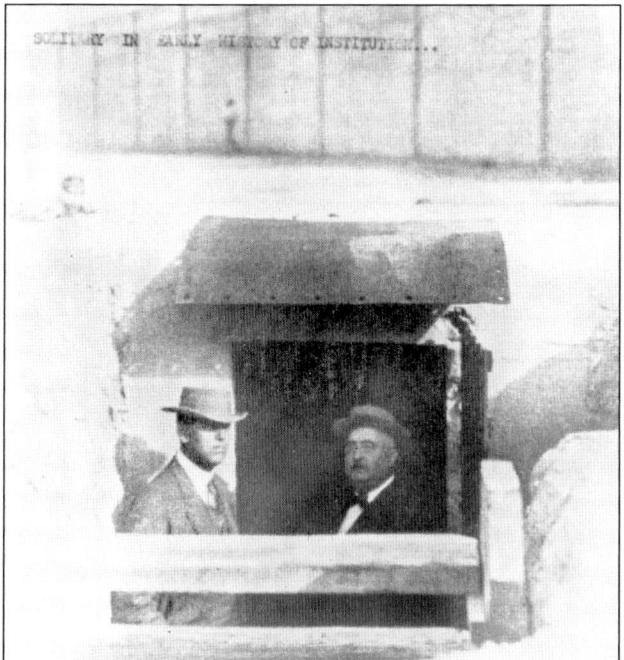

Governor Hunt (right) is pictured around 1918 in the solitary confinement area of the prison called the "Snakes." Inmates were sent there for punishment and had only water to drink and bread to eat. Hunt, however, believed in the education and rehabilitation of inmates. He did away with prison stripes and initiated a plan by which prison labor was used for building highways on the two-for-one plan.

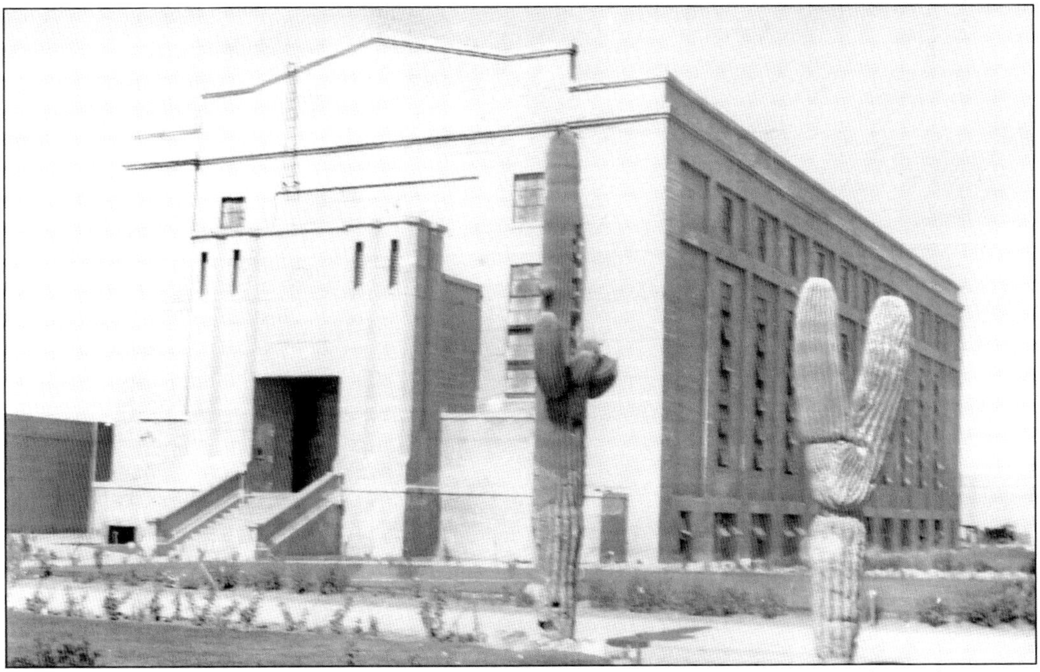

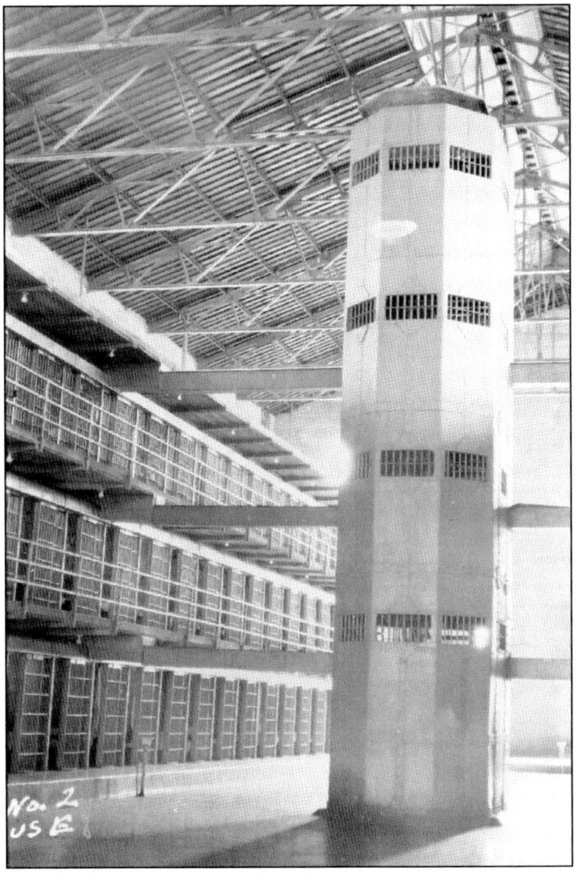

In 1930, what is now Cell Block 2 was constructed with three tiers of cells. The 26 doors on each tier were designed to all open or lock at the same time, but the lock system did not always work. The basement was a cageless dormitory for the aged and ailing inmates who could not climb the stairs.

The two-man cells were 15 by 8 feet with upper and lower bunks, a small sink, and a seatless toilet. The four-man arrangement of Cell Block 1 had not worked. Longtime warden Frank Eyman wrote in a report that, in his opinion, each cell should house a single inmate. Overcrowding at the prison made this difficult to achieve.

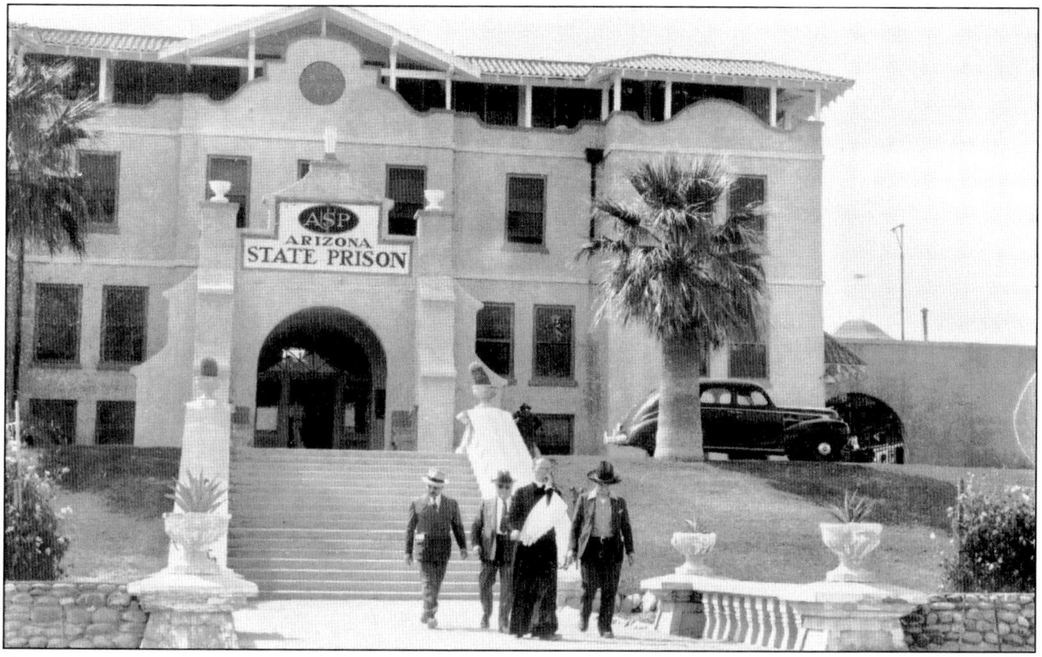

A visiting priest leaves the administration building. Note the top floor of the building, which was constructed for a time when it might have to be used as an emergency fort. It was more often a screened break room or sleeping porch for guards. Eventually the screens were taken down, some windows were blocked in, and the area was used for storage. Later the space was divided into offices.

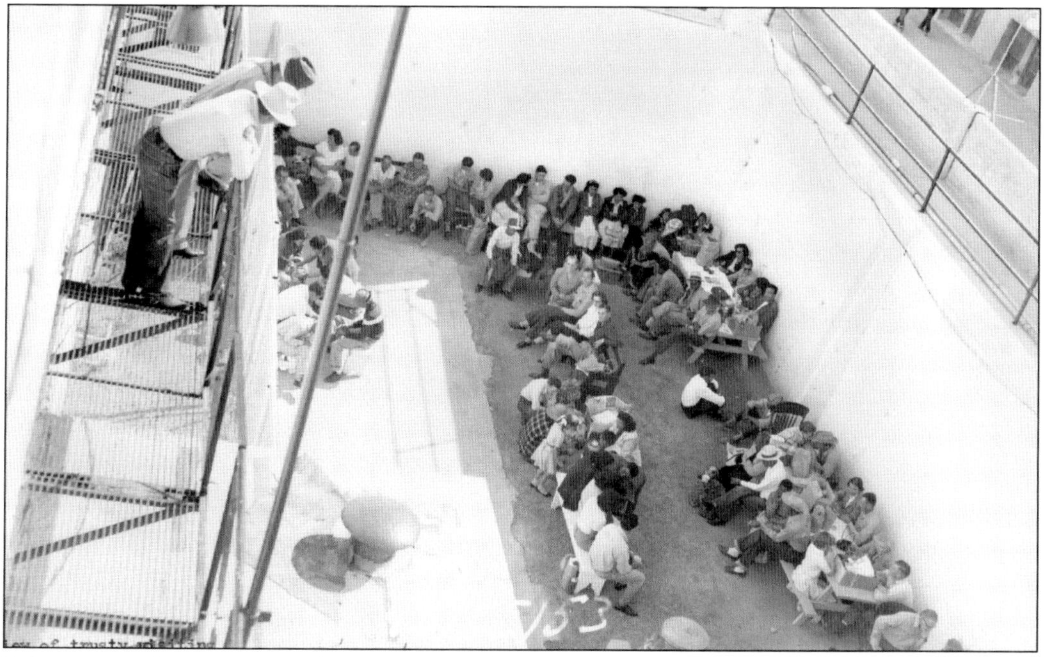

Of course, as in any prison, the most awaited activity for inmates is visitors' day. Here groups of inmates and visitors meet in the yard, watched over by "wall men." These guards must be alert to anything signaling trouble.

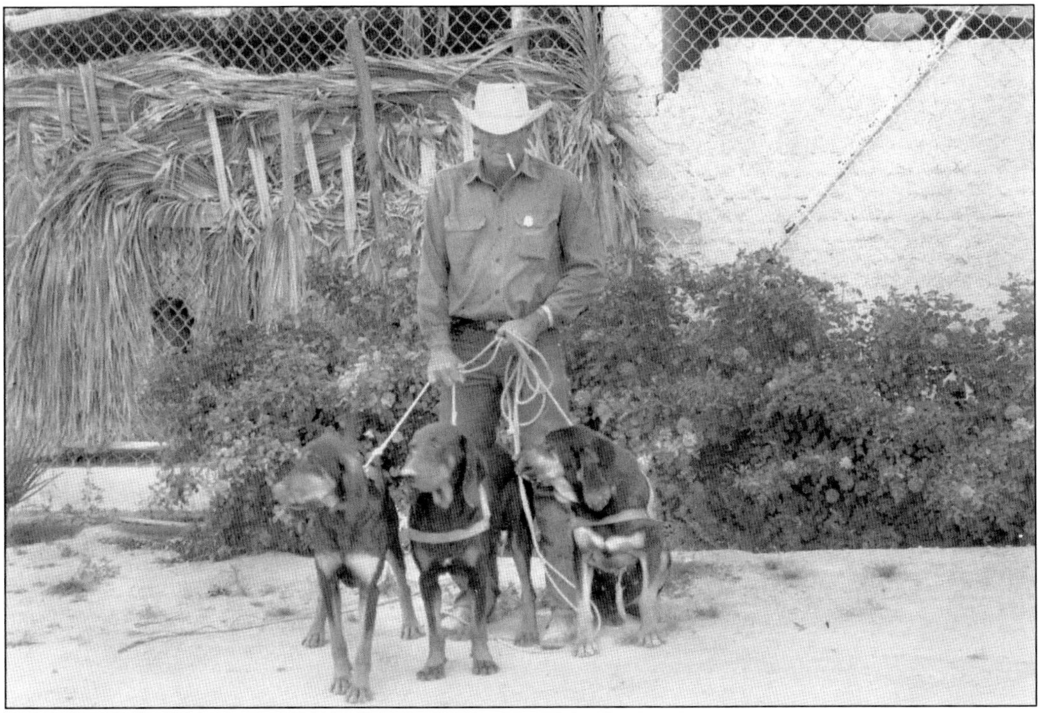

The bloodhounds and their handlers are on call 24 hours a day to go on the hunt for a prison escapee. Leashed hounds are still used today.

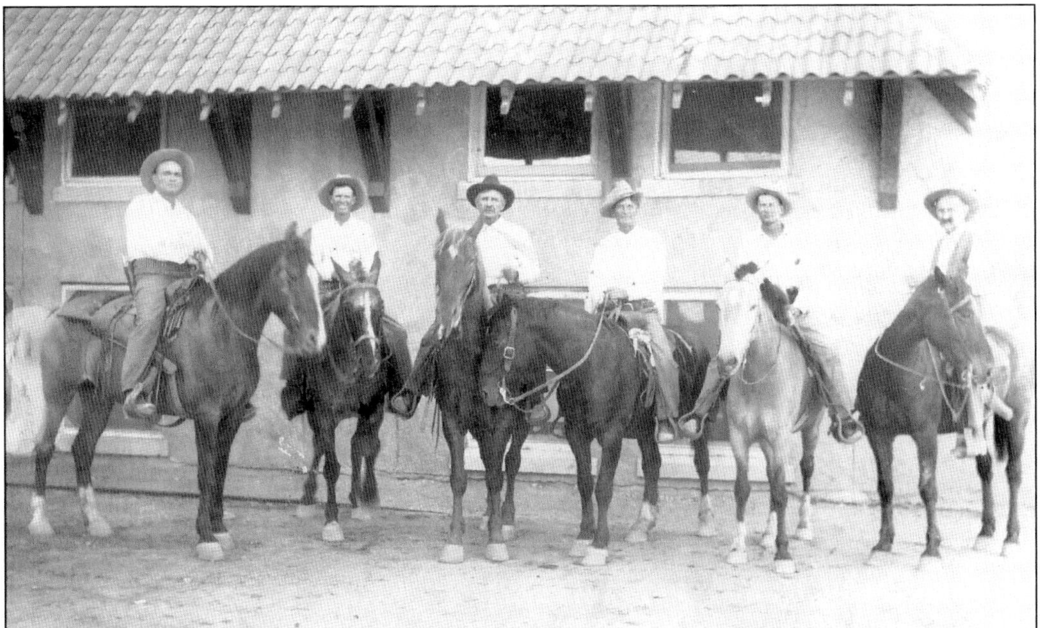

Mounted guards were indispensable to this prison, located on the desert with mountains on its border. The guards had to have a thorough knowledge of horsemanship and the handling of firearms. Pictured around 1944, from left to right, are Wesley Cates, William "Mike" Sims, Fred Jones, Seth Pyeatt, Edward Van Haren, and Capt. Jack White.

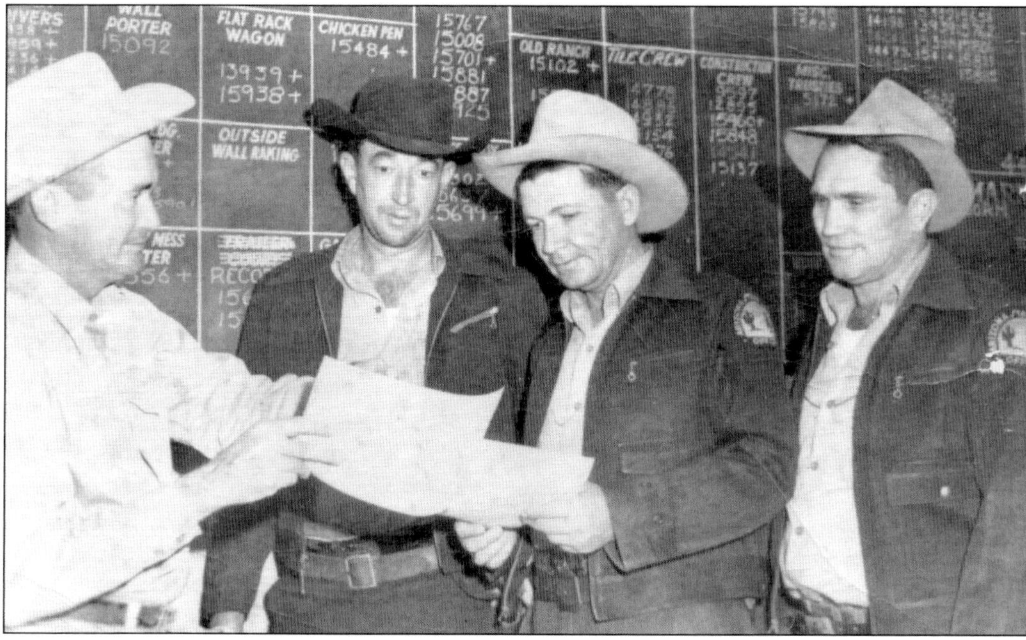

In this photograph, guards are receiving their assignments. For many years, guards worked seven days a week on whatever shift was assigned. Unless there was an escape, they were allowed to go home at night. It was hard to make ends meet on the salary paid to prison workers, who also had to buy their own uniforms. With few unskilled steady jobs available, sometimes it took political influence even to get hired.

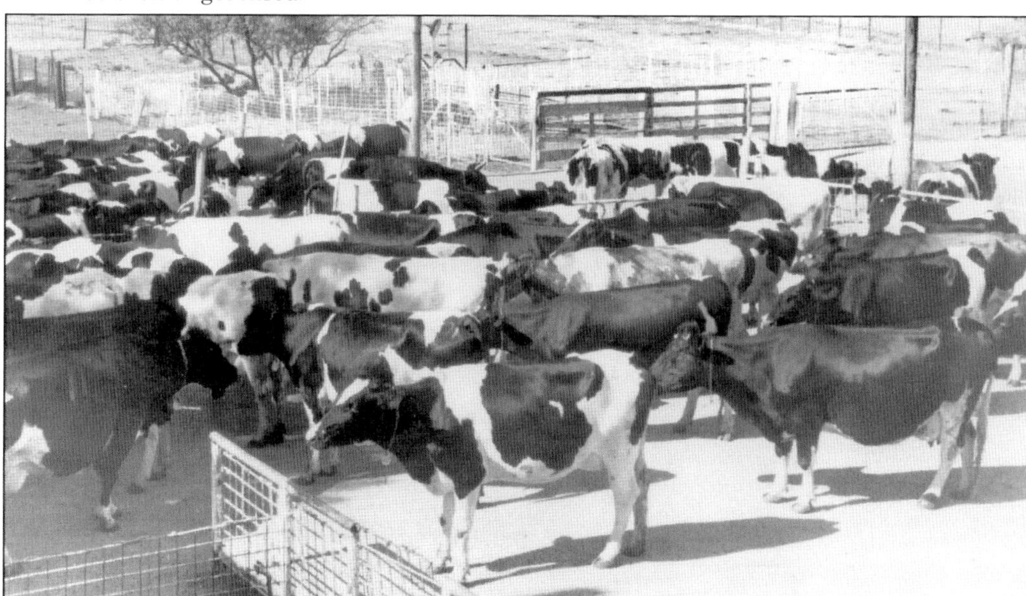

The dairy farm at the prison was one of the largest operations in the state of Arizona. Most cows were milked three times a day, and their milk was pasteurized at the prison. Thousands of half-pint cartons of milk were produced for prison inmates' consumption. Any surplus went to such institutions as the Pinal County General Hospital, the Immigration and Naturalization Service Center, and several school districts.

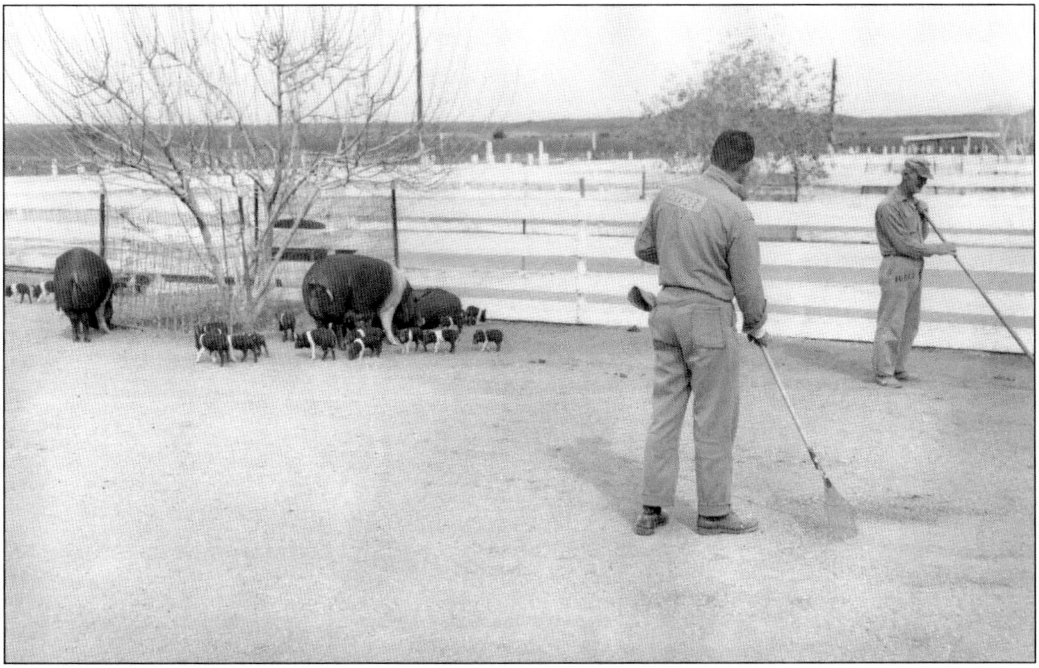

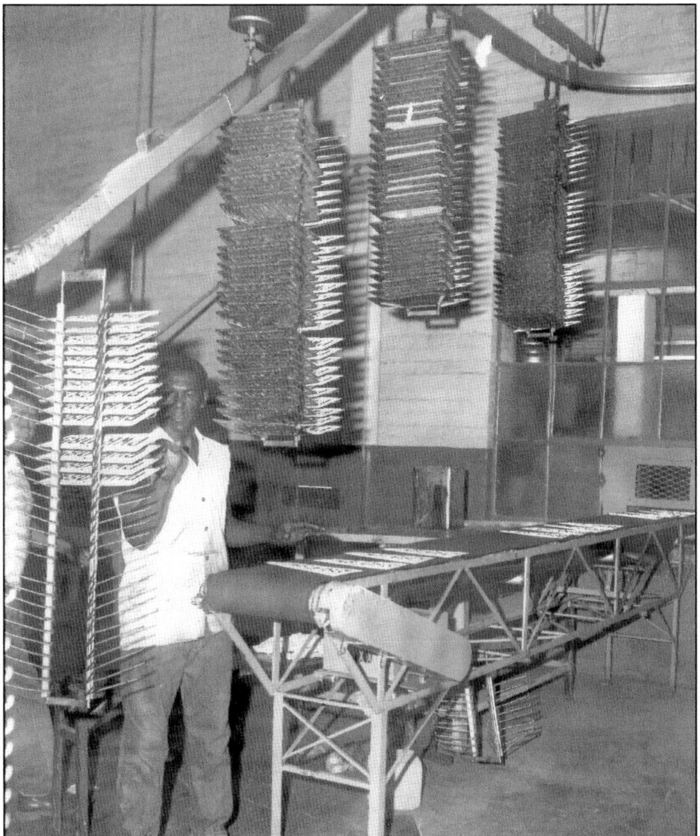

For many years, pigs were raised at the hog farm three miles down the road from the prison. Originally assigned to work at the farm as punishment, inmates grew to enjoy the task. After about five and a half months, a hog grew to the slaughtering weight of 215 to 225 pounds. Pork was consumed within the prison walls, and the excess was sold to other institutions.

The prison produces license plates for all mobile equipment in the state. Each vehicle had a plate for the front and one for the back, so pairs of plates with the same combination of letters and numbers were made. Today only one plate is required. At one time, letters on the plate were assigned according to each county.

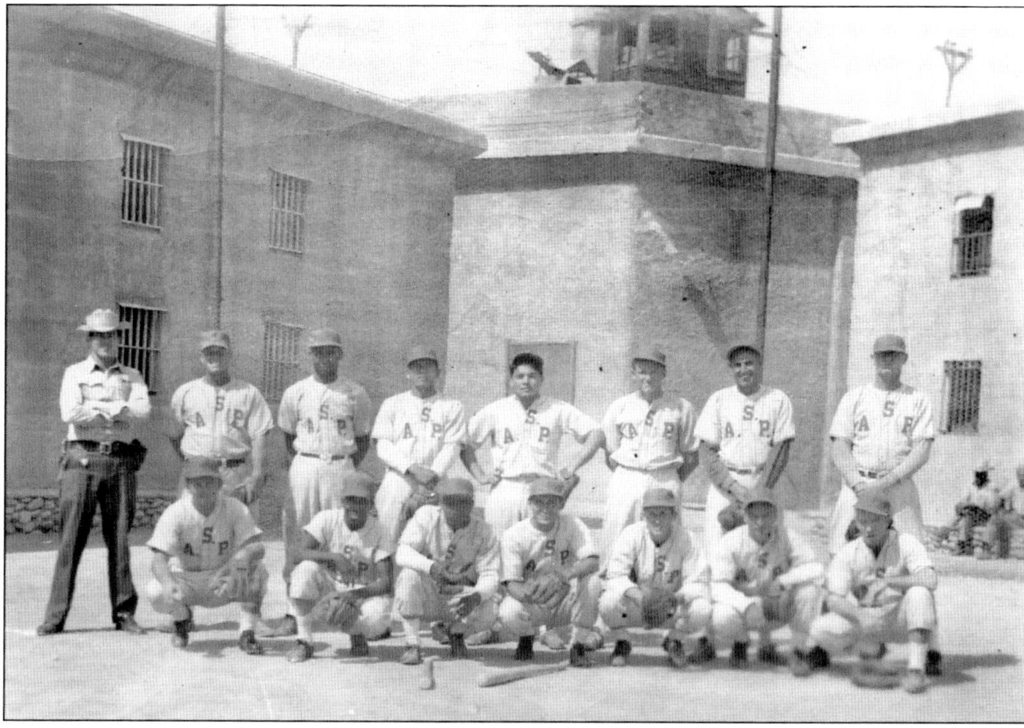

Even during the first days of the Florence prison, the administration allowed inmates to play sports. When the first buildings were constructed, a ball ground was laid out. Eventually there were also a gymnasium, basketball court, and fight ring. Pictured above is the 1944 baseball team. Outside teams were often brought in to compete with the inmates. According to the *Arizona Republic*, "All such contests were greeted with enthusiasm." Boxing equipment included weights (sometimes prison-made), bags, and shoes supplied by the state. Below, fighters stand in front of the fight ring as visiting spectators look on from the top of the walls. A recreation hall was provided as well.

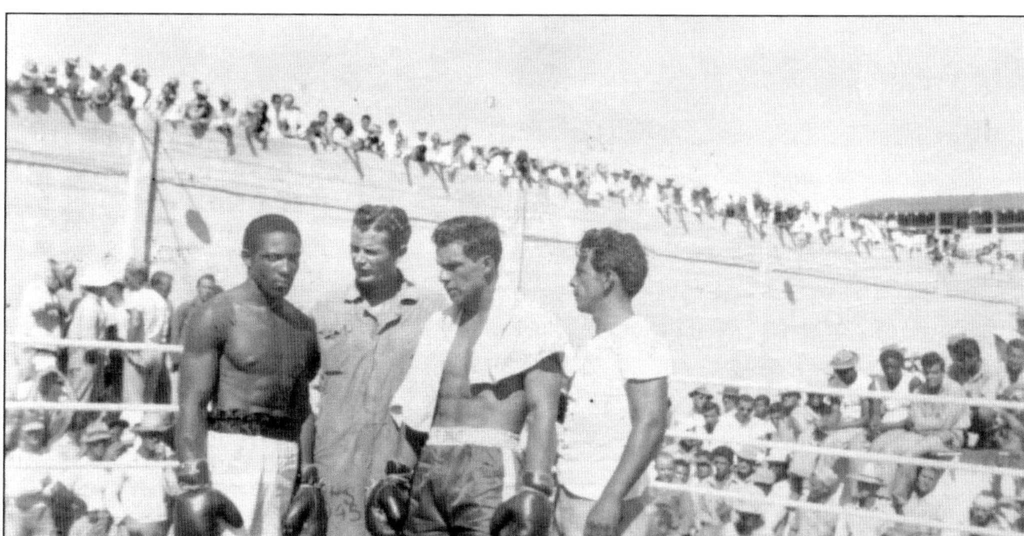

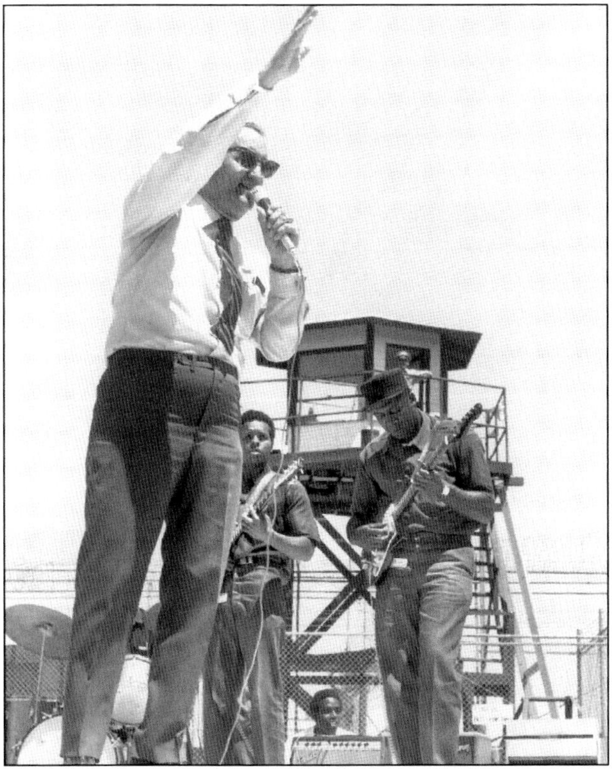

Not as well-known as his brother (famed Southwest artist Ted DeGrazia), the talented Frenck DeGrazia worked as a music teacher at the local high school for years. DeGrazia also taught music at the prison. His prison band, known as Stars Behind Bars, practiced daily for its performances at prison sports events and the Junior Parada. Here DeGrazia directs the band, with the guardhouse in the background.

A crew films the Paramount movie *Riot* at the prison in 1968. Starring actors Jim Brown and Gene Hackman, the movie was about inmates taking over a prison and holding guards hostage. It was the first film to be premiered in a prison. The audience, according to the *Los Angeles Herald Examiner*, consisted of "pros and cons." The pros were responsible for the movie, and the cons—well, they were the inmates.

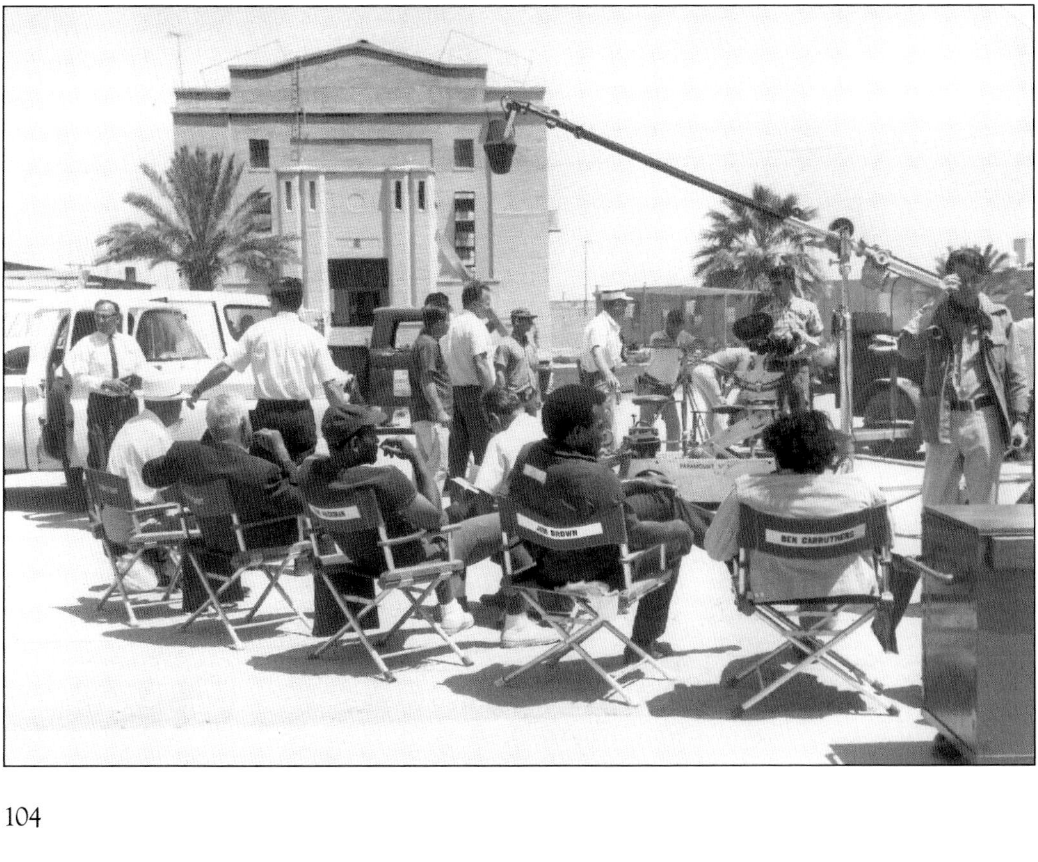

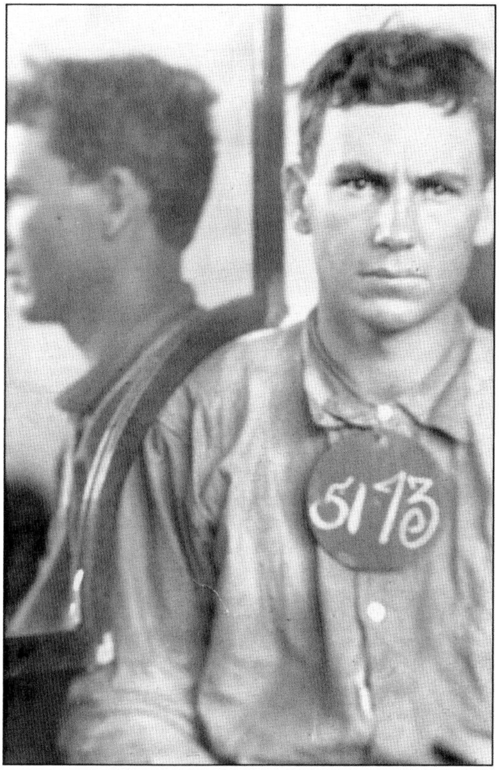

During World War I, a posse tried to arrest brothers Tom (right) and John Power at their cabin in the Galiuro Mountains for being draft dodgers. A gunfight ensued. Of the four men in the posse, only one man returned alive. The citizens of the nearby community of Safford were incensed. When the brothers fled, 3,000 men, including U.S. Cavalry troops from Fort Huachuca, searched the mountains of southeastern Arizona. Tom and John were cornered in Mexico, about 40 miles from the border. There was no death penalty at the time, so the Powers were sentenced to life in the state prison in Florence.

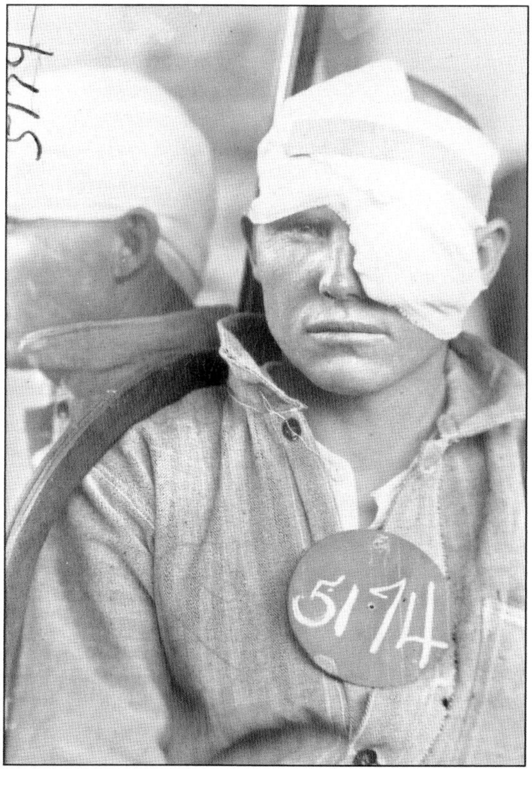

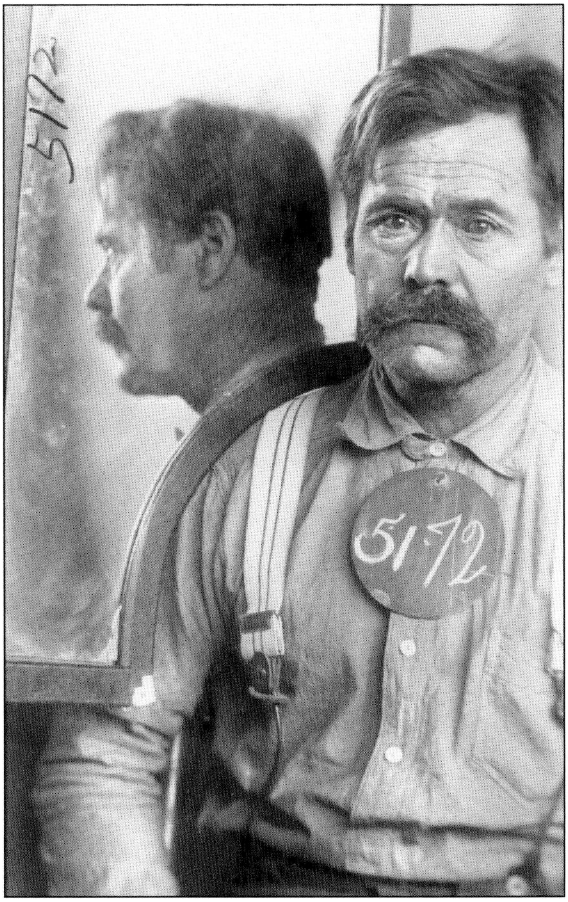

Tom Sisson, a former army scout and the partner of the Power brothers' father, fled with Tom and John. He and the brothers were considered "cold-blooded killers." In 1957, Sisson died in prison of heart disease at the age of 86. He had testified in an affidavit that he "did not advise the Power brothers to not sign up for the draft." He left $10,000 saved from his army pension to John Power.

After 42 years in prison, the Power brothers were given a full pardon. Cooler heads had realized the contradictions in the stories of the gunfight. They settled in Klondyke, Arizona, near where they had lived before. Tom (left) and John are pictured in front of the post office of the mountain town. Today the brothers are buried in the Klondyke Cemetery.

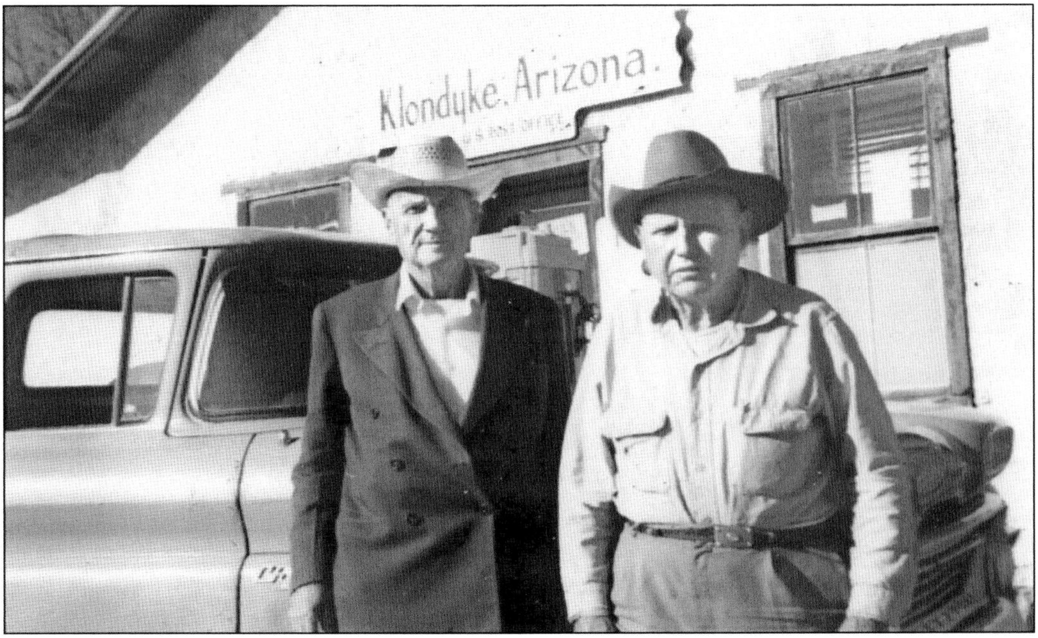

Eva Dugan had been arrested out of state for stealing her Tucson employer's car. When the employer's body was found, Dugan was then brought to Tucson to be tried and sentenced for his murder. The first woman to be hanged at the prison, she was also destined to be the last. At the February 21, 1930, hanging, her head snapped from her body, which prompted an end to the practice. Dugan's mug shot is framed by the noose.

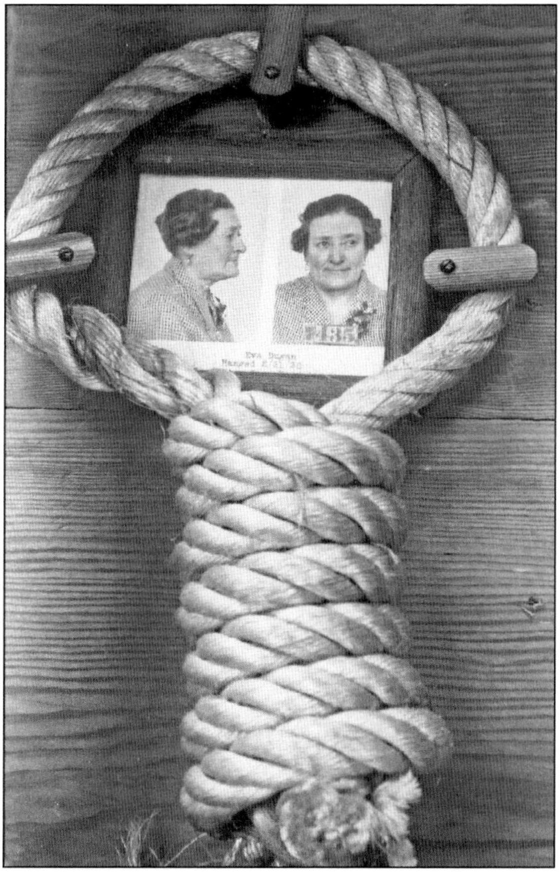

In 1934, brothers Manuel and Fred Hernández were the first men sentenced to die from lethal gas in the state of Arizona. It was also the first double execution by lethal gas in the country. Convicted of murdering a prospector, the brothers were executed within 18 months of the crime. The double chair is on display at the Pinal County Historical Society Museum. (Courtesy P. E. Guerrero and D. Legler.)

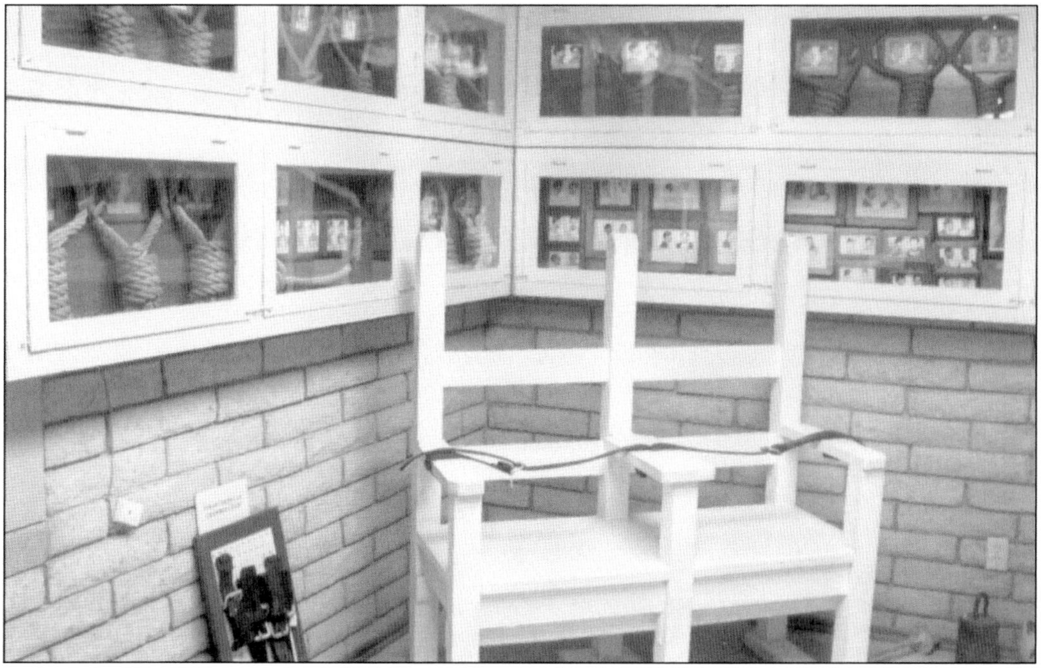

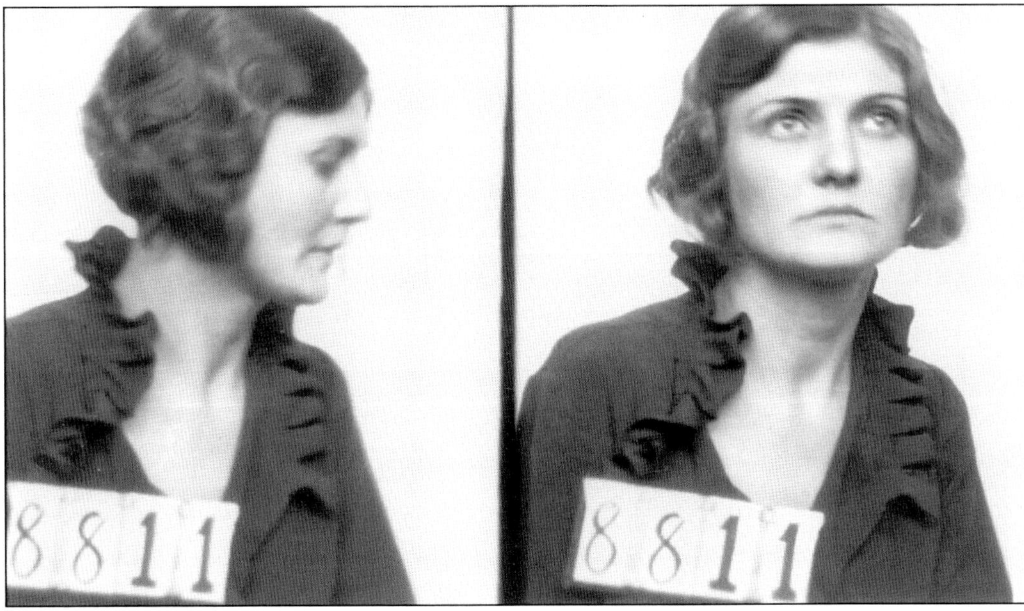

Winnie Ruth Judd, Arizona's notorious "trunk murderess," was convicted of killing two close friends, cutting up one of the bodies, and shipping both in trunks to Los Angeles. Apprehended, Judd was brought back to Arizona, tried, and sentenced to death. At a sanity hearing in Florence, she was found insane and committed to the Arizona State Hospital in Phoenix. Shown here are Judd's prison photographs from 1933.

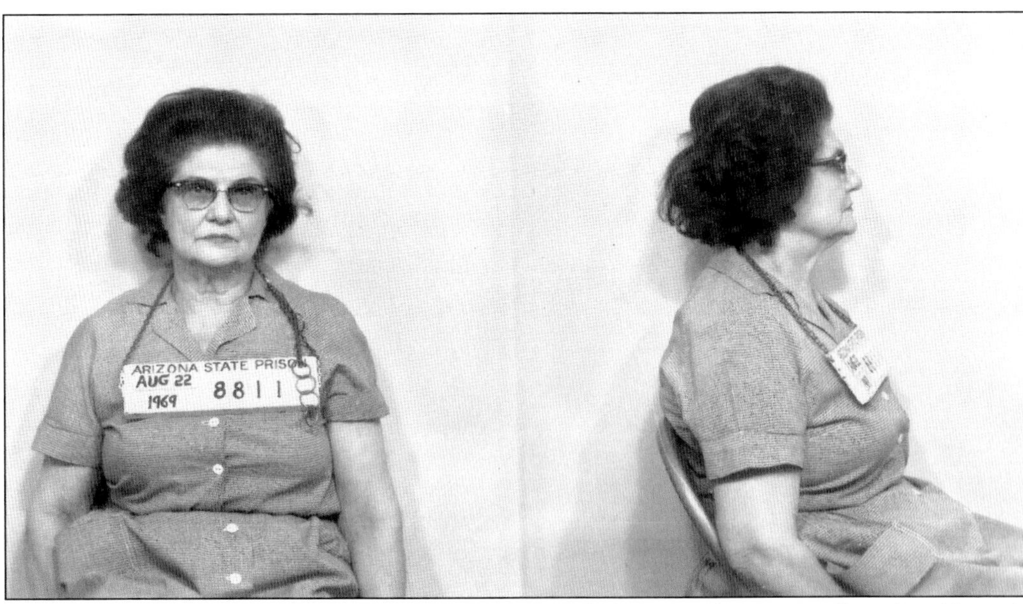

Judd was a model patient at the mental hospital, except for her periodic escapes. Found and brought back to the hospital many times, in 1962, she escaped and remained missing for over six years. Discovered working as a housekeeper in Northern California, Judd was returned to Arizona and incarcerated at the Florence prison, when these photographs were taken. Judd was eventually paroled and lived out her life near Stockton, California.

Eight

WAR COMES TO FLORENCE

During the Civil War, Union soldiers from California came through Arizona to keep the territory from the Confederates. Eventually some people who had sympathies for one side or the other became citizens of the new desert town. Some 30 years later, citizens of Florence participated in the Spanish-American War. Then, at the beginning of World War I, Germany let Mexico know that if that country would be their ally, it would give the United States' southwest back to Mexico. Simultaneously, Pancho Villa created problems on Arizona's southern border. Arizona soldiers went south to protect the border, and some left for war in France as part of the American Expeditionary Force.

With World War II came changes to Florence. Many young men and some women joined the military, leaving farmers shorthanded in the fields. In 1943, a prisoner-of-war camp was established just north of Florence and the Gila River. Camp Florence, which originally held Italians and later Germans, had the reputation of being well run. Many of the POWs were assigned to work in the fields to help the labor-strapped farmers. A Japanese relocation camp was also located near the Pima Indian Agency town of Sacaton. Military personnel came from all over the nation to assist local personnel in operating the camp. After the war, some of those posted at the camp remained in Florence. Where the camp was, there is a retirement community today.

Both Florence residents and their neighbors, the Pima Indians, joined the military. Two Florence citizens were rescued from sinking ships in the Pacific and lived to tell the tale, while another was imprisoned in a German POW camp. Returning veterans were given the benefit of an education through the GI Bill. Arizona's U.S. senator Ernest W. McFarland, who wrote the home and business loan sections of the bill, was later referred to as the "Father of the GI Bill."

Many Florence residents continue to participate in America's wars.

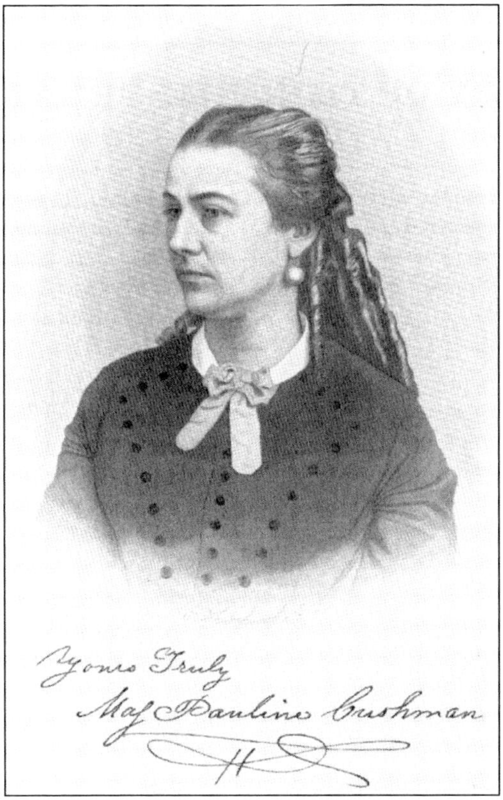

Born in New Orleans, Pauline Cushman became a successful actress during the Civil War. Recruited as a Yankee spy, she was captured by Confederate forces and sentenced to hang but rescued by Union troops. After the war, she traveled the country performing a one-woman show about her war exploits. She eventually settled in an adobe house on Florence's Granite Street while married to Sheriff Jeremiah Fryer.

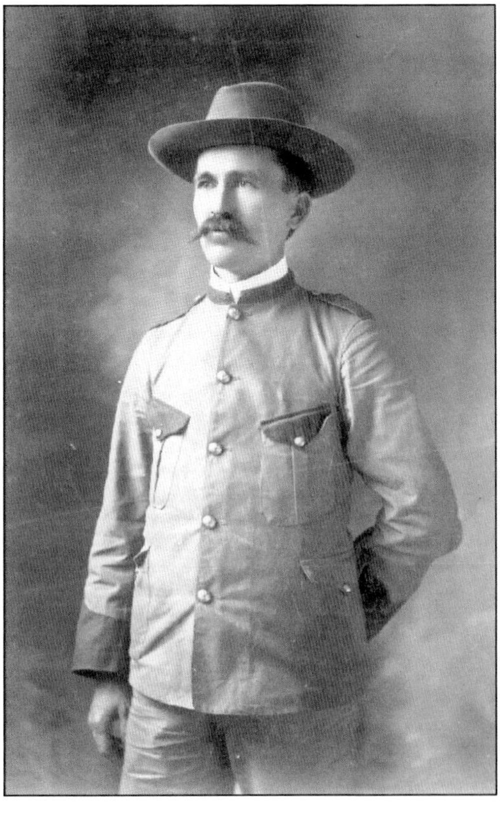

George Eggleston Truman was the only Pinal County resident to enlist for the Spanish-American War and serve in Teddy Roosevelt's famed Rough Riders. The youngest of eight children from Oneida County, New York, George followed his older siblings West to seek his fortune. Arriving in Florence in 1890, he began raising cattle and mining. George married Mary E. Collingwood, raised three sons, and held several elected offices as a Democrat.

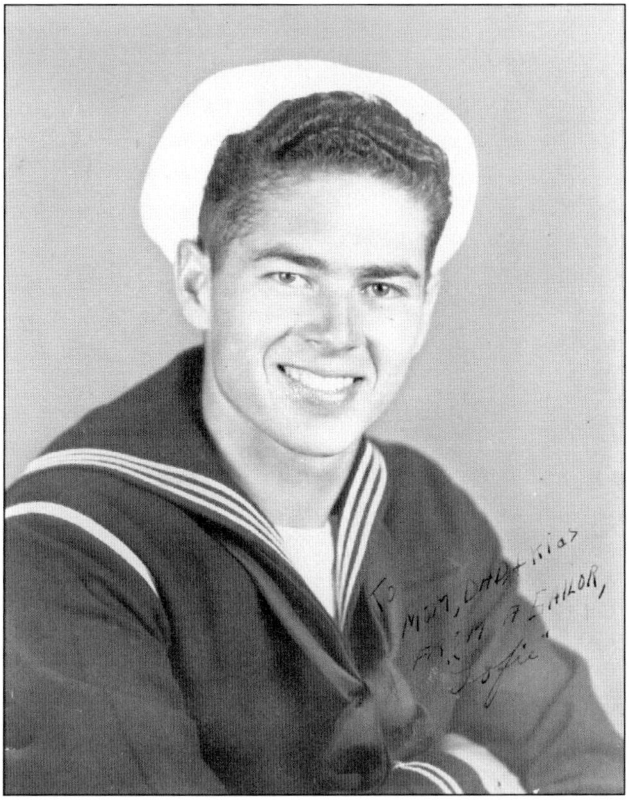

Rudolph Moraga joined the navy at 17 "to see the world." He found himself on the escort carrier *Bismarck Sea* supporting the attack on Iwo Jima. Considered the "Gateway to Japan," the island was heavily defended. Japanese kamikaze (suicide pilots) flew themselves into the ships. The *Bismarck Sea* was hit by kamikaze on February 21, 1945. Badly wounded, Moraga was rescued after four terrifying hours in shark-infested waters.

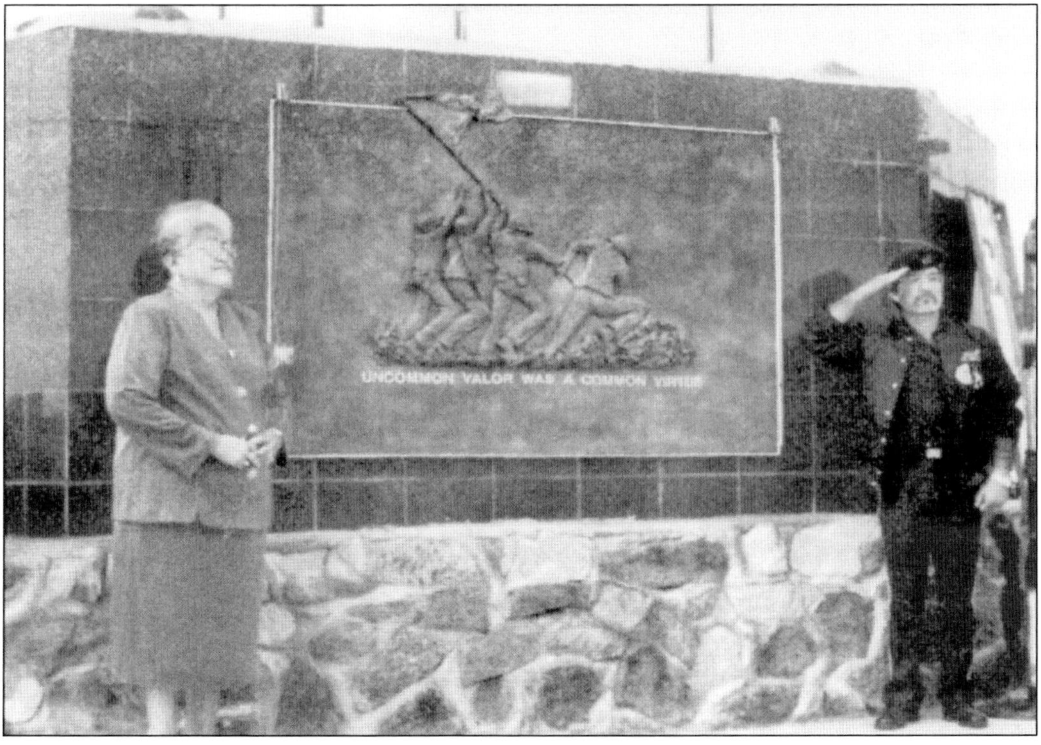

Former governor Mary Thomas and sculptor Oscar Urrea unveil the Ira H. Hayes Monument at a park in Sacaton 55 years after the February 19, 1945, attack on Iwo Jima. Hayes, a Pima Indian born on the reservation, earned fame as one of the six men photographed raising the American flag at Iwo Jima during one of the bloodiest battles of World War II. (Courtesy *Casa Grande Dispatch*.)

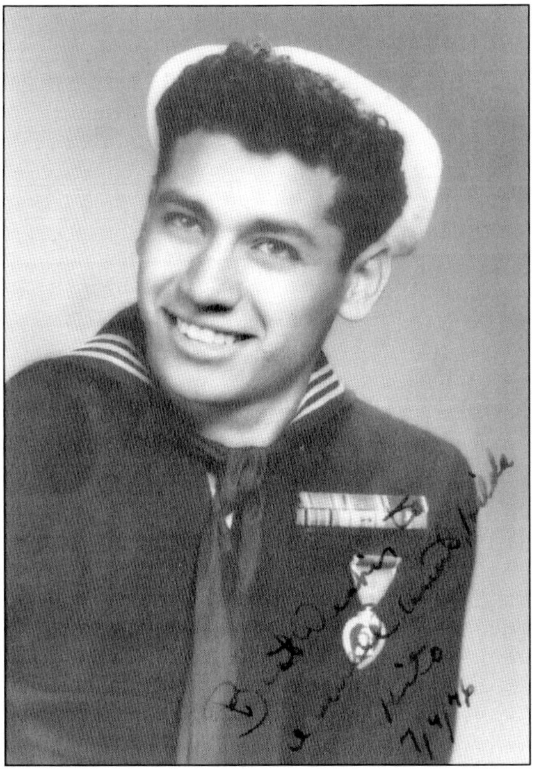

Florence's 17-year-old Adolfo "Harpo" Celaya was among the survivors of five days in shark-infested waters after his ship, the USS *Indianapolis*, was sunk in the Pacific. The cruiser had delivered the components of the atomic bomb later dropped on Hiroshima. The crew members' SOS was not heard, and combined with other blunders, they were not located until only 316 of 1,196 remained alive.

Patriotic children pose with their mother, Natalia Michea White (seated), who holds her grandson David, during World War II. Seen here from left to right are Benjamin and Dolly (the parents of David), Fredric II "Buzz," Martha (who did not enlist), Mary, and Gene. Missing from the photograph is John, who had already gone to war. All returned home safely.

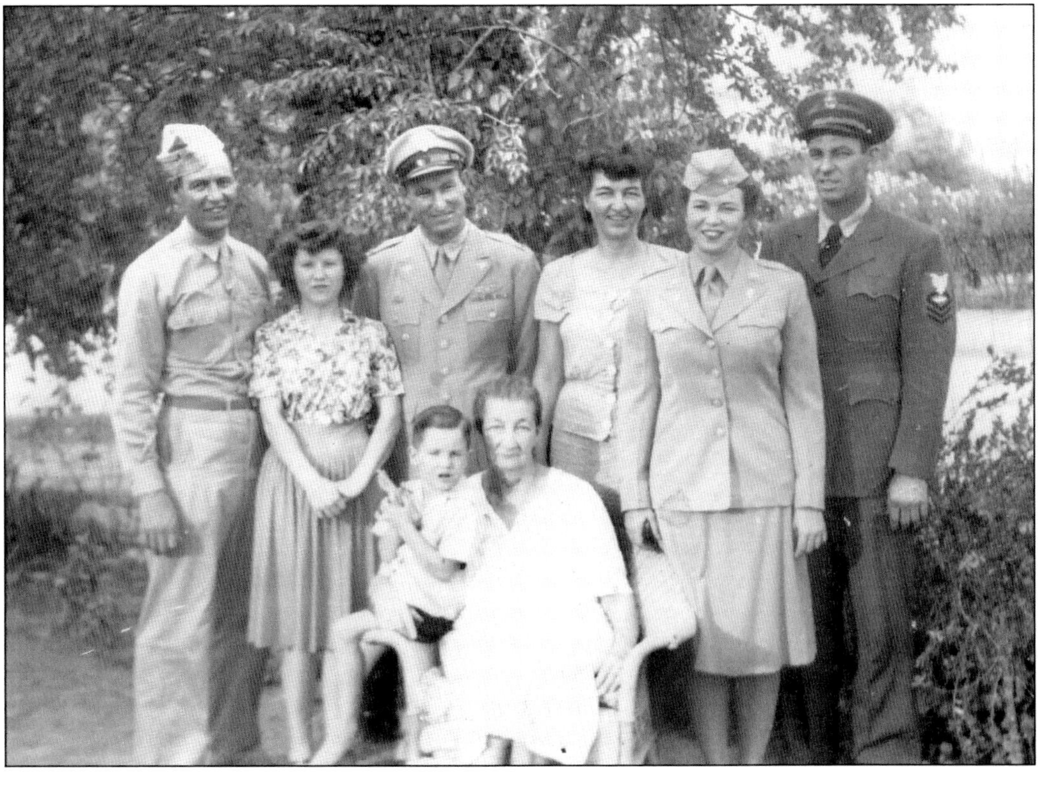

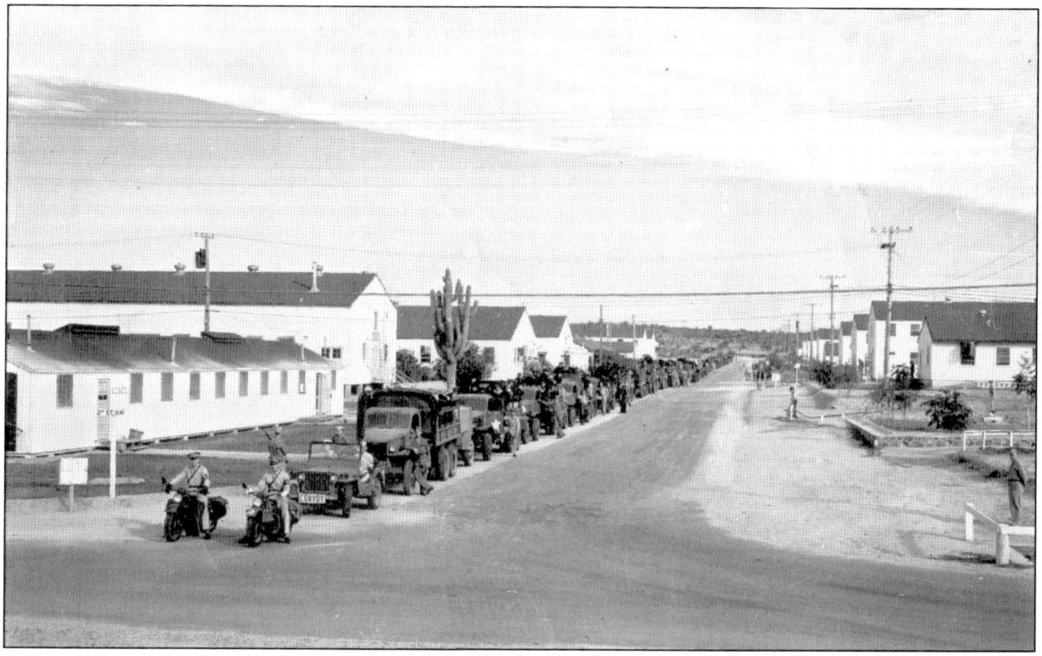

One of the largest POW camps in the country was built in Florence during World War II. Over 13,000 German and Italian prisoners were held there. Florentines worked civilian jobs at the camp. Staff were entertained by USO dances held at the Florence Woman's Club. Prisoners picked cotton on area farms since local men were off at the war.

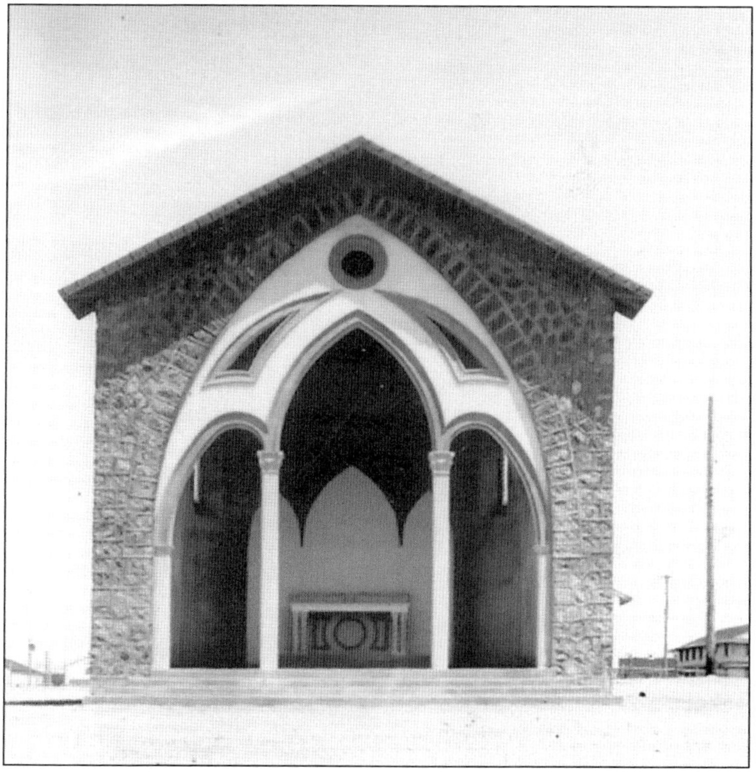

This chapel stood in unique contrast to the POW camp surroundings. Constructed by Italian prisoners in 1943, the chapel included artwork on the interior walls. Services conducted by Florence clergy were held for the prisoners. The camp's site is now a large retirement community. Some of the residents hope to build a replica of the chapel near its original location.

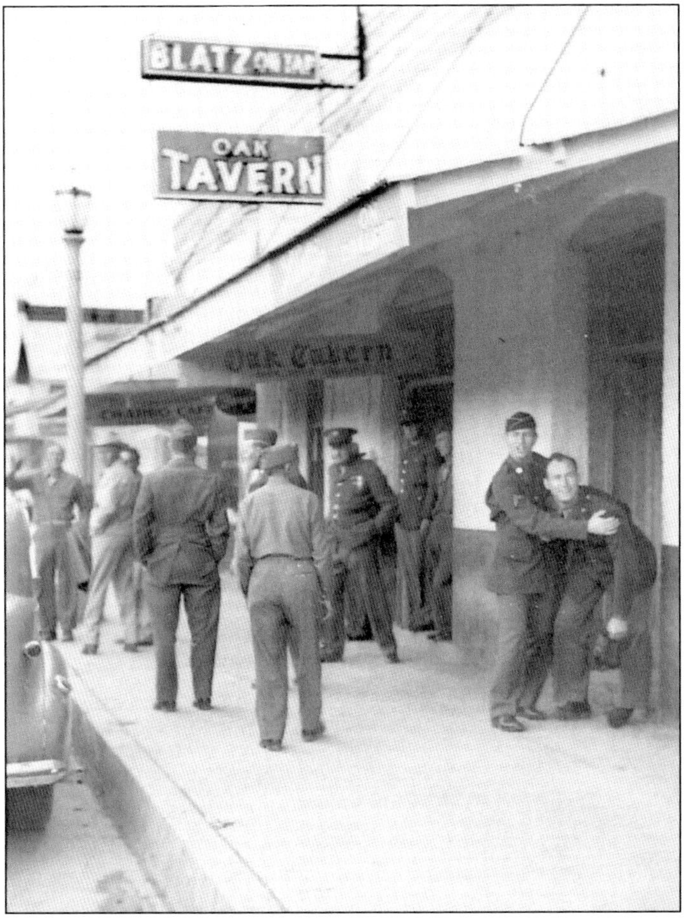

Military men are pictured in front of the popular Oak Tavern on Main Street. Most of the soldiers were stationed at the POW camp north of town. At right, army air corpsman Hendrik "Heine" Schewel Jr. holds up his friend Fredric "Buzz" White II. After White's airplane was shot down, he would spend 19 months in a German POW camp. Happily he would return home when his Stalag 3 was liberated.

A young bride, Dorothy "Dottie" Borree is teased by friends Heine Schewel (left) and Buzz White II. They told her that they would steal her while her husband, Jim, was away at war. Jim Borree flew reconnaissance out of Florence, Italy, and attempted to alert her where he was by underlining "Florence" in her addressed mail. Neither the censors nor Dottie caught on to his code.

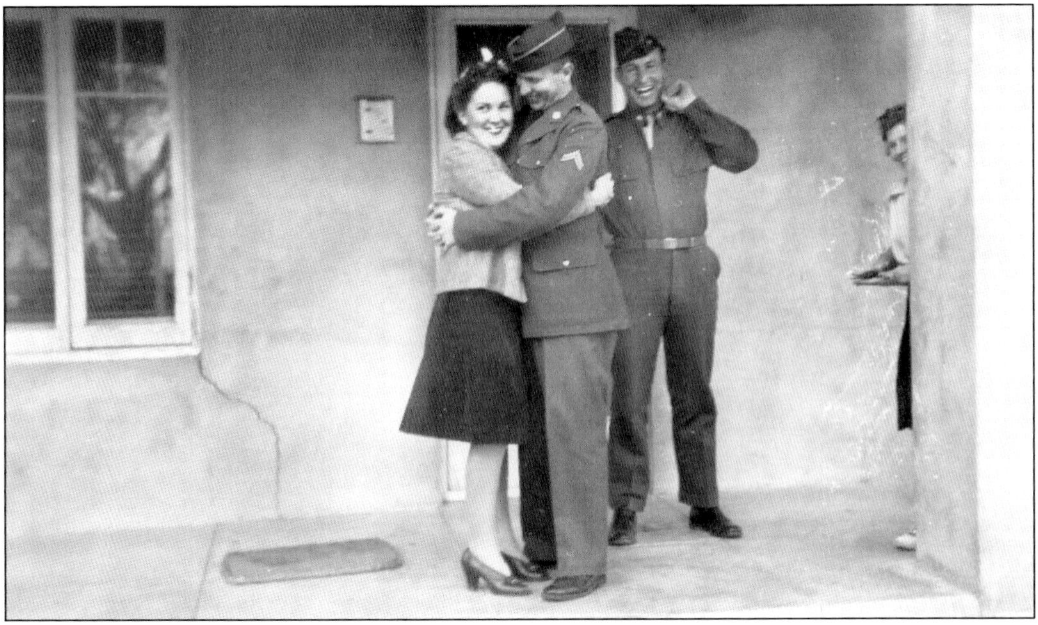

During World War II, Gene Autry worked as a technical sergeant at Luke Field near Phoenix. Here he visits at the home of rancher and rodeo producer M. Twain Clemans and his wife, Rose, around 1943. The couple's daughter Barbara sits on Autry's lap. Barbara thought of him as an uncle. When seeing him on the movie screen, she was disappointed he did not wave to her in the audience.

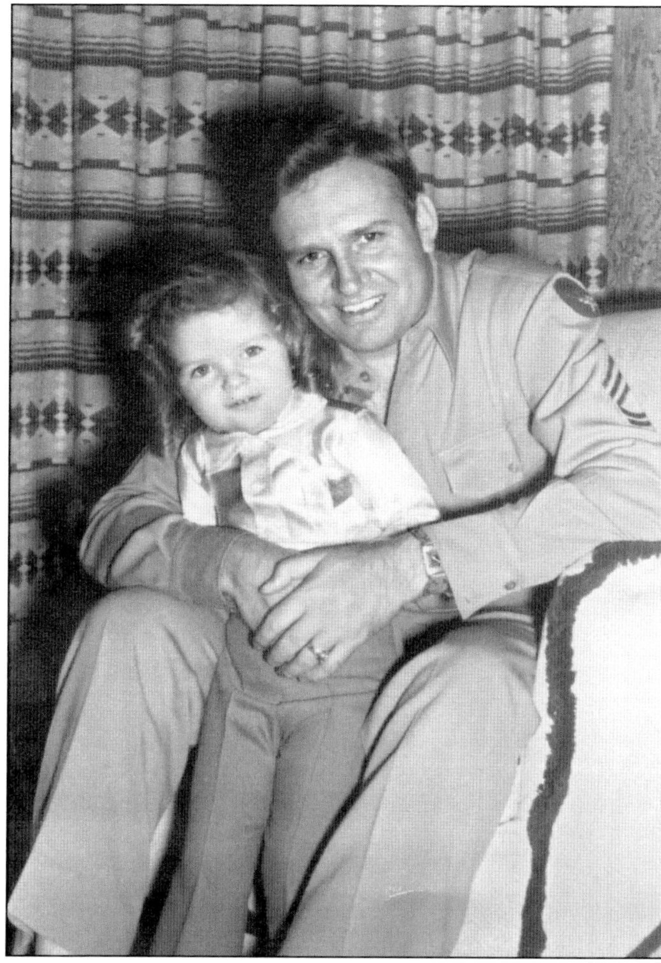

The American Legion was formed as a national organization in 1919. Immediately Florence formed what is now Post No. 9 in the Arizona Department. The McLellan-Parsons Post was named after two local citizens who went off to World War I and did not return. Today the post is headquartered in the former Joseph Collingwood and Company store, one of the most historically significant buildings in Florence, as shown here in an early photograph.

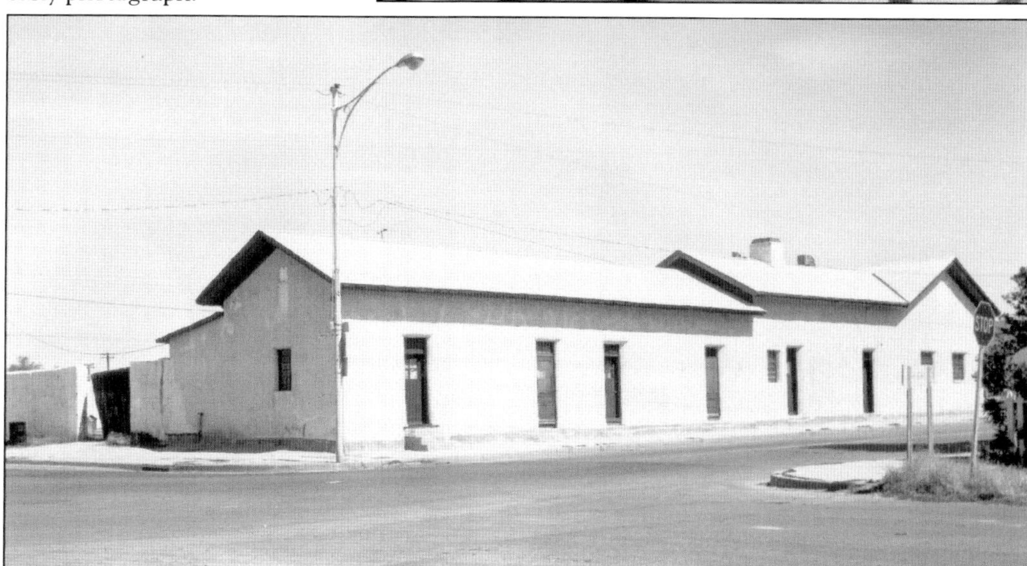

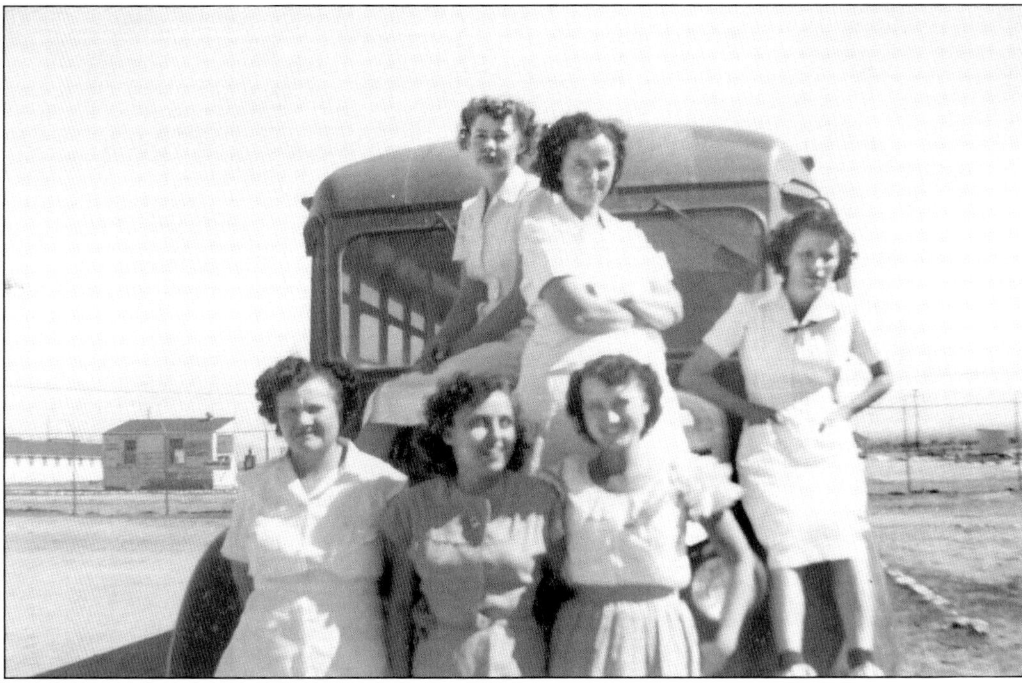

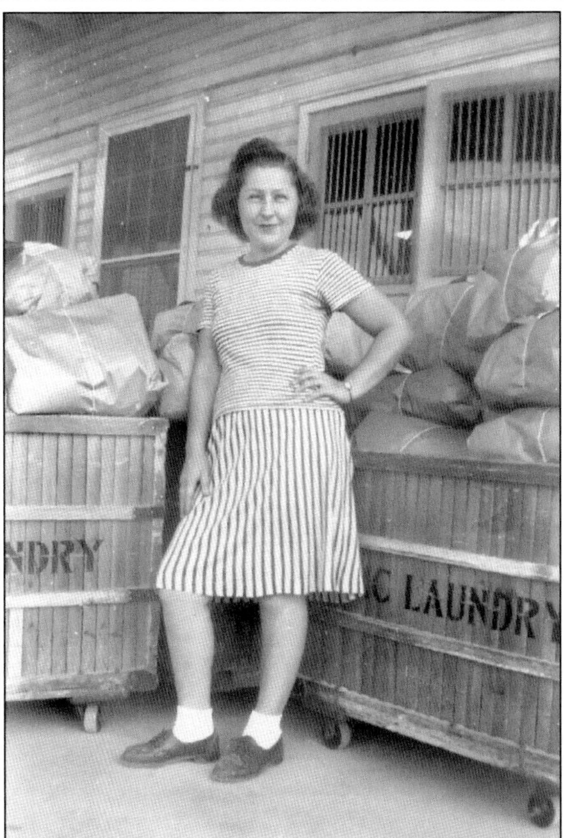

At the close of World War II, the POW camp, empty of prisoners, became a laundry for the air force. Women were picked up at their homes and transported to Florence Camp to do the laundry for Williams Field in Maricopa County and Davis Monthan Air Base in Tucson. Above, Mardell Long (front center) and Esther Rhodes (top right) are the only identified women on the truck. The women were allowed to use the facilities for their own family ironing. Rhodes often laughed that her son was complimented at school for having perfectly pressed pants. At left, a woman only identified as Billie is pleased to show off large bins of wrapped bundles of finished laundry.

Nine

Keeping the Past Alive

The continued boom that Florence anticipated never quite materialized. Quiet, modest growth developed instead, with the employment opportunities and revenue the county seat and prisons afforded. The absence of unbridled new growth in the heart of the downtown allowed many of the historic structures to avoid the wrecking ball, but weather and time were beginning to take their toll.

By the 1960s, many old adobe buildings were knocked down by order of the county health department. Local residents, alarmed, wanted to begin the preservation of these unique structures. Organized efforts started in the 1970s, and the old adobes and early commercial buildings were no longer seen as crumbling eyesores, but rather as potential diamonds in the rough. Many endangered buildings were saved and restored. Dr. Harris Sobin and Associates published an extensive survey and history of the town and architecture. The drive to save Florence's historic buildings had begun in earnest. The downtown was listed as a National Historic Site, and private homes were added to the National Register. The Town of Florence created an advisory commission to oversee the historic district, enforcing guidelines for changes to historic structures, new construction, and signage. Arizona State Heritage Grants have been used to help with a number of projects.

One can see a variety of architectural styles and materials while visiting the historic district. Among the eclectic blend are examples of Sonoran, Early and Late Transitional, American Victorian, American Bungalow, and mission revival architecture. The historic district has been re-surveyed and expanded several times, and many more buildings have been identified and protected. Pedro E. Guerrero, who now owns a home in the district, was once a photographer for Frank Lloyd Wright. He and the author and photographer Dixie Legler photographed most of the buildings included in this chapter.

An annual tour of historic homes and buildings is held on the second Saturday in February. Through preservation efforts and continued interest, Florence remains an authentic and original slice of Arizona history.

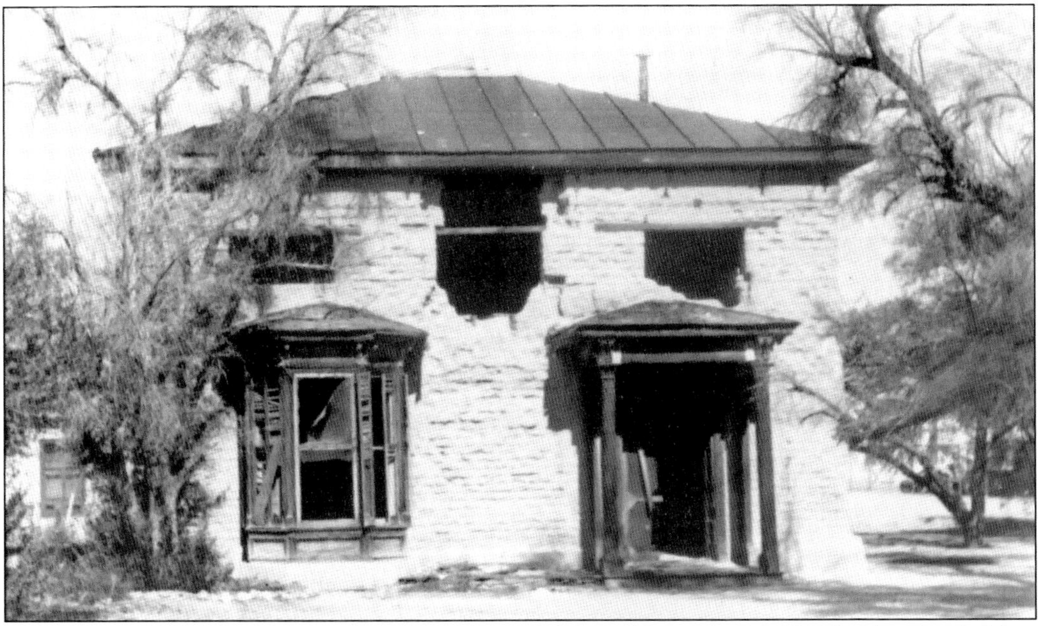

A widow, Ella Clarke lived in the Clarke House with her nephew Nott Guild. After her death, Nott remained there alone until his own death in 1956. The house sat vacant and vulnerable to the elements, a deteriorating eyesore on Main Street. Many residents were horrified at the condition of this historic structure. The Clarke House Foundation was established to save the building.

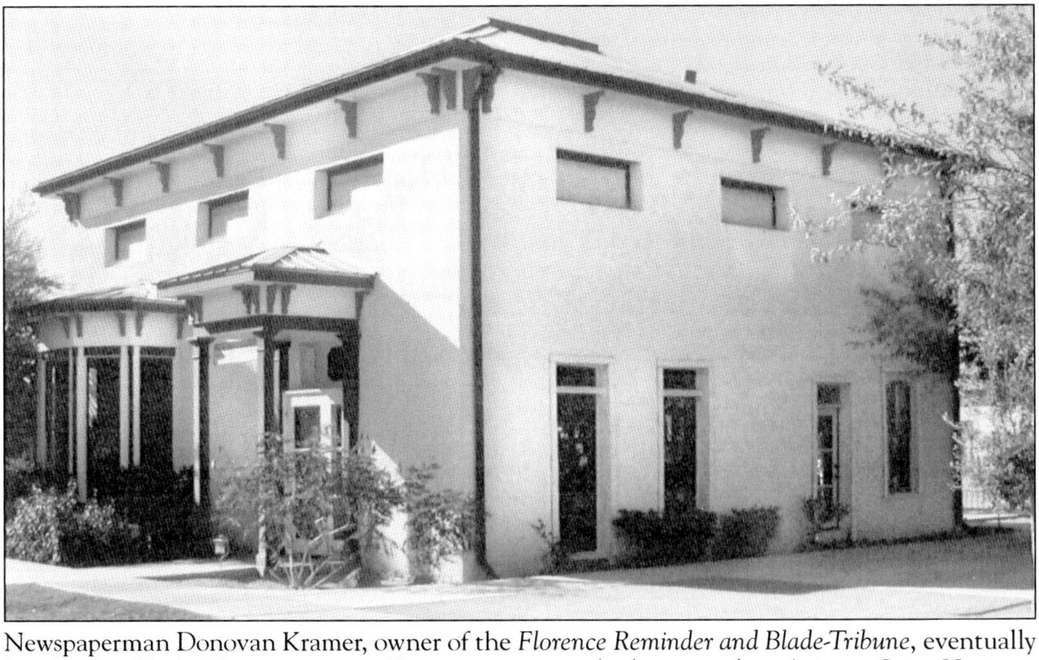

Newspaperman Donovan Kramer, owner of the *Florence Reminder and Blade-Tribune*, eventually bought the Clarke House property. His investment in the house and an Arizona State Heritage Grant provided the means to restore the building to become his newspaper's office. Often included on the annual historic tour of Florence, it is a highlight of the historic district. The building has also been the scene of ice cream socials and town gatherings, much like it was in its earlier day. (Courtesy P. E. Guerrero and D. Legler.)

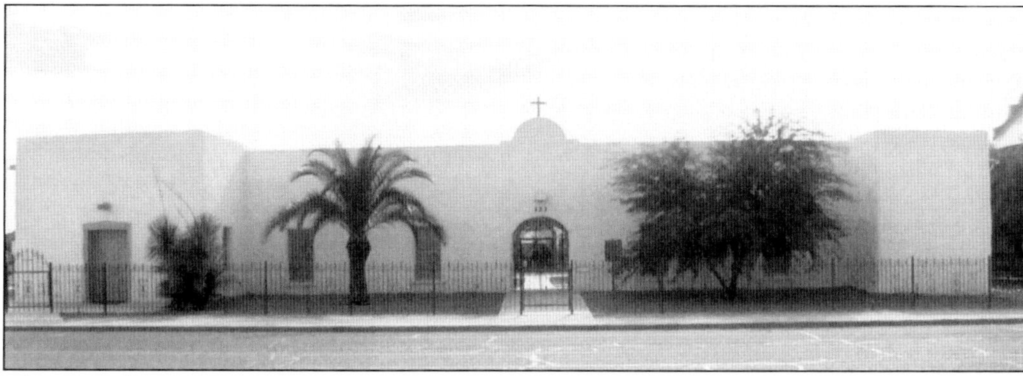

The Chapel of the Gila partially collapsed in 1993. Days before slated demolition, the Arizona State Historic Preservation Office was contacted and a campaign to save it began. Its historical and architectural importance inspired many entities to join forces and provide finances to restore it. Several entities contributed to its preservation, including the local church community, French and Catholic organizations, and the State of Arizona. It is the only surviving mission church of the territorial period in central Arizona. (Courtesy P. E. Guerrero and D. Legler.)

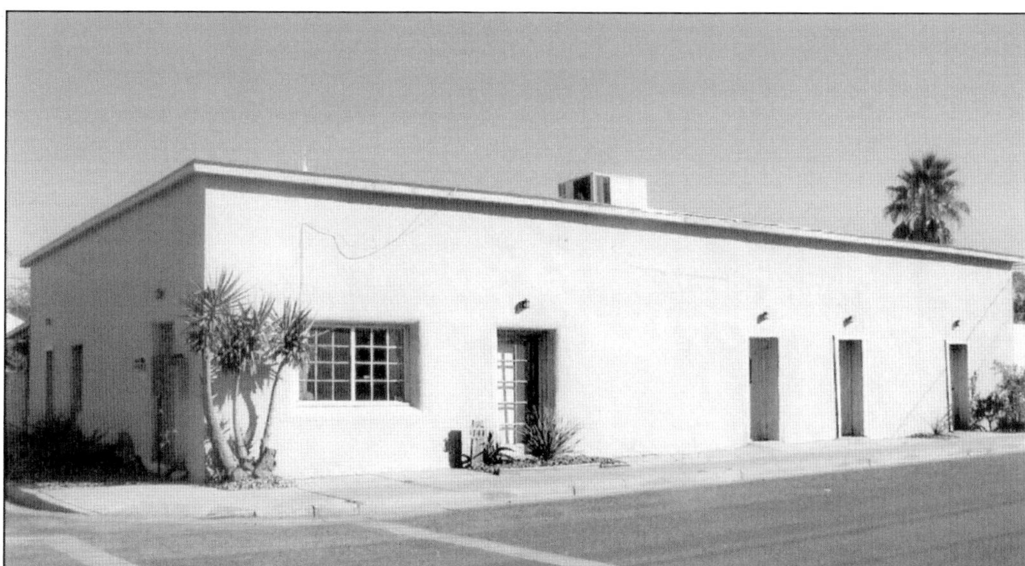

One of the few remaining intact corner Sonoran row houses, the c. 1880 Jesus Preciado de Luna House exhibits the typical thick stucco on sun-dried adobe brick walls, a flat roof, and a street facade built directly on the property line. A garden patio is in the rear. The interior overhead construction is of round vigas (cottonwood beams) and saguaro ribs. Juan de Luna put the house title in his wife's name, a Mexican tradition. (Courtesy P. E. Guerrero and D. Legler.)

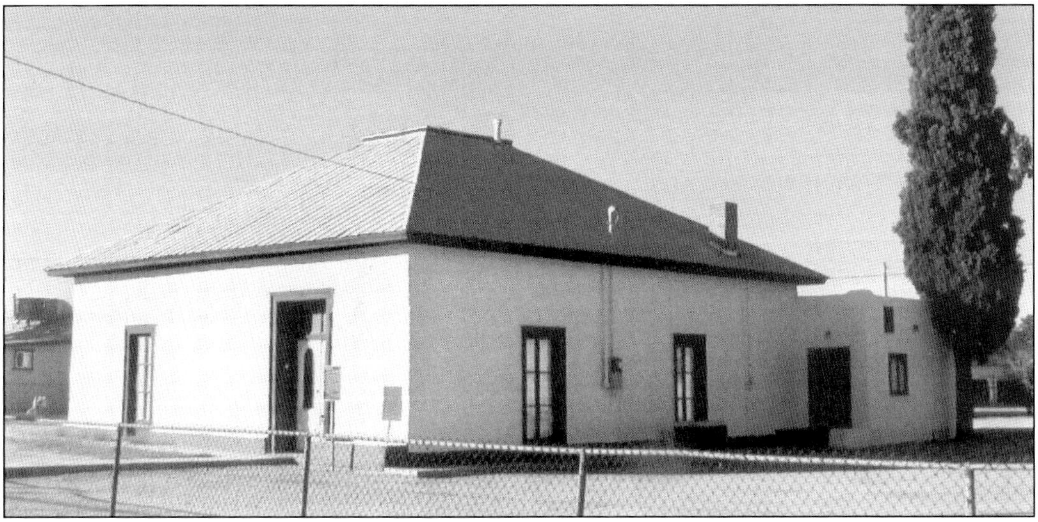

The 1878 John Clum residence is a foursquare Late Transitional–style adobe house with a pyramidal mansard timber-framed roof and 10-foot setbacks from the property line. The tin roofing most likely replaced original wood shingles. The interior includes casement windows, transoms, and an elegant marble fireplace. Architect Harris Sobin's assessment concluded that features of the house suggested a possible influence of the architecture of U.S. Army installations in Arizona, of which Clum would have been familiar. (Courtesy P. E. Guerrero and D. Legler.)

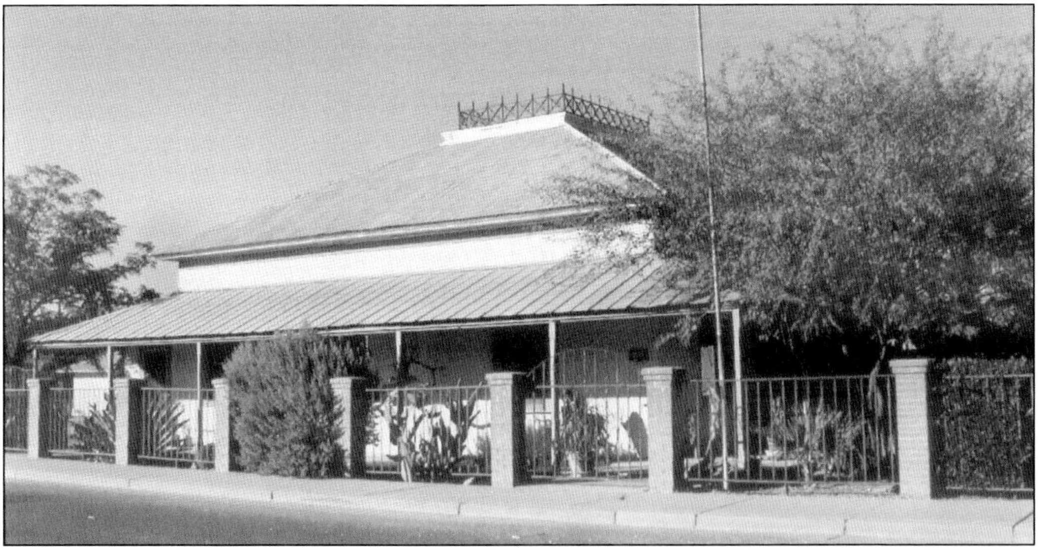

The 1888 adobe Jacob Suter House originally contained a foursquare plan with a central zaguan (center hall). The zaguan and door and window placement provided cross ventilation to cool the house. Typical Late Transitional–style details include the mansard roof and a veranda added in 1889. A many-sided veranda allowed one to find shade throughout the day. Suter was a tinsmith and hardware merchant. The tinwork on the roof is representative of his craft. (Courtesy P. E. Guerrero and D. Legler.)

As people with other architectural preferences arrived, many Sonoran adobes were transformed with the addition of pitched roofs covered with wood shingles. This improvement helped protect the adobes from monsoon rains. This Early Transitional style is reminiscent of Greek revival farmhouses of the East. The Isabella Cosgrove House was built about 1880. Added elements are a brick veneer over the original adobe bricks and a tin roof. (Courtesy P. E. Guerrero and D. Legler.)

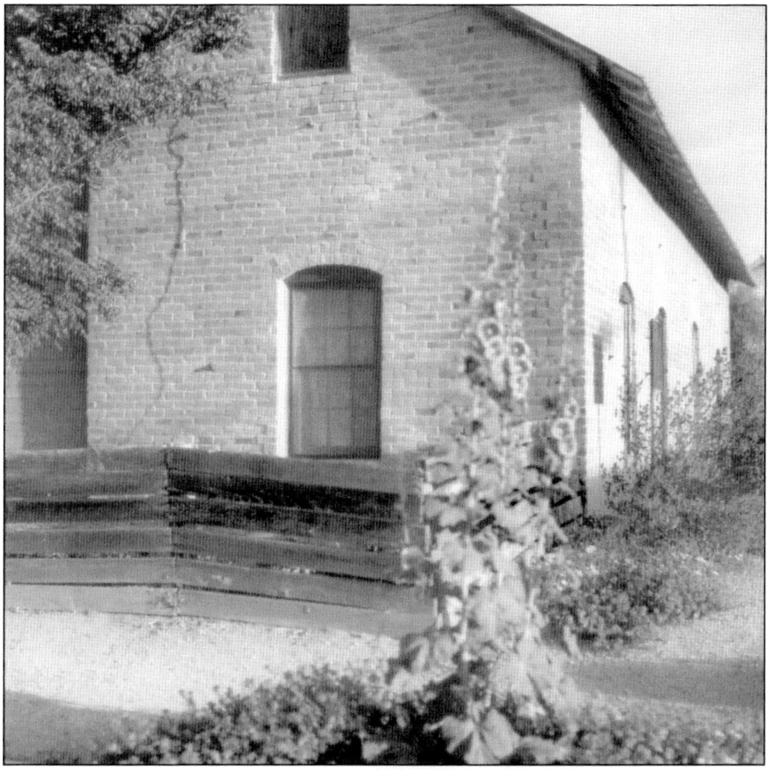

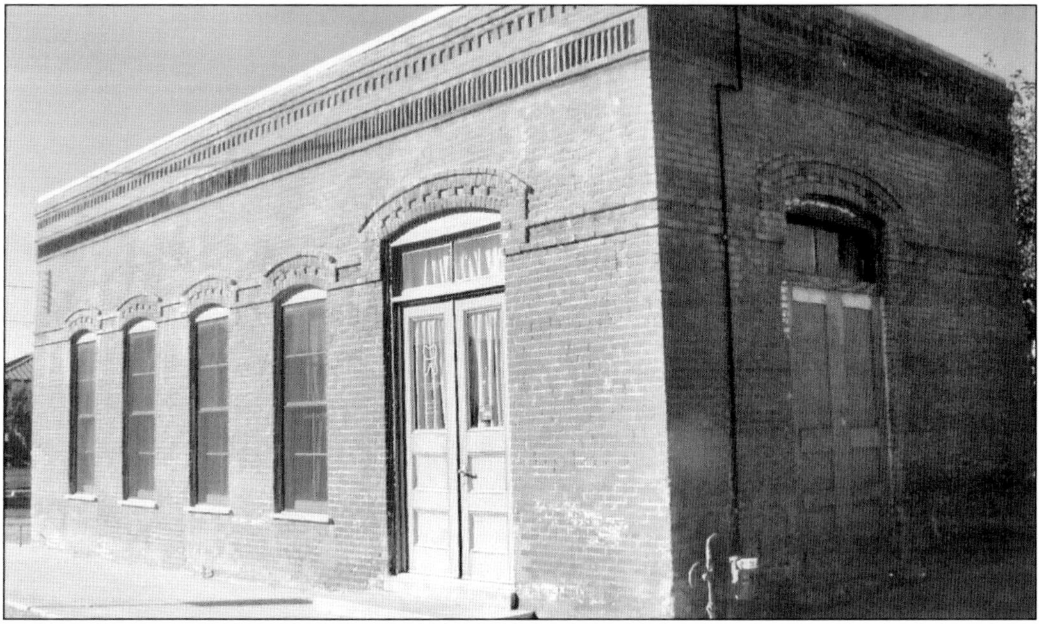

The John Nicolas Second Saloon and Beer Hall, constructed around 1888, may be Florence's earliest sand-struck brick structure still existing. A flat-roofed American Victorian–style commercial building, it is built flush to two property lines and is one of the few structures with a basement. Sophisticated brickwork and detailing suggest a professional architect's design. (Courtesy P. E. Guerrero and D. Legler.)

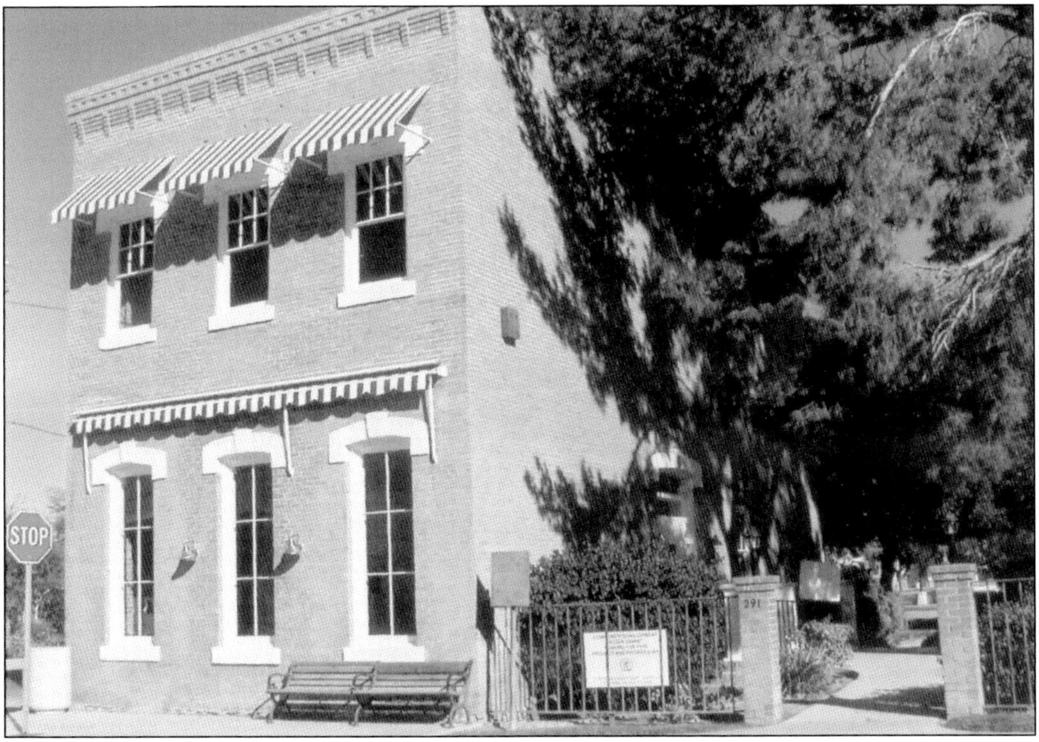

The Brunenkant Bakery is a two-story sand-struck brick American Victorian commercial structure built about 1889. It includes a basement, and ornate brickwork and parapets give it a distinctive character. The most recent restoration effort was performed by the Town of Florence with the help of an Arizona State Heritage Grant. The building now serves as the Florence Visitor Center. (Courtesy P. E. Guerrero and D. Legler.)

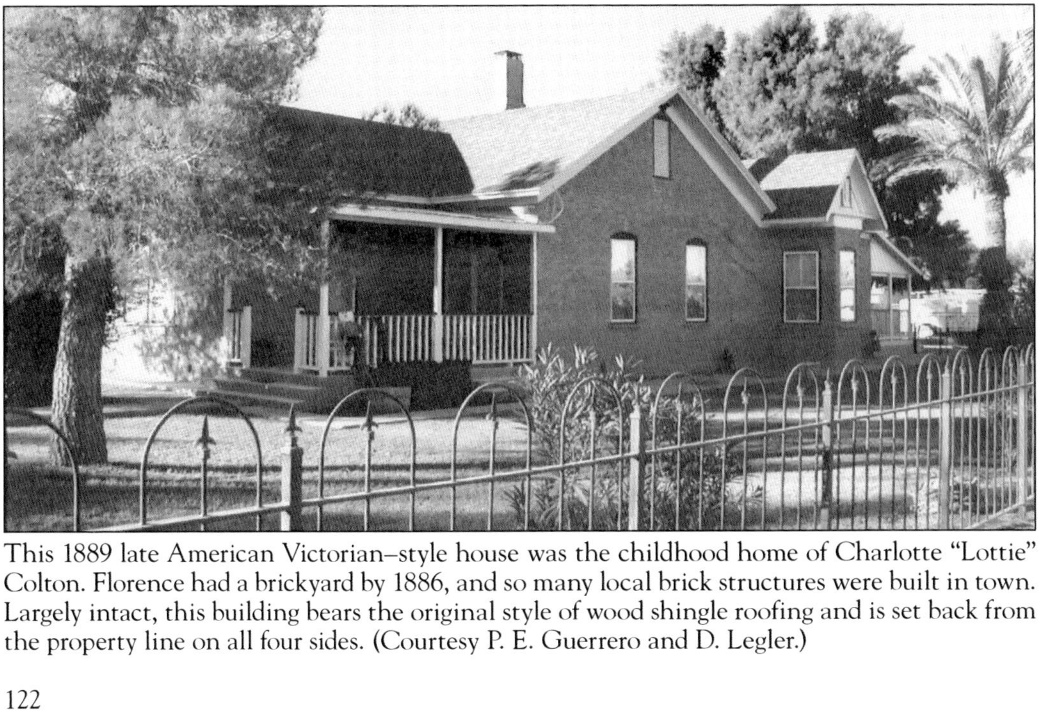

This 1889 late American Victorian–style house was the childhood home of Charlotte "Lottie" Colton. Florence had a brickyard by 1886, and so many local brick structures were built in town. Largely intact, this building bears the original style of wood shingle roofing and is set back from the property line on all four sides. (Courtesy P. E. Guerrero and D. Legler.)

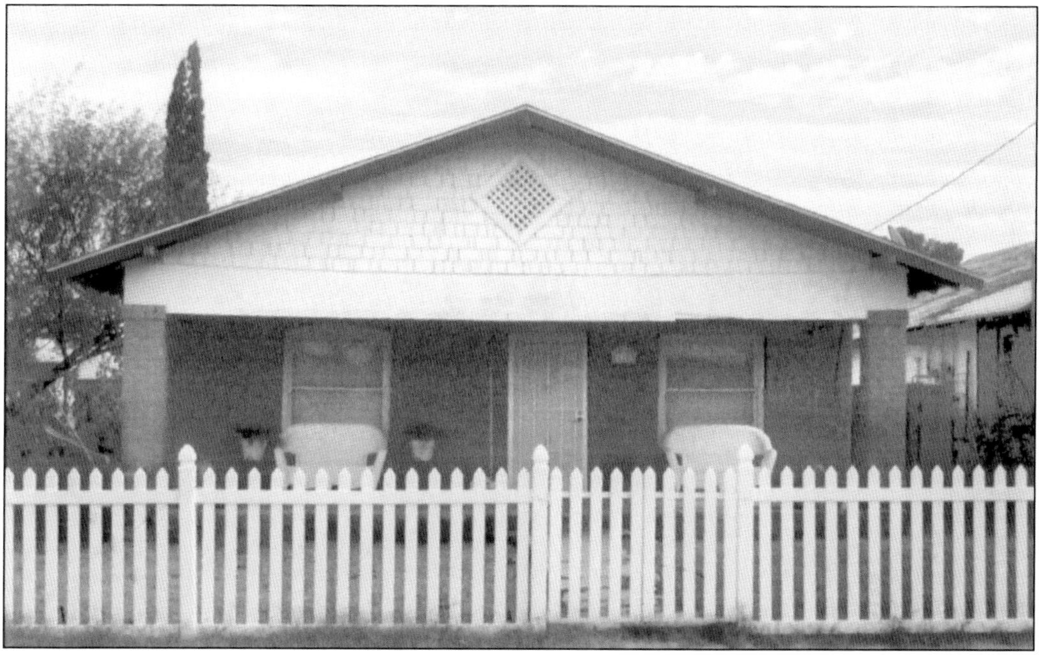

The 1908 Emma Monk Guild House, constructed of locally made brick, is one of the first Bungalow-style homes in Florence. A modest residence with cantilevered eaves, full porch, and wood-truss construction, it is an example of the modernism that provided many with affordable housing. The roof line is perpendicular to the street. (Courtesy P. E. Guerrero and D. Legler.)

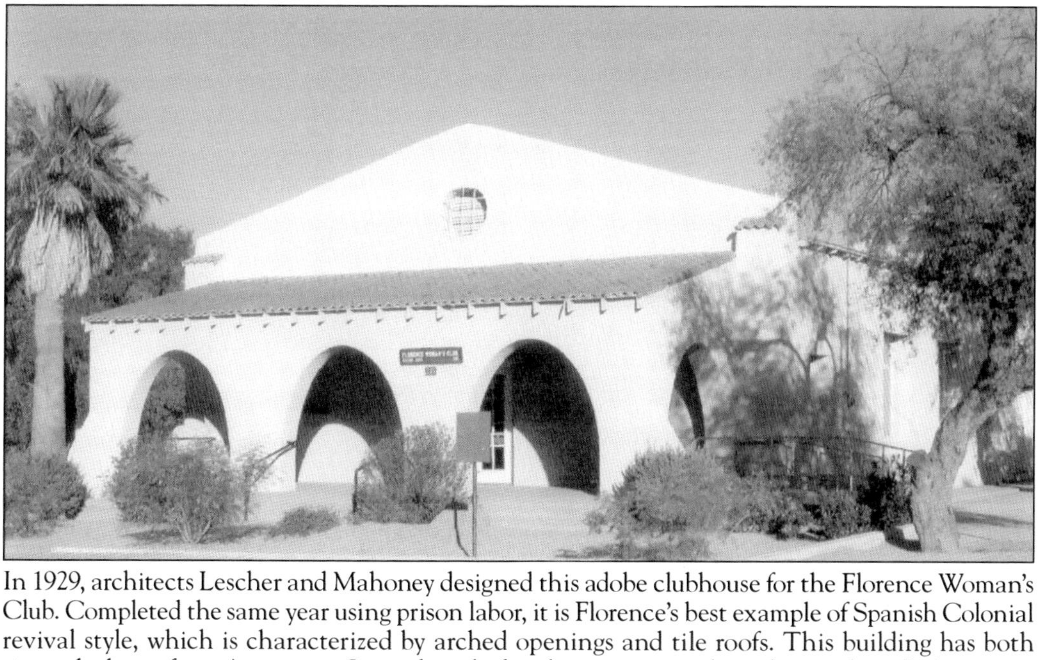

In 1929, architects Lescher and Mahoney designed this adobe clubhouse for the Florence Woman's Club. Completed the same year using prison labor, it is Florence's best example of Spanish Colonial revival style, which is characterized by arched openings and tile roofs. This building has both tin and tile roofing. An ornate Spanish-style fireplace is centered on the south wall. (Courtesy P. E. Guerrero and D. Legler.)

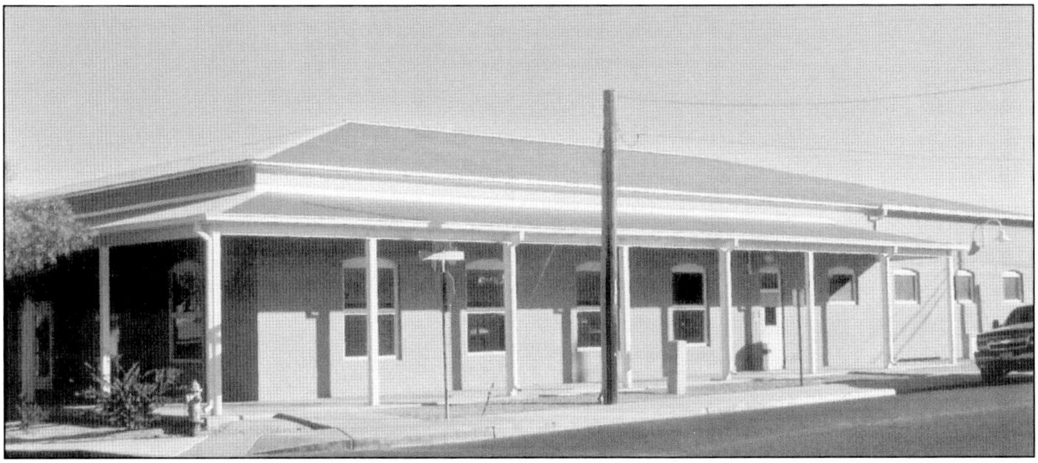

This modern U.S. Post Office was built to blend into the historic district, echoing the architectural feel of Florence. The town authorized an advisory commission to oversee its historic district. Even now, buildings and signs need to complement the historic character of the district. The group also facilitates the acquisition of historic markers. (Courtesy P. E. Guerrero and D. Legler.)

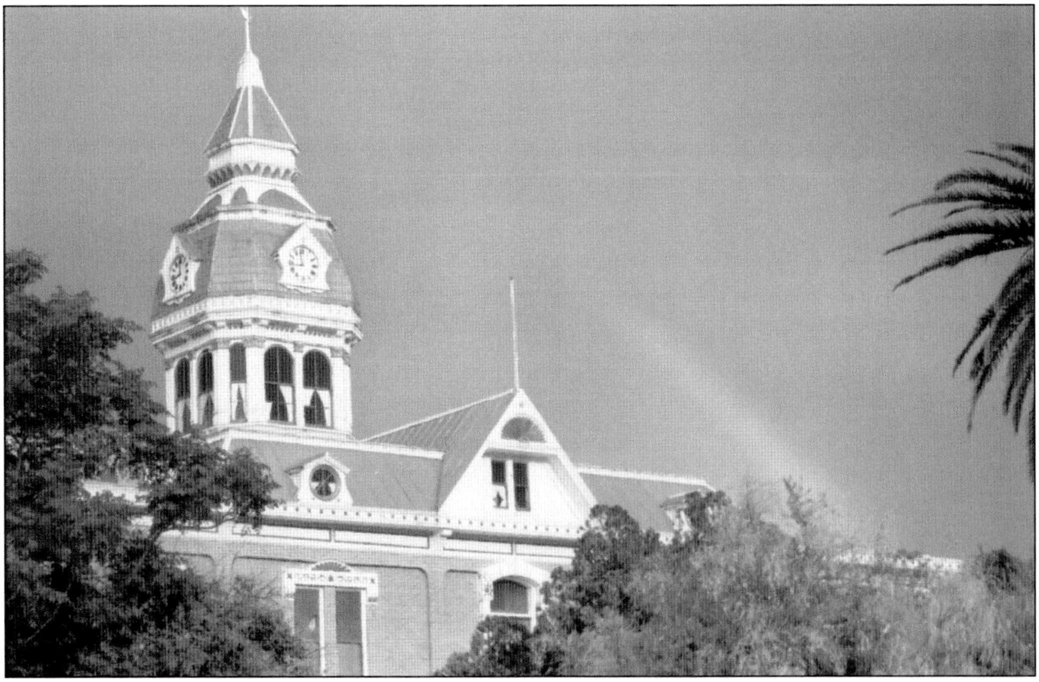

By 2006, all county offices had been moved from the 1891 courthouse building. Restoration has begun and plans are in motion to restore the empty structure for a new use. An important and easily recognized Florence landmark, the courthouse also illustrates the long and often difficult process of preservation as its future is contemplated. The rainbow over the tower symbolizes the hope for the future of the courthouse and the town of Florence itself. (Courtesy P. E. Guerrero and D. Legler.)

Ten

The Pinal County Historical Society Museum

In the late 1950s, a group of private citizens banded together to create a historical society and museum that would preserve and present the history of Pinal County. Located in Florence, the group was the only faction at that time working to preserve the area's history. Since then, a number of other communities have created their own historical preservation organizations. The Pinal County Historical Society has, therefore, narrowed its focus to Florence and the immediate surroundings. The emphasis is upon events and people who most directly influenced the growth and development of the town. The museum collections showcase displays and artifacts that bring these stories to life.

Visitors can view the actual bullet holes from the Peter Gabriel–Josephus Phy shootout and the knife Phy used to stab a bystander as he lay dying in the street. They can see the stuffed monkey doll that Winnie Ruth Judd made for the Arizona State Prison chaplain's daughter. It is included in a display along with her execution order, which was ultimately overturned by her plea of insanity. The artifacts of the law-abiding citizens vary from Ella Clarke's 1884 square grand piano to a foot-pedal dental drill and chair from Dr. Ferdinand Brockman. He would offer patients a swig of whiskey before pulling their teeth. Outdoor exhibits include a 1920s homesteader cabin, Alex Gay's blacksmithing equipment, Florence fire trucks, and old-time farm equipment.

Many researchers and writers find the library and archives invaluable resources for rare documents and photographs. Families seeking Florence connections come to do genealogy research. Many, in turn, offer their precious photographs and family histories to add to the museum's archives.

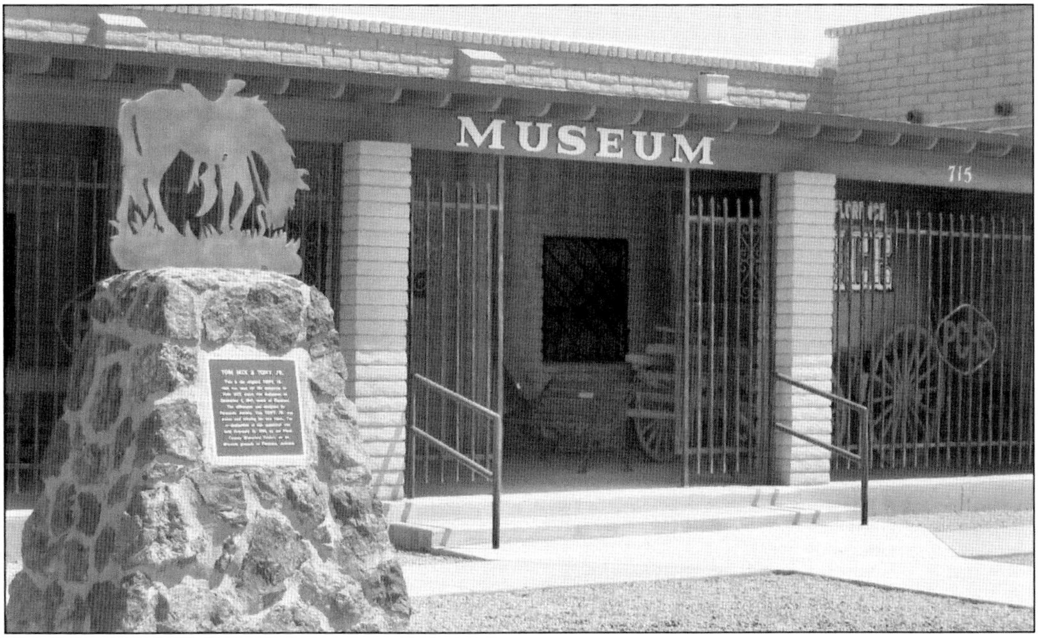

The Pinal County Historical Society Museum is located at 715 South Main Street in Florence. It provides a good orientation for visitors before they continue on to the historic district. Visitors will then have an overview of one of the oldest towns in Arizona. The historical society is a nonprofit organization, and admission is by donation.

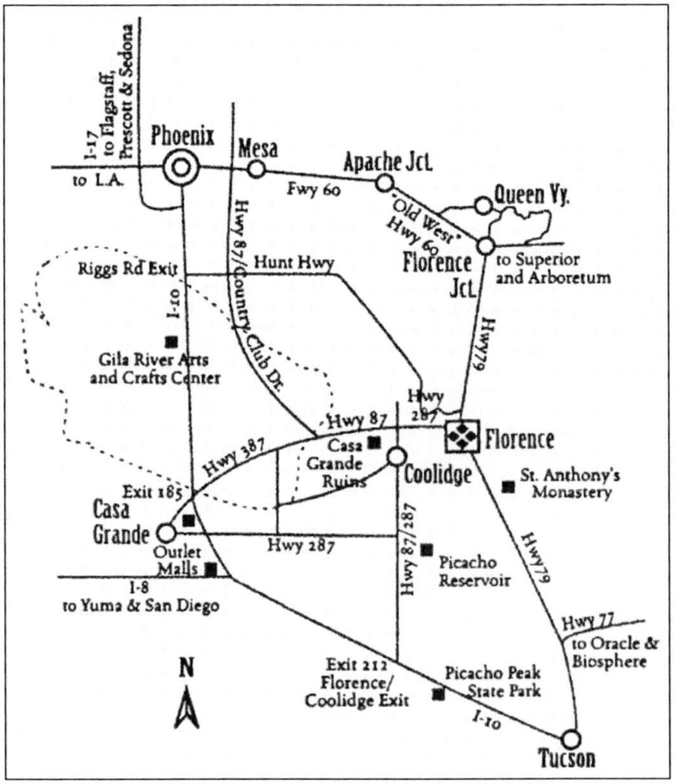

Florence is halfway between Phoenix and Mesa to the north and Tucson to the south. The Pinal County Historical Society Museum, which offers a free speakers' program during the winter season, is open six days a week: Tuesday through Saturday 11:00 a.m. to 4:00 p.m. and Sunday 12:00 to 4:00 p.m. It is closed from July 15 to August 31, Easter Sunday, Independence Day, Thanksgiving Day, Christmas Day, and New Year's Day. The museum is certified by the Arizona Historical Society.

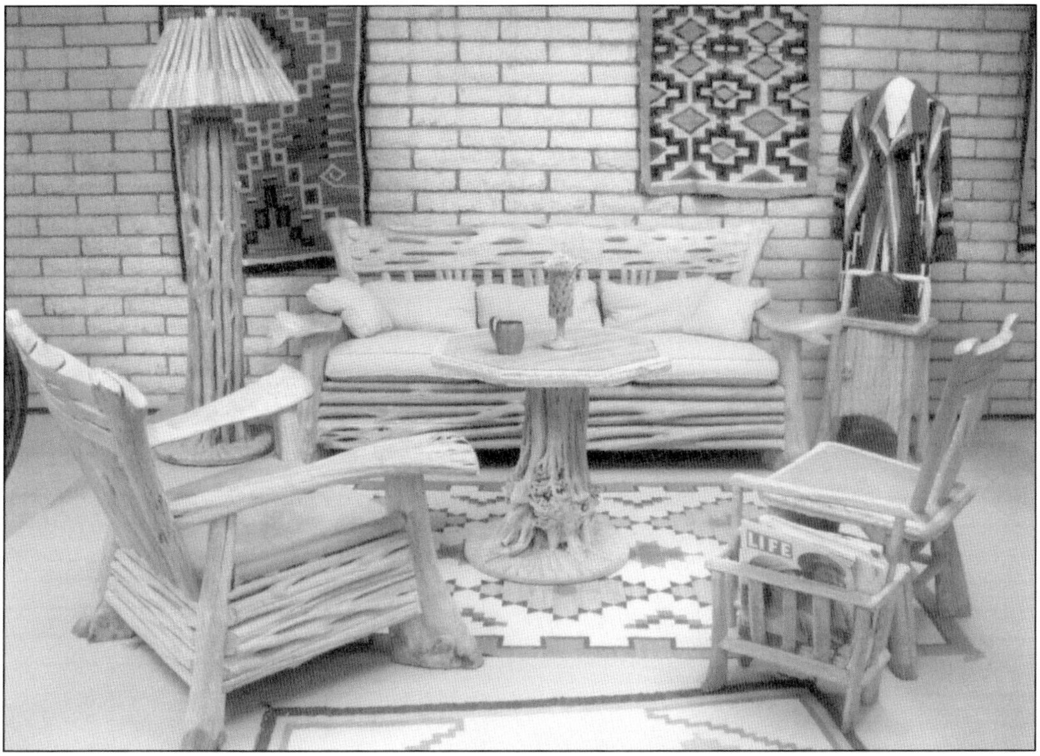

This unique living room suite is made of the inner woody ribs of the saguaro cactus. Produced in the 1930s when the Depression encouraged creative solutions, this set was used in a house at the nearby Eleven Mile Corner community. Now the saguaro and other cacti are protected, and craftsmen can no longer harvest them freely from the desert. (Courtesy P. E. Guerrero and D. Legler.)

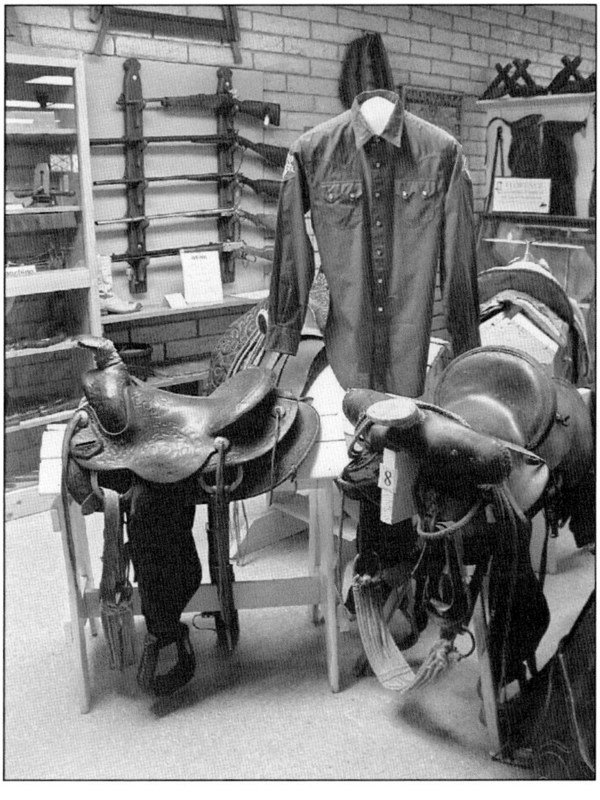

Cowboy and ranch life is portrayed in this exhibit of saddles, firearms, and chuck wagon gear. Many early ranching family brands are displayed. Of note are the horsehair ropes, branding irons, and extensive barbed-wire collection. Ranching and the cowboy lifestyle were important parts of Florence's early history. An extensive bullet display and the Collingwood Gun Collection may also be seen at the museum. (Courtesy P. E. Guerrero and D. Legler.)

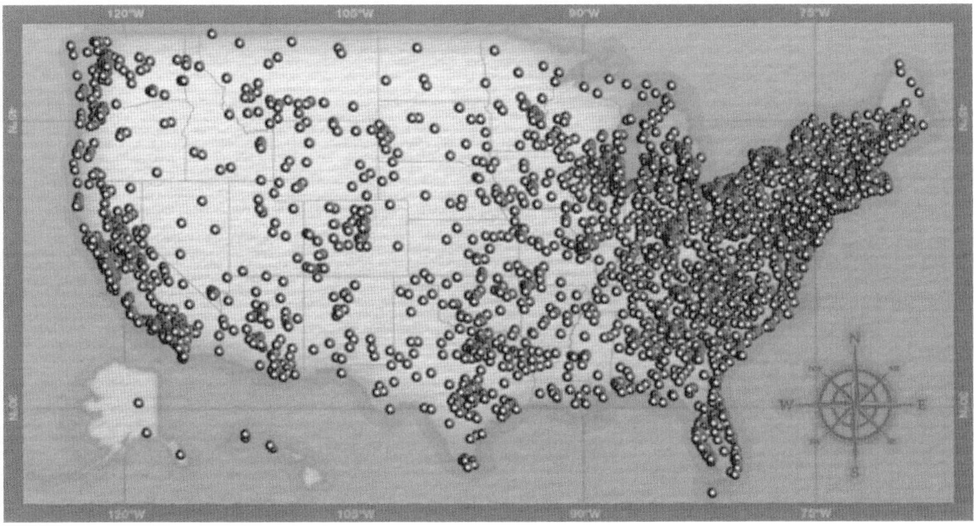